CHASIN' FREEDUM

"Those who say it can't be done are usually interrupted by others doing it."

- James Baldwin

"I am no longer accepting the things I cannot change. I am changing the things I cannot accept."

- Angela Davis

"Believe you can, and you're halfway there."

- Theodore Roosevelt

"If there is no struggle, there is no progress."

- Frederick Douglass

"I am America. I am the part you won't recognize. But get used to me. Black, confident, cocky; my name, not yours; my religion, not yours; my goals, my own; get used to me."

- Muhammad Ali

"If you have no confidence in self, you are twice defeated in the race of life."

- Marcus Garvey

"Character is power."

- Booker T. Washington

PRAISE

"Quawntay Bosco Adams has become a modern day legend and this book shares his superhero origin story."

- The New York Independent

"Shawshank Redemption was a special story but Chasin' Freedom was especially great because it's a true story."

- The Los Angeles Tribune

"This is a story that transcends borders, oceans, languages and even cultures. It's a true story of Triumph!"

- The London Digest

"Sometimes there is no good guy or bad guy. This isn't that story."

- The Miami Chronicle

Chasin' Freedum: The True Story of Bosco

Paperback ISBN #978-1-959473-04-6

(Originally published by Jailhouse Publications, 2015)

quawntaybadams@gmail.com

www.quawntayboscoadams.com

TOP TALENT
PUBLISHING

SELF-IMPROVEMENT, BUSINESS DEVELOPMENT BOOKS

CHASIN' FREEDUM

THE TRUE STORY OF

BOSCO

QUAWNTAY "BOSCO" ADAMS

CONTENTS

DEDICATION

This book is dedicated to the people and the struggle, and my ladies—my Grandmother (R.I.P.), my mother, my daughter.

ACKNOWLEDGMENTS

Please allow me to acknowledge and thank everyone who helped me put this book together. Of course, I must thank my mother, who has always been there for me no matter the occasion or circumstances. I would also like to thank my cousins Mykeah, Raven, and my sister Tameka, for typing my handwritten manuscript. And last but not least, I want to thank Monika, who allowed her beautiful soul to spill out into the creation of the book cover, and Shanee, who came through when I most needed and helped me clear the final hurdles. If I left anyone out, thanks.

INTRODUCTION

While I was confined to a small cell in the booking area of the Marion County Jail in Salem, Illinois, a guard came to my door and informed me that a woman with a sexy British accent was constantly calling the jail in hopes of speaking with me. The words *sexy, woman*, and *British accent* were enough to pique my interest. I later discovered the woman to be Rebecca Cody, a movie producer who, along with her partner Sam Brown, was interested in creating a documentary based on an ingenious jailbreak I executed years earlier. They were determined to get me to sign on and share my story with them. They were so impressed with my escape that they were willing to go forward without me and produce the documentary from public documents if I weren't willing to talk.

Why—why me and my escape? I asked. Certainly, I wasn't the only prisoner to escape confinement in the twenty-first century. True, Sam agreed; however, I was the only one to do so ingeniously and while under constant surveillance, he said. This was long before El Chapo's underground escape.

Initially, I refused to talk, for I was apprehensive about putting my name, face, and life before the world. But after several days of pondering, I hesitantly agreed to talk to Sam and Rebecca and authorized them to produce my story into a documentary titled *Break Out*, which premiered in early 2010.

Ever since then, people from all around the world have written to me to express condolences and amazement. The documentary has thrust me under a lens that has given me a degree of fame that I, a quiet introvert, never wished for. By the same token, it has provided a reason for people from all walks of life to empathize with and commend a lawbreaker for breaking the law—which says more about the law than the people.

Surprisingly, the documentary and the scant narrative of my chase for freedom were sufficient enough to intrigue people and make them want to know more about me and my story. So in response to the many requests, and to provide answers to many questions, I decided to open up and write the following memoirs to give people a broader view of my story.

Writing this book was both easy and difficult to complete. It was easy because I simply put my thoughts and memories on paper in a chronological order; however, it was difficult because I had no experience in writing on a scholastic, much less professional, level, and I had no idea where to begin. Nevertheless, I set my mind to it, blocked out my hunger pains and the constant ruckus occurring around me in solitary confinement, and, using a small flimsy ink pen that either dripped or stopped working every other word, applied myself and came up with an interesting book.

Since an ambitious heart can't be denied, I present my story.

PART ONE: MODERN DAY SLAVE

CHAPTER 1

DIVINE INTERVENTION

Have you ever felt as though you've been here before? It's sort of like your life continues to repeat itself. You dream of incidents long before they occur, experience the past in the present, and yet repeatedly make the same mistakes over and over again. There has to be a meaning behind all of this. What is the purpose? Everything in life has a meaning and purpose; therefore, everything that happens in life happens for a reason. There are no coincidences. So when my life fell apart on the leap-year night of January 23, 2004, I was forced to reflect and ask myself *why*.

Actually, it all began eleven days earlier when I flew out to St. Louis, Missouri to await the arrival of people and things that never seemed to arrive—at least not how I expected them to. First, my friends who were hauling a load of marijuana for me were busted on I-40 as they sped through the Texas panhandle. Then Yeyo and Twinky, my crime partners, who had no knowledge of or involvement in the panhandle bust, had mysteriously fallen from the face of the earth as they were facilitating the shipment, and my consignment, of 1,000 pounds of marijuana from Yeyo's uncle in Mexico.

All of this should have been my warning that the universe was conspiring against me and that perhaps I was in the wrong line of business at the wrong time. Certainly, there were more opportunities out there for me; after all, I was still young and handsome, and although I was quiet, I was charismatic and influential with the ambition of a devil. Unfortunately, though, I never considered taking the time out to stop, think, and heed the message the universe was throwing my way. I was moving too quickly, bound at the heart and mind, in a world of destruction, a world of invisible bars that I had inadvertently constructed and confined myself to. I should have heeded the signs.

I *was* on the verge of heeding the message, inadvertently and for the moment, for after several days of awaiting Yeyo and Twinky's arrival, and four days of unsuccessfully trying to reach them by phone, I gave up on them and the deal, and booked a flight back home to L.A. They'd given me reason to depart the cold, snowy, and gloomy mid-west for sunny southern California where beaches and less risky, white-collar hustles remained available to me. I canceled my plans to leave and considered the deal back on.

I hopped in my rental car and went to meet Yeyo and Twinky at a Taco Bell on the outskirts of St. Louis. The second I entered the restaurant and joined them at their table, I experienced an eerie feeling that something was wrong. They had deadpan facial expressions, and their body language was incongruous with their words. Simply put, they were behaving extremely peculiarly. Granted, the fact that they were in the midst of a big deal in a foreign city with a huge African American population was enough reason for the jitters; however, they were beyond nervous. Yeyo seemed burdened and worried; Twinky appeared to be downright terrified; and they both seemed to be hiding something.

When I asked about their immense delay in arriving in St. Louis, they claimed that while traveling east on I-40 they were involved in a terrible accident that left them stranded without car or cell phone chargers in a small town somewhere along the Texas panhandle; however, neither had a scratch to show for it. When I inquired about their ride to St. Louis, they gave me a cockamamie story about hitching a ride with a friend who just so happened to be traveling through Texas to Chicago for a wedding. This sounded like a script specifically prepared for a state trooper. When I asked about the friend, they said that he dropped them off and continued north. Nevertheless, a peculiar Mexican man was sitting at a back table, slowly munching on a taco and peeking at me. *Something's wrong.* But instead of heeding my intuition, I invited Twinky and Yeyo to my apartment.

We exited the restaurant and hopped in my rental car, Twinky in the passenger seat and Yeyo in the back. As we began to pull out of the parking lot, I caught a glimpse of the stranger in the Taco Bell rising from his table and hastily making his way to the exit. Suddenly my mind was overcome with anticipation of mischief. My heart began to palpitate, and I told myself that I was making a big mistake by proceeding with these two weasels.

I maneuvered the car through the parking lot of a nearby shopping center, trying to not only evade the stranger but also keep an eye on him. I watched as he exited the restaurant, entered a blue Chevy Lumina, and began to drive around in circles as if he were lost.

From the backseat, Yeyo nervously looked around, presumably in search of the stranger. Suddenly, his phone rang, but instead of answering it, he told Twinky in Spanish to turn up the radio, believing that the music would drown out his conversation. He then flipped open his phone and began to talk into the mouthpiece while looking in the direction of the Taco Bell. All the while, I was spying through the rearview mirror.

Fearing the stranger to be either a fed or the grim reaper, I abruptly parked the car in front of a department store. I warned Yeyo and Twinky that we were being tailed, hopped out of the car, and scurried into the store. While I roamed the aisles, pretending to be a shopper, Twinky and Yeyo entered, also pretending to be shoppers. They tried to inch near me to discretely inquire about my observation and suspicion, but little did they know that I was trying to elude them as much as I was the stranger.

I managed to distance myself from them and slip out the back door. With no particular place to go, I sought temporary refuge in the lobby of a nearby hospital. Once inside, I pulled out my phone and summoned a ride. While I sat there waiting for my ride, Twinky repeatedly called my phone, but I refused to answer. Instead, I shut it off. I was extremely paranoid and feared the calls were solely intended to reveal my location through the phone's GPS.

When my ride arrived, we drove around the area and searched for signs of the feds, but found none. We didn't see cops, Twinky, or the stranger in the Lumina. I then began to think that perhaps I was overreacting.

Later on, while packing my bags for the second time that day, I turned on my phone and was greeted by a dozen messages from Twinky. Hesitantly, I decided to return his calls and confront him about the suspicious activity. Quite naturally, he swore that they were not trying to set me up, but he did admit that the man in the Lumina was with them. He was part of Yeyo's idea of having me tailed to see if I were up to any funny business of my own.

And their cockamamie story about being in a terrible accident and stranded, without wheels or cell phone chargers, in a small town? Twinky admitted that the accident was minor and resulted in them spending a few days in an immigration detention facility. He said that they didn't want to tell me about the arrest because they feared I might call off the deal. Although

I was still a little skeptical—just a little—Twinky's explanation seemed to make sense.

All of the lies and smokescreens were Yeyo's idea of security. He didn't want me to know everything because he didn't trust me completely; nevertheless, he needed me. The marijuana business in the South and the Midwest was very lucrative, and I was his only connection to the region. He needed me, not only to help distribute his merchandise but also to help clean his face. He was already a million dollars in debt with the guys in Mexico, and there was more money tied up in this deal. He was counting on the deal and several more to clear his debt and save his ass. As he put it, the wheels on the tractor-trailer hauling the marijuana were already rolling, and if it were to arrive in St. Louis with nobody to accept it, there would be heads rolling. And it was very likely that one of those heads would be his.

Ultimately, I agreed to accept the load. I did so not only to help Yeyo climb out of his financial jam—and prevent his head from rolling—but also to recoup some of my own and to fulfill some of the commitments I'd made to people. I'd promised my uncle $25,000 to save his business; I'd promised to pay my friends᾽ lawyer fees; and I'd promised many other people the world; therefore, I was determined to fulfill my obligations, even if it killed me. Considering all of this, it was hard to walk away from the prospect of selling 1,000 pounds at $1,000 per. That alone was enough to lure me back in.

Although it was Sunday when Yeyo claimed that the wheels on the semi were rolling, the pot didn't arrive until Thursday night. This should've been the reason for questions, but asking myriad of questions in the illegal drug business is sort of a taboo. And although trust is rare, some degree of it is essential to making a deal less complicated. Therefore, I kept many of my doubts and questions to myself and reluctantly trusted that Yeyo and the gang had my safety, as well as everybody else's, in mind.

Also arriving in St. Louis that night, via airplane, was another Mexican dude, Angel, whom I had never seen before. As a facilitator in the transportation of marijuana for the guys in Mexico, Angel's job required him to find and recruit truckers to haul marijuana to various destinations in the U.S. and to ensure that every stem and leaf safely reached its destination.

Yeyo and I picked up Angel at the airport and took him to a scrap yard in East St. Louis where we planned to unload the marijuana from the tractor-trailer. Moments later we were joined by two Spanish-speaking Caucasians in a tan sedan, who, according to Angel, were the truckers that hauled the marijuana from Texas. I sat inside the car while Yeyo, Angel, and the truckers walked around the scrap yard, surveying it and discussing the delivery. Ten minutes later, Angel and Yeyo returned and announced that the delivery would take place the following morning.

"Something ain't right," my cousin Rat tacitly warned when I returned to the apartment. "This game is give and go, but this give is taking too damn long." Rat's comment was my first presentiment of the night, but since he was an extreme pessimist, I disregarded his comment as another one of his glass half-empty remarks. My second presentiment came when Simone, a woman I'd dated, said that I was too sexy and intelligent to be a pot dealer. She essentially laughed and refused to believe that I could be so stupid. She made me promise to meet with a friend of hers in the modeling industry and to at least give it a try. Although I had refused many scouts before, I had a feeling that it probably was now the time to stop being so macho and to give it a shot. Then later that night, I received a call from Lorrie, whom I hadn't talked to in three weeks; she called to give me my third and greatest presentiment of the night: She was pregnant.   I suddenly had an epiphany that I was in the wrong place at the wrong time.

The morning came and went, but the weed still had not been delivered. The truckers now claimed that we needed to find another location because they did not believe they could maneuver the tractor trailer through the narrow alley leading into the scrap yard. This should have been another warning. But I was too desperate to perceive this delay ominously.

Later that evening, while we sat around thinking of alternative locations to unload the marijuana, Angel received a call from the truckers saying that they had unloaded the marijuana into a U-Haul van and that it could be picked up at the Gateway Truck Stop in Granite City, Illinois. Yeyo, Angel, and I quickly set out in my rental car while, unbeknownst to Angel, Twinky and the stranger from Taco Bell covertly tailed us in a similar U-Haul van. We planned for Twinky and the stranger to provide surveillance on the truck stop, then transfer the marijuana from the truckers⊡ van into our van.

However, fate had a different plan. Ten minutes into the twenty-minute drive, Yeyo received a phone call that apparently didn't sit well with him. His eyes enlarged and he furtively looked at the passing street signs, struggling to read them, while his free hand turned up the volume on the car stereo. He then conspicuously whispered into the mouthpiece of the phone. It was like deja vu, reminiscent of the scene at the shopping-center parking lot earlier that week when he tried to discretely reveal our location to Stranger. Only this time he sat in the passenger seat. It didn't take long for me to infer that Twinky and Stranger were lost.

Seeing Yeyo's frustration, I tried to distract Angel, by talking to him, while Yeyo futilely tried to reveal our location to Twinky. Unfortunately, though, Yeyo was unfamiliar with the streets we traveled, and worse, he couldn't speak or read a lick of English. Even if the signs were in Spanish, he still wouldn't have been able to read them, for he had grown up on a marijuana farm in Mexico and had never spent one day in a classroom. Once he reached his zenith of frustration, he gave me the phone. But this too was futile, for Twinky and Stranger were two airheads who couldn't even navigate their way through a Taco Bell parking lot, much less a foreign metropolis.

Having arrived at the truck stop, I parked next to the truckers, who were sitting inside a sedan parked next to a U-Haul van. Angel exited and walked over to the truckers, who quickly exited and stood beside the sedan. At this moment, Yeyo called Twinky and openly inquired about he and Stranger's whereabouts. They were clearly lost and confused, so when Angel returned with an uncertain expression on his face and the ignition key to the van and asked who'll drive, we had to change our plans. I thought about how valuable the merchandise was and figured I would be the best option. I took the key from Angel, exited the car, walked over to the van, opened the door, hopped in the driver seat, inserted the key into the ignition, and tried to start the van, but nothing happened.

My heart instantly dropped into my stomach, and images from the previous night quickly flashed through my head, starting with Rat's warning, then Simone's flattering comments, and ending with Lorrie's pregnancy revelation. I was now convinced that the deal was a trap. I immediately opened the door and prepared to flee, but a swarm of federal agents surrounded the van like bees on a honeycomb. There was nothing I could do, nothing but laugh. I laughed like a deranged man as I exited the van and lay on the pavement with the weight of the U.S. Government on my back, including a DEA agent named Fox.

It was now January 24, 2004, and I felt as though I were at the rim of a drain and my life was on the verge of being poured down into it. I was confined to a small congested, melancholic holding cell that wasn't much bigger than a horse's stall. It was dimly lit just enough for the jailers to see inside, and it reeked of urine, bad breath, and alcohol seeping from the pores of detoxifying prisoners who hadn't showered in days. The back cinder-block wall was chilly from the freezing temperature outside, but the inside of the cell was warm and humid with body heat and respiration. The conditions were foul and depressing, yet they were the least of my concerns.

I guess I'm not as intelligent as Simone assumed, I thought, as I blindly gazed at the ceiling of the holding cell, struggling to think coherently. My mind was drained and distracted by my battered emotions. My psyche was stuck somewhere between the emotional junction of laughing and crying, but unable to do either. I was disappointed, angry, and confused. Disappointed in myself, angry with my alter ego, and confused as to where to place the blame. I blamed Angel for failing to have the truckers tailed. I blamed Yeyo for confusing my visceral alarm system with all of the secrecy and smoke screens. I blamed my alter ego for getting me caught up in such a deal. And above all, although my pride begged to differ, I blamed myself for being such a fool. After all, it was I who failed to heed my foreboding anxiety. It was I who couldn't suppress my natural traits of trust, even when my own survival depended on it. And it was I who naively showed up at a truck stop to do a drug deal with three-and-a-half strangers. It was all my fault. I wasn't so smart after all.

On the other hand, if there is any truth in the doctrine of Divine Intervention, perhaps my arrest was the result of something much more profound than stupidity and intelligence. After all, whenever a blessed man loses sight of his purpose and fails to utilize his natural gifts productively in accordance with universal law, the Higher Power will intervene. Perhaps my arrest was really the result of divine intervention.

How else could I explain the portentous timing? Eight years earlier during the wee hours of January 24, 1996 (also a leap year), I was arrested in Oceanside, California, in a dragnet drug sting directed by a DEA agent named "Fox." Either the timing and name were purely coincidental, or there was something creepy and mystical about foxes and leap years during the twilight between the 23rd and 24th of January.

Per the Higher Power, 2004 might have been the perfect year to snatch me from society and teach me a lesson, but to me, 2004 was supposed to be my year of opportunity and prosperity. Just twenty-four days earlier, I resolved to make 2004 my last year of dealing marijuana. I planned to cross over to real estate investments and other legitimate businesses. It seemed that promising real estate opportunities were being thrown at me, and suddenly after 28 years, my quiet charisma—charisma I never knew existed until now—began to attract friends, associates, and supporters from all walks of life. Considering the opportunities popping up in the year 2004, it was definitely the wrong time to be doing time.

I had even enrolled in an expensive real estate class to learn all of the tricks and skills necessary to make the business work for me. I even devised a strategy of my own which I referred to as *Follow the Rich White Man*. Gentrification proves that whenever a rich white man ventures into inexpensive urban real estate, he uses his wealth and political connections to reduce crime, drive away poor people, and, thereby, increase the property value. I was no smart man, but I knew that I couldn't go wrong in real estate by following the rich white man.

On a minor note, I also resolved, as part of my New Year's resolution, to delete the phone numbers of most of the women listed in my cell phone; to get dressed more often, rather than running around all day in comfortable sweats, tee shirts, and sneakers; to be more selfish and use the word *no* more frequently; and to stop giving away my fast earned money so freely. In other words; I had resolved to make 2004 my most prosperous year yet. A year dedicated to self-empowerment.

However, there I was twenty-four days into the year, and I hadn't made good on any one of my New Year's resolutions. I hadn't deleted any numbers from my phone, but added plenty; I still ran around all day in gym clothes; I still couldn't muster up the courage to say "No!"; I still opened my wallet to anyone who asked; I still tipped waitresses twenties and fifties as if I were rich; and I hadn't made one attendance at my real estate class. Instead of attending class, I was busy attending the streets. I had lost focus. I even lost sight of the rich white man and started following the path of a rich Mexican man. One who couldn't even speak English.

I had failed to use my gifts and natural traits of trust, benevolence, altruism, charisma, and wisdom in a manner productive to humanity. I had failed to recognize and follow the path that the universe had laid out for me; instead, I naively walked the illusory path that the ghetto laid out before me, a path that placed the ego over the soul and self over humanity, a murky path that only led me further away from my purpose in life. Consequently, the universe intervened. Divine Intervention!

CHAPTER 2

CAGED IN

Psychologically drained, I found a spot on the floor of the holding cell with Yeyo and Angel, and dozed in and out throughout the rest of the night, disturbed only by my incessant thoughts and the frequent sound of the heavy, steel door opening, and slamming shut whenever a new prisoner entered.

By noon, the holding cell resembled the basement of a 17th century slave ship—it was filled beyond capacity with distraught black men in desperate need of showers. Except for Yeyo and Angel, everyone in the cell was black. Had I not known any better, I would've thought that I was incarcerated in Haiti instead of the predominately white county of St. Clair, Illinois. Judging from the holding cell, white folks either didn't commit crimes or didn't get arrested for them, and that began to worry me all the more.

In spite of the circumstances, though, the holding cell had its spurts of humor. The highlight was a crack-head jokester whose teeth were much too large for his mouth. Every time he opened his mouth, the holding cell erupted with laughter. His jokes were funny, but his smile was even funnier. Every time he smiled, it appeared that he was showcasing a set of ivory dominoes.

The jokester's main target was a teenager who was both humorous and disturbing. Having been arrested on minor charges, he harassed his grandmother with exorbitant number of collect calls, pleading with her to raise money for his bail. The poor old lady tried her best, yet when she failed to move at the youngster's pace, he had a tantrum and began shouting at her.

The youngster's coarseness with the old lady became rather disturbing, and the fact that he was sporting gold-plated teeth, fancy clothes, and expensive shoes, but still couldn't come up with $300 to get out of jail, was even more disturbing.

Exacerbating the situation, the crack head suggested that the youngster pawn his gold-plated teeth to raise the $300. He even offered to smuggle them out and cash them in for him. This caused the cell to erupt with more laughter, and the youngster with anger.

Awakened by the laughter, Angel sat up and looked around bewilderingly. It appeared that he was expecting to awake and find that the previous night had been a nightmare. He got up and walked to the lone stainless-steel toilet in the front of the cell and shamelessly dropped his pants to his ankles and took a crap in broad view of whoever didn't look the other way. This caused the cell to erupt with more laughter, and Angel instantly became the butt of the crack head's jokes. Although I laughed along with the rest of the prisoners, I had an eerie feeling that Angel's weak bowels was ominous that the three of us were in serious shit.

I laughed, worried, and cried inwardly until 8 o'clock Saturday night when we were processed into the jail. At that moment, I was forced to swap my comfortable sweats and sneakers for an orange jumpsuit and a pair of plastic slippers. Sadly, after more than $200 worth of collect calls, the youngster still hadn't raised the $300 he needed to secure his bond. Consequently, he too was forced to trade in his expensive sneakers for slippers.

With the change of clothing, we officially became prisoners, an unnecessary expense to the taxpayers and a burden upon our families and everyone else willing to support us and accept our collect calls. The only winners were the cops, the jailers, and the phone companies, all who stood to profit to the detriment of humanity and public resources.

We were fingerprinted and photographed, and our mug shots revealed that we weren't too happy—the only person smiling was the crack head. After being issued bedrolls we were escorted down a long corridor to our housing units.

Yeyo and Angel were assigned to an open dormitory, and as luck would have it, I was taken to a more secure unit at the very end of the corridor. The unit was small and square with two tiers and two-man cells—ten cells on the top tier and ten on the bottom. The center of the unit served as a dayroom, with nothing more than a couple of metal tables and stools for prisoners to sit around, play table games, watch TV, and wait on the courts.

I stood outside the unit with my bedroll tucked under my arm and stared through a huge Plexiglas window at the prisoners as they watched TV and played table games. They seemed to be unaware of my presence until the electronically operated door began to slide open. The prisoners stopped what they were doing and stared at me, and the dayroom became quiet, except for the TV. The rare quietude caused more prisoners to spill from the cells to investigate. After a brief moment of silence and stares, the prisoners resumed their activities. Several smiled as though they were happy to have a new companion to share in their misery. Based on their reaction, it was safe for me to assume that the sliding door was not a revolving one.

After the dayroom returned to its usual noisiness, I heard someone call my name. I looked around and spotted a familiar guy leaning over the rail of the upper tier. He flashed a nervous gold-capped-teeth grin and expressed shock in seeing me. The guy was Steve Caraway, a fortyish black dude who resembled a taller version of Rapper/Singer Cee-lo Green. Steve was part of a prominent family in East St. Louis who were invested in everything from tire shops to record labels. I first met him in the early part of autumn through his cousin Dominique, and a business relationship immediately ensued. Unfortunately, our business quickly ended in late December when he was indicted by the feds on myriad of drug related charges.

I dropped my bedroll on my bunk and went upstairs to talk to Steve. The first thing he asked me was: "What happened?" I was too embarrassed to tell him that I'd fallen for the marijuana-in-the-disable-van trick, so I gave him a slightly twisted version of the facts. I lounged in Steve's cell for about an hour, swapping tales and legal advice. His cellmate, Bud (also from East St. Louis, with gold in his mouth, and facing federal drug charges), listened and added his two cents; he also provided me with the number of an attorney. As I got ready to leave Steve's cell, I contemplated asking for the $20,000 he owed me; instead, I settled for a bar of soap, a tube of toothpaste, and a few dollars' worth of snacks.

On my way down the stairs, I was stopped by B.G., a tall youngster with an afro who looked like a slightly taller and darker George Forman back in his *Rumble in the Jungle* days.

"You ball?" he asked. I contemplated lying, but I remembered hearing about a gym downstairs in the basement. "Not really," I replied, knowing that the truth would eventually come to the light—it always does.

As I walked away, I couldn't help but think about the many times people asked me if I play basketball. Because of my 6'4" 195-pound frame and agile swagger, people often mistake me for a ball player. White people really profiled me as such. I couldn't walk the beach or sit next to a white person on an airplane without them asking: "Do you play basketball?" Often, if the inquirer was an attractive woman, I'd lie and say yes. Truthfully, even if they weren't attractive and a female, I'd say yes. It was much easier than telling the truth.

Locked in the cell for the night, I snacked on potato chips and became better acquainted with my cellmate, Lorenzo Rodriguez. I called him "Lorro." He was a 26-year-old Mexican national with fair skin, long black hair, and dark, angry-looking eyes. He reminded me of one of the characters in the 1980s TV show *Kung Fu Theater*. He spoke very little English, but since I spoke a little Spanish, we were able to communicate well. Lorro's journey to jail began when he received a call from a childhood friend promising to make him a rich man if he were to come to America. He accepted the offer and migrated North of the border to St. Louis, where he found himself providing security and collecting debts on the behalf of his friend's organization. Eventually, they were indicted and arrested on a huge cocaine-conspiracy charge. Funny thing, his friend who promised to make him a very rich man fled to Mexico and was never apprehended, nor did he send Lorro a dime for commissary or lawyer fees.

Full of potato chips and Mexican drug tales, I drifted to sleep without even brushing my teeth—something I hadn't done in years. Another thing I hadn't done in years was dream. But on this night, I dreamt non-stop. I dreamt that I was free, dreamt of Lorrie choking me and making me promise that I wouldn't go to prison, and dreamt of Simone telling me that I was too sexy and intelligent to be a drug dealer. My dreams were so vivid that I expected to awake and find that they were my reality and that my reality was just a bad dream.

That dream, however, was shattered early in the morning by the sound of cell doors buzzing open, bringing me back to my dismal reality. But instead of facing such reality, I skipped breakfast and resumed sleeping. Over the following few days, I slept and dreamt like never before. The dreams came incessantly as if they were my brain's natural defense to my horrid reality.

Tuesday morning, four days after our arrest, we were taken to the federal court building in East St. Louis for our initial appearance. We were transported to court the same way we'd been transported to the St. Claire County Jail Friday night—Yeyo and Angel in the back seat of a police cruiser, and I in the passenger seat of a gray Ford F-150 driven by a black officer whom I refer to as "The Champ."

As The Champ gripped the steering wheel, I notice that he

was wearing a Super Bowl ring he'd won playing for the 1986 Chicago Bears. He hadn't been wearing the ring the night he dropped me off at the jail, which made me suspect that he was wearing it this day just to impress the people at the court building. Certainly the ring would enhance his status and pique the interest of any big-wig court official hip enough to discern the significance of such a ring. By the same token, in a courtroom full of white folks, his hardware (the ring) and my hardware (handcuffs) might've supported the stereotype that most well-to-do black men are either athletes or drug dealers.

As we waded through the early morning traffic, The Champ accepted a call from one of his informants and openly discussed setting up a local drug dealer. The Champ planned to provide the informant with prerecorded currency to pass to the unwitting drug dealer, and then he and his posse would raid the drug dealer's house in search for the money and more contraband. The details of the conversation were somewhat disturbing, particularly because the informant, the drug dealer, and the cop were black. In the racist War on Drugs, I naively half expected that black cops wouldn't be so supportive. To a degree, I felt that, after 400 years of slavery and setbacks, black cops in an all-black town like East St. Louis should turn a blind eye to drug dealers and consider the hustle as self-reparation for the set-backs of slavery.

When the Champ terminated the call, I asked him how common it was for people, particularly black men, to assist as informants in the War on Drugs. Shockingly, he said that it was very common, and that some did it for money, and others to get out of trouble. I was quickly learning the truth about the War on Drugs and how cutthroat it made the business. I had heard stories of people snitching and setting up drug dealers in their community, but I had a hard time believing that it was so prevalent—probably because I was so use to trusting people and giving them the benefit of the doubt.

Even still, considering that the War on Drugs primary

goal was to overpopulate prisons with black men, I couldn't fathom how another black person could voluntarily support such injustice. To me, The Champ and his informants were no different than the negroes who helped capture runaway slaves.

What's the purpose? I wondered. It wasn't like all of the snitching and drug busts were stemming the flow of drugs and reducing consumption. It all seemed futile and senseless, wasting hundreds of billions—if not trillions—of dollars, and millions of persons via incarceration, just to try to stop an adult from getting stoned. There had to be a hidden agenda that only Congress, President Reagan and Bill Clinton knew about; after all, no government is so stupid and arrogant to continue wasting precious lives and resources fighting a losing war. Somebody other than foreign cartels, cops, and correctional officers had to be winning. What's the purpose? There has to be one.

Having arrived at the court building, The Champ parked in a garage underneath. Two minutes later, as I sat in the passenger seat of the F-150, talking to The Champ, appearing as if I were a free man, Angel and Yeyo arrived, gazing suspiciously at me from the back seat of the police cruiser. To them, it might have appeared that I was cooperating and receiving special treatment. In hindsight, I now believe that the scenario was staged as a part of the fed's divide-and-conquer strategy. I wouldn't be surprised if I were to learn that the phone call between The Champ and the snitch was staged as a means of trying to seduce me into cooperating.

Thus far, my incarceration had been filled with lessons and culture shocks, and upstairs in the courtroom, I received another cultural shock. Although the court building was in East St. Louis, a predominately African American city, everyone in the court building, other than The Champ, the usher, and the criminal defendants, was white. The prisoners at the jail had told me that all the judges were white, but I still expected to see black clerks, marshals, and lawyers. Seeing so many white faces only galvanized my fear of injustice.

The purpose of the hearing was to inform us of the allegations charged in the criminal complaint, something I'd been waiting all weekend to find out. As suspected, the truck drivers were the weak link. To my surprise, though, they were also undercover ICE agents who'd been investigating Angel for years. After reading the criminal complaint, I looked over at Angel with fury.

When we first met, I perceived Angel to be a professional marijuana trafficker, but now I perceived him to be the stupidest man in the world. He not only made the mistake of hiring two undercover agents to transport the marijuana, but also failed to have them tailed even though they were absolute strangers transporting more than a million dollars' worth of merchandise across the country. More reason to gripe was the fact that he and they guys in Texas didn't know how to count. Instead of loading 1,000 pounds onto the truck, they added an extra 400, thereby placing us in jeopardy of longer sentences.

Since we didn't yet have lawyers, a lady from the public defenders' office stood in for us. When she introduced herself, and began to brief us on the hearing, Angel pretended to have difficulty understanding English, so an interpreter had to be assigned to assist him and Yeyo. The lady asked if we wanted the court to appoint us attorneys, and Angel said yes. Yeyo and I, however, were planning to retain the lawyer Bud referred. When I relayed such plans to the public defender, she looked surprised.

"Don't waste your money," she advised me. "He can't get you any better deal than I can."

I had no interest in copping a deal—I wanted to go home!

"What are the chances of a bond?" I asked, changing the subject.

"That's not going to happen; the judge isn't going to let

you out on bond," she retorted, bursting my bubble of hope.

I leaned back in the chair and pursed my lips, thinking of a way to get around the pessimistic public defender. It seemed that every question I asked was met with a negative response.

According to her, I didn't have anything coming, and she didn't even know the facts of the case. In fact, she wasn't even my lawyer; she was just some pessimistic lady standing by to ensure that I understood the charges alleged in the complaint.

When the judge entered the courtroom, all talking ceased and we all senselessly rose to our feet only to return to our seats a few seconds later. He simply asked if we had read the complaint and understood the charges. He then ordered that we be interviewed by the probation department and returned before him two days later for a detention hearing.

After the hearing we were locked in a bullpen down in the basement to await an interview with someone from the probation department and, then, our ride back to the jail. Since we now knew that everything was Angel's fault, and that there was no way out for him, I urged him to take the rap and tell the feds that I had no idea what was inside the van, and that I was simply chauffeuring them around.

He said that he'd take the rap, but at the same time, his nerves sent him to the toilet to take a crap, just like the time in the holding cell at the jail; only this time, it was no laughing matter.

Back at the jail I was bombarded with questions as soon as I stepped into the unit. Steve and Bud were the primary inquirers. Ironically, although Bud seemed overly interested, he'd already learned most of the details of my case from his attorney. He seemed to know more about my case than I did. Apparently, he and his attorney talked right after the hearing, for he knew that the truckers were in fact undercovers, and that the marijuana weighed 1,400 pounds rather than 1,000.

Knowing what I now know, I'd say that Bud and his lawyer were snooping on me with ill intent. But at that time, I assumed the lawyer was connected and capable of pulling the right strings to get me out of jail. I didn't hesitate to call the lawyer and inquire about his representing me and Yeyo. Although he agreed to take the case, he could only represent one of us. And being that Yeyo had the most money, he chose to represent Yeyo and referred me to another lawyer who met with me the following morning and demanded $40,000 up front.

Two days later when we returned before the magistrate, Yeyo's sixty-thousand-dollar attorney was at his side, the pessimistic public defender was beside Angel, and I was alone. The public defender leaned over to me and whispered: "I don't know why your partner wasted his money on this guy—he's going to get the same results as my client." Since I didn't have a lawyer, and the lawyer whom I intended to retain was sitting in the gallery, the magistrate asked him if he'd represent me under the Criminal Justice Act (at the court's expense). Not wanting to offend the man in the black robe, the lawyer reluctantly agreed. Later, he informed me that I wouldn't receive the same service as a paying client. I offered to throw him a few extra dollars under the table, but he declined.

Allowing time for the paperwork to be processed, the court postponed my detention hearing and allowed Yeyo and Angel's to proceed. To my surprise, the public defender representing Angel appeared to be a much better litigator and advocate than Yeyo's expensive attorney. I soon learned that she was no pessimist at all. In fact, she was simply a realist; everything she said would happen actually happened.

CHAPTER 3

HEAD BUSTER

"We some head busters...We some head busters... We will knock a hater out ... We some head busters" a rowdy group of prisoners chanted and sang along to the lyrics of a rap song blaring from the TV. They were so hyped that, had I not known any better, I would have thought they were actually intent on busting someone's head. As I entered the unit, I silently, yet sarcastically, prayed that I wouldn't be mistaken for a hater.

I safely made it through the dayroom without being attacked by anyone but Bud and Steve, who drilled me with questions about my case. Being in no mood for talk, I gave them vague answers and continued to my cell where I could be alone, engrossed in my thoughts, and worry myself to some type of solution; or better yet, sleep the days away and dream that I was elsewhere.

Initially I found that sleeping and dreaming was better than facing reality, but as the days passed and I grew tired of dreaming and worrying, I began to hang out in the dayroom more often. Many prisoners found this to be the perfect time to spark conversations about their case and to search for information about mine. Most of the prisoners were facing extremely lengthy sentences for nonviolent drug offenses, and it seemed that hope and dope (dope in the form of antidepressants and other medication) were their only means of coping. Many prisoners liked to talk to me because I had sympathetic ears, strong shoulders, and a little understanding of the law. In talking to me, they found a sense of hope.

Ironically, I had the ability to provide hope even when I myself didn't have any. I guess it was my ability to empathize—which was fueled by my own fears and curiosity—that made me the ideal prisoner to vent to. Little did the other prisoners know, I secretly sought answers of my own, and the more they talked and vented, the more I learned about my new environment and the legal web I'd become tangled in, a web that entangled us all as brothers of a common struggle.

Our common struggle as prisoners of the War on Drugs created an automatic superficial bond amongst us. We were able to relate to each other's sorrow and anguish; therefore, we often supported each other in a hospitable way. For example, we shared books, commissary, information, advice, etc., and respected each other to a certain degree.

However, by no means were our relations all fine and dandy. That same common struggle that bonded us also divided us. Many prisoners plotted against one another and sacrificed each other in hopes of gaining favor from the prosecutor and the court. For most, a reduced sentence was the only conceivable means of getting out of the trouble they found themselves in—they called it "helping myself." As a result, we were like a bunch of crabs in a bucket crawling over each other and pulling each other down in hopes of getting out.

The misperception that prisons are filled with buff, angry guys who despise all snitches was now being proven to be just that—a misperception. The feds had a way of turning the toughest wannabe gangster into a snitch. To return to the illusory life style depicted in most rap videos (the flashy clothes, fancy cars, shallow women, and egotistical behavior), many prisoners were willing to secretly be the snitch that most rappers claimed to despise. The experience was mind boggling.

The cutthroat, snitching culture was new to me, and it started getting close to home one morning when a prisoner named Leandro returned from court with good news and bad news. The good news was that he'd pled guilty and was granted release on bond pending his sentence. The bad news was that he'd seen Angel at the court building with two federal agents. We didn't have any court hearings, and weren't expecting any until the indictment, in which the prosecutor had 30 days from the date of arrest to file. So the only logical assumption was that Angel was cooperating and debriefing. Upon hearing the bad news, I immediately began to worry, almost to the degree of panic.

To ensure that Angel wouldn't renege on his promise to help vindicate me, I desperately asked Leandro to make a call and relay a message for me upon his release. "Call my homeboy and tell him that I believe the dude from Texas is snitching, and that I need him to get at the people in L.A. to make sure that he keep his mouth shut," I told Leandro. He agreed to relay the message upon his release the following day, but he also told Bud about the situation. Later that day, Bud approached me and offered his assistance in getting a message to Angel, and the streets if necessary. Bud was scheduled for a visit from his attorney that evening, so he offered to sneak to Angel's unit en route and slip a note under the door if I wanted. He also offered to relay messages to the streets through his visits. I declined the latter, but I did give him a non-incriminating note to pass to Angel.

Bud left for his attorney visit around 7 p.m. and returned 40 minutes later. I was sitting in the dayroom talking to Amad, another prisoner from L.A., when Bud walked into the unit shaking his head and indicating that something had went wrong.

With little regard for Amad's presence, he came straight to the table and gave me a spiel about a guard walking up behind him and confiscating the note as he was attempting to slide it through the gap underneath the door to Angel's unit. He then told me not to worry because he was in the process of trying to get the note back.

"Maybe he will get it back," Amad later joked. "After the feds make a copy of it." He went on to warn me that I needed to be careful with Bud because he was suspected of being a "head buster." Misunderstanding what he meant by the term *head buster*, I replied that I too was capable of busting heads.

Sensing my lack of understanding, Amad explained that the term "head buster" was another word for snitch throughout the federal prison system. According to Amad, many of the prisoners in the unit were head busters, including Bud and Steve. Snitching is so prevalent in the feds that there is a saying that goes: 85 percent do, and the other 15 percent will soon wish they would have done so.

Although I kept hearing about head-busters, I didn't really realize the significance of the term until a prisoner named Benny returned from court one evening rubbing his head. Benny was a red-faced, scrawny, white dude from rural Missouri. Benny liked to refer to himself as "white trash," which seemed to suggest that in the criminal justice system, he fared only slightly better than the black prisoners. According to him, his troubles began when he visited a friend's house in the boondocks of southern Illinois. While he and his friend sipped beers and caught up on old-times, a dozen local and federal law enforcement officers raided the house and arrested both of them.

According to Benny, he had no idea that his friend was manufacturing and selling meth from his home. One of the sales had taken place during Benny's visit. "Don't worry ol' buddy—I'll let 'em know you had absolutely nothing to do with this," were the last words Benny had heard from his friend. Soon thereafter they both were indicted by the feds.

Having gone a month without hearing a word from his court-appointed attorney, Benny was taken to court expecting to have some type of status hearing. When he arrived in the basement of the court building, however, he was issued a pair of black slacks, a white button-up shirt, and a pair of black hard-bottoms which were two sizes too big for his feet. Dressed in oversized hand-me-downs, a baffled Benny was hustled into the courtroom where his attorney greeted him with a superficial handshake and a practiced smile.

"Ready to rock-n-roll?" the lawyer asked.

"What's going on?" Benny inquired.

"Today's the big day—we're going to pick a jury here shortly," the attorney replied.

Stunned, confused, and apprehensive, Benny tried to talk the lawyer into slowing things down and giving them a moment to talk about it. But the lawyer looked Benny square in the eyes and gave him two options: Either plead guilty or let the trial proceed. With trembling legs and a crackly voice, Benny bravely sat back and let the trial begin. After all, his friend would get him out of this mess—he was sure of that.

A little past 6 o'clock, a beet-red Benny stumbled into the unit sporting a sorrowful expression and rubbing the crown of his head.

"How'd it go?" a nosey prisoner asked.

"Started trial," Benny mumbled.

"What!" Benny's cellmate exclaimed, upon overhearing the conversation. Benny nodded, and an inaudible "yea" escaped his lips.

Going to trial is extremely rare in the feds; in fact, 97 percent of federal cases result in a plea of guilty. So as word of Benny's trial quickly spread through the unit, prisoners began to form a crowd around him and ask how it was going.

"Not good," Benny somberly replied.

"What about your friend?" his cellmate asked. "Isn't he going to testify for you?"

"The no good bastard testified, alright," Benny replied, animated and angry. "The son-of-a-bitch testified against me!"

Benny's response sucked the air out of the unit and caused everyone to gasp as if they'd just witnessed a baby falling from a tenth-story balcony.

While Benny carried on about how his friend lied and accused him of helping manufacture and distribute meth, Amad tauntingly winced and clutched his head as if he'd been whacked in the head. "Ouch!" Amad sardonically interjected. "Somebody get Benny a bandage."

Unable to hold it in, the crowd erupted with laughter at Amad's sardonic sense of humor.

The following day, Benny returned from court and went directly to his cell and slept for weeks. That's when I really began to understand the meaning of the term *head buster*. It was like Benny's friend had crept up behind him and whacked him in the back of his head with a sledge hammer.

CHAPTER 4

CAN'T DO IT!

It had been well over 30 days since our arrest, and I still hadn't heard anything about an indictment being filed. According to the Speedy Trial Act, the government had 30 days from the date the criminal complaint was filed to file an indictment or set me free. On the 29th day, I began to feel optimistic; on the 30th day, I was upbeat; on the 33rd day, I was walking around with a smile on my face; and on March 2nd, I was taken to court and arraigned on an indictment that had been filed, unbeknownst to me, two weeks earlier on February 18th, 2004. Count One charged that Angel, Yeyo, and I, as well as others known and unknown to the grand jury, knowingly conspired to possess with intent to distribute in excess of 100 kilograms of marijuana. Count Two charged the three of us with possessing marijuana with the intent to distribute. Both charges carried a statutory sentence of 5-40 years.

I was dismayed by the charges and the penalties they carried. I had absolutely no idea that a person could be sentenced to so much time for marijuana. Had I known, I would've found me another hustle and left the marijuana business to the drug cartels. I honestly thought that the most a man could get for marijuana was five years. I found myself wishing that I had murdered someone and been caught for it—at least then I wouldn't have been facing so much time behind bars.

Now that the charges were officially pending, my mother retained an African American lady from St. Louis to represent me. Initially, I wasn't buying the advice from the public defender lady who said that all attorneys were the same. But after a couple of visits from my new attorney, I found myself wishing that I had taken the public defender's advice. My attorney was no different than any other attorney. The only thing unique about her was her physique. She had the body of an African goddess, and I enjoyed peeking at her derriere more than I appreciated her legal advice.

Perhaps I was in a state of denial and didn't want to believe what she was saying, but I felt that she was trying to scare me into pleading guilty. According to her, my statutory sentence range would be enhanced due to a prior drug conviction. Instead of 5-40 years, I was looking at anywhere from 10 years to life without parole. And let her tell it, I would likely be sentenced in the range of 30 years to life. Overall, she advised me to cooperate and plead guilty or be prepared to lose in trial and spend the rest of my 20s, all of my 30s, all of my 40s, all of my 50s, and perhaps the rest of my life behind bars. Refusing to take her advice—or even further entertain it—I wanted nothing more than for her to shut up, stand up, and sashay out of the interview room. I liked her much better when she was standing and leaving than sitting and talking.

The days following my attorney's bad news, I found myself subconsciously repeating the phrase: "Can't do it!" I said it so much that several other prisoners started mimicking it. Before long it wasn't unusual to see several prisoners walking around saying: "Can't do it!" The difference between my saying it and their saying it, however, was that they were simply saying it because it was a catchy phrase; whereas, I was saying it because I really meant it—I couldn't do it!

I constantly thought about Lorrie being out there alone pregnant with my child. The thoughts were driving me crazy. I understood the difficulties and pains associated with being a single parent, and the child of a single parent. Parenting is the most exhausting job in the world; it is a 24-hour duty that requires undivided attention and support beyond food and shelter. It involves constant monitoring of the child's daily activities to ensure that he or she isn't being exposed to people, places, and things that could lead to unhealthy thoughts and behavior. And, then, if somehow exposed to such an unhealthy environment, a parent must be observant and wise enough to recognize the effect it might have on the child's psyche, and know what it will take to counter it. This is why raising a healthy and productive child often requires more than one parent can offer. I often worried that any negative traits or behavior by my daughter at the age of seventeen would fall squarely on my own conscience. For that matter, and for the sake of my child's well-being, I couldn't sit behind bars. I couldn't do it.

Most of the other 39 prisoners in the unit couldn't do it either. But although they constantly whined and moped–something I didn't do–they were actually complacent and defeated. They shuffled about the unit all day in their orange jumpsuits, often consumed with playing table games and watching TV like zombies. The only time they seemed to be alive was when they were either playing dominoes or watching rap videos, at which times the few white prisoners would become disgruntled and storm to their cells where they'd try to sleep the day away. Very few prisoners exercised, read books, or tried to conjure up a way out, and all of them routinely formed a single-file line at the door to receive medication from the nurses when they made their rounds twice a day.

This was my new environment and perhaps my new life, and the sights and thoughts of it were depressing. I couldn't do it. I couldn't accept the thought of spending the next several decades in such a somber and debilitating environment, especially for nothing–I hadn't killed anyone. And although prisons were usually better than county jails, I couldn't do them either. I couldn't see myself doing 30 years of terrible food, thin mattresses, loud noise, unnecessary violence, restricted movement, unnecessary strip-searches and punitive shakedowns. I couldn't accept being trapped on a concrete island without beaches, tropical fruit, or women, an island with nothing but rotten apples, rotten souls, rotten egos, and men–too damn many of them. I couldn't imagine spending the remainder of my days trapped in a world that lacks purpose, one without tomorrows and where yesterdays are just that— yesterdays. I was hardened and sickened by the thought of enduring such cruel and evil existence for decades, all because of a natural leaf that was on the verge of being legal. I couldn't do it.

On the other hand, I didn't have many options. A simple guilty plea likely would have saved my 50s and a year or so of my 40s. But I wasn't willing to voluntarily forfeit 20 years of my life for something so harmless and victimless as entering a disabled van containing marijuana. I'd wasted too much of my life, and I couldn't afford to waste another twenty years, especially at the crossroads of my life. And again, I certainly wasn't willing to do so voluntarily.

Another option was to cooperate. Snitching would've saved my 40s and possibly some of my 30s, depending on the value of the information I were to provide, the amount of property seized, and the number of arrests and convictions resulting from such information. However, I couldn't do that either. I wasn't selfish and coward enough to intentionally sacrifice dozens of lives and families for the sake of my own.

Furthermore, I didn't agree with the War on Drugs, and certainly couldn't find myself supporting it under any conditions. I'd rather rot than assist the government in a racist war that was arguably designed to overpopulate prisons with nonviolent, financially-oriented black men. I can't do it!

My only other option at the time was to put my fate in the hands of a predominately white jury that likely wouldn't know more about a young black man than what they've seen in *The Wire, Gangland*, rap videos, and other stereotypical "jiggaboo" negro TV shows. Having witnessed the results of what such a jury did to Benny, I was convinced that I couldn't stand a chance. In fact, sadly to say, I preferred to be carried by 6 blacks than to be judged by 12 whites.

CHAPTER 5

A WAY OUT

Having concluded that I was neither pleading guilty nor going to trial, I began to search for an alternative. I didn't know what that alternative would be until it came to me one sunny afternoon while I was looking out the window in the back of my cell. As I sat on the top bunk, gazing at freedom, thinking about the fact that Lorrie was indeed pregnant with my child, and cursing myself for the opportunities I'd squandered, the tantalizing sight of freedom fused with my fear of injustice induced thoughts of breaking out of jail.

When I had first looked out the window nearly two months earlier, there was snow on the ground. Now the snow was gone and the winter had rapidly melted away, paving the way for spring and my dreadful May 3rd trial date, which was quickly approaching. My only refuge was outside the window on the other side of the razor wired fence. Thus, my only hope of escaping what I feared to be injustice was by escaping jail altogether, by finding a way to get on the other side of the window and disappearing like the winter.

The window was a long and narrow structure running horizontally from one wall to the other. Vertically, it was only 16 inches. The 16inch space would've been more than enough for me to slip through had there not been a hollow, rectangular bar running horizontally across the middle. *Only if that bar wasn't there*, I wished. But wishing wasn't enough–I needed to find a way to make it disappear. Although I hadn't the slightest idea how, I did have a strong will. And I knew that wherever there's a will there's a way–an ambitious heart and mind is half the way to success. So, guided by desperation and determination, I sought out ways to break out of jail.

I started by seeking information; for after ambition comes

knowledge and application. In my quest for info, I discreetly picked the brains of other prisoners for details about the jail, the surrounding neighborhood, and anything else that could be useful to my cause. Surprisingly, I was no longer the naturally shy and quiet introvert who only entertained conversations of humor and substance. In my desperate search for information, I found myself entertaining frivolous conversations and subtly steering them in the direction of the jail, the neighborhood, and demolition and construction of homes and buildings. I even surreptitiously pried for information that might lead me in the direction of a piece of metal that could be used to chisel through the cinder-block wall, or a stone that could be used to grind and saw through the bar in the window.

One day, while talking to a prisoner named "Haystack," who'd spent most of his life working construction jobs, I learned about a tool which he referred to as a *Saw-Zaw*. He described it as an electrically-operated hacksaw, and claimed that it could be used to cut anything from plastic to metals. I had never seen a hacksaw blade before, but I'd heard of them being used to saw down the barrels of shotguns, and I once had my car stolen by someone who used a hacksaw to cut my steering wheel and remove the security club. Other than that, I knew nothing about hacksaws, let alone a *Saw-Zaw*. Nevertheless, when Haystack told me that the blades for the magical *Saw-Zaw* came in a variety of sizes, I began to think of ways to smuggle one into the jail.

It didn't take long for me to figure it out. After observing how mail was being delivered at the jail, I devised a plan to smuggle a saw concealed inside a package of confidential legal mail. Specifically, I noticed that on Saturdays, when the regular mail officer was off duty, random guards would pass out mail, and they did a poor job of inspecting it. The lady who normally passed out mail, Monday through Friday, routinely flipped through the pages of the incoming legal mail; whereas, the random guards who distributed it on

Saturdays simply opened the envelope and peeked inside.

Using a series of coded letters and phone calls, I reached out to my cousin for assistance in smuggling the saw. I instructed him to conceal a five-inch reciprocating saw blade between two sheets of pasted papers, and to place the pasted papers in the middle of a stack of more papers and documents. Per my instructions, the stack of documents was placed inside a large manila envelope with the return address of an unwitting attorney and mailed to me via priority mail. It was mailed Thursday morning and due to arrive Saturday.

Coincidentally, that Friday several prisoners were transferred to the Federal Bureau of Prison, thereby freeing up a cell on the top tier. Without hesitation, or permission from the guards, I moved into the cell. It was the perfect cell for me to escape from. The window in the back was Plexiglas and much easier to escape through than the tempered glass in most of the other cells. It was also facing the back of the jail, which was obstructed by trees and shrubs, and invisible to the pedestrians and motorists travelling the streets around the jail—the only eyes that frequented the back of the jail were those of the deer that occasionally sipped water from a creek on the other side of the razor wired fence. More importantly, I was the only person in the cell, leaving nobody but me to witness my escape.

My first night in the cell, I was awakened in the middle of the night by a bright spotlight beaming through the back window. I was sleeping on the top bunk, so the light reflected off the ceiling and shined onto my face. I awoke, startled and confused, and slowly rose to look out the window and investigate the source of the light, but I couldn't see anything because the bright light blinded me. It wasn't until the light began to move that I realized it was a searchlight attached to the side of a police cruiser making perimeter checks around the jail. I prayed that it was routine or random, because anything else could've meant that the cops were aware of my escape plans.

Fearing the worst, I stayed awake most of the night, looking out the window. The police cruiser never circled the jail again that night, yet my nerves remained edgy, and my mind was seized by rampant worries that the saw had been discovered in the package. Every thirty minutes when the guards made their routine cell checks, I half expected them to pull me from the cell and take me to the hole. I didn't stop worrying until Saturday afternoon when a guard entered the unit with a white bin filled with mail.

While most prisoners crowded around the guard, I stayed inside my cell and spied from the narrow window on my door. The guard sat the bin of mail on a table in the dayroom and yelled out "Mail Call!" as if we weren't already aware. He then pulled out a stack of mail and started calling out names. Peeking out the window, I found myself subconsciously trying to locate my package within the stack—as if that were possible. When he pulled out a large manila envelope, my heart began to palpitate with concern and excitement. At that moment I knew the saw had arrived.

The guard called out my name, but, not wanting to give the impression that I was anticipating the package, I stayed inside the cell and pretended that I hadn't heard him. I let the guard and a nosey prisoner call my name a few times before emerging from my cell with a whimsical expression on my face. I was nervous, but also excited and prepared for the worst.

The package was sitting on the table when I arrived downstairs. The guard picked it up, and after weighing it in his hand and commenting on its heaviness, he asked if he could take a look inside, as if I had a say in the matter. I shook my head, indicating that I didn't mind—which I didn't as long as he wouldn't inspect the pages. He tore open the envelope and pulled out a stack of papers that had to be at least two inches thick. At that moment, I stepped closer, preparing to snatch the papers and run to the nearest toilet and flush them if necessary. But instead of flipping through the papers, he simply shook them and handed them to me. I grabbed the papers and began to walk away.

"Adams," the guard yelled, stopping me as I began to climb the stairs.

"You want the envelope?" he asked, with a quizzical expression.

I had been so ecstatic about receiving the package that I forgot the envelope sitting on the table. I grabbed the envelope and calmly walked up the stairs two steps per stride.

Once inside the privacy of my cell, I hastily combed through the papers and found the saw taped between two sheets of paper that were pasted together. I eagerly ripped the saw from the paper and stared at it as if it were a jewel. I then tested it on the edge of the bunk and was overcome with joy when the teeth of the saw grinded against the metal edge of the bunk, slowly turning it to metallic sawdust. It was hard to believe that such a tiny thing could actually set me free. It was now just a matter of sweat and time, something I had plenty of.

For the most part, I was confident in my plans—I had gone over them in my head many times. I'd cut the end of the bar, then the Plexiglas windowpane, and escape by climbing out of the window and onto the roof of the jail where I'd be less visible. Once outside the jail, I'd go to a payphone up the street and call Dominique (whose sister lived nearby) for a ride. It was that simple.

My only concern was the other prisoners in the unit. By now, I knew that most of them were snitches in desperate search for information to report to the feds in hopes of receiving a reduced sentence. I particularly worried about a group of prisoners whom I called the "Rat Pack." Comprised of Steve, Bud, a 400-pound snitch named "Heavy," and several other prisoners, the Rat Pack held daily meetings and exchanged detailed information about crimes, drug deals, and other prisoners' cases. They would then alter the facts, tailoring them into criminal tales of great interest to the feds, and then present them to the feds individually so that they seemed more credible. In essence, they were duping the government by exchanging fabricated tales for reduced sentences. They even went so far as to encourage their friends and family to gather and provide information about drug dealers in society on their behalf. Sadly, some cops and prosecutors didn't mind that the stories were fabricated, as long as they helped secure convictions.

To me, the Rat Pack were some of the lowest breed of humans. They were not too far above rapists and child-molesters. I couldn't stand them. But I did appreciate two things about them. One, between them and the phony truckers, I realized how cutthroat the drug business was, and how selfish and cold-blooded one must be to prosper in it. The Rat Pack didn't care how many dudes they helped bury in prison, nor who it was, as long as it helped shorten their stay. The second thing I appreciated about the snitches in the unit was their propensity to be extremely noisy. Every day, they would gather in the dayroom, talking loudly, arguing over nothing, and slamming dominoes on the metal tables. While they spent their days in the dayroom behaving raucously, I spent mine in the cell noisily sawing through the bar in my window. I appreciated them dearly for that.

There was a moment, though, when I came close to killing one of the snitches. I had been in my cell for hours with the window on my door covered when a nosey prisoner barged in. The prisoner wasn't my friend. I'd rarely spoken to him, and we had nothing to talk about. Therefore, he had absolutely no reason to enter my cell, especially while I had the window on my door covered. He pretended that he was just checking on me, but I suspected otherwise. When I looked out into the dayroom, I saw the other snitches looking up at the cell as if they'd sent him to investigate my secretive behavior. Obviously, he was snooping around, and that was cause for me to saw his head off with the saw—at least punch him in the face—but I had too much to lose to risk being placed in the hole at the moment. Instead of punching him in his mouth, I suppressed the urge and simply scolded him about entering my cell.

When I first started sawing, I expected to be done within a week, but I encountered several obstacles that set me back. First, the saw broke two days after I started sawing, forcing me to order a new one and wait nearly five days for it to arrive. Then, when I resumed sawing, I encountered a solid, narrow, cylindrical bar inside the hollow, rectangular bar. And, to my dismay, the cylindrical bar seemed impossible to cut.

Stuck at a dead end, I desperately consulted my unwitting advisor, Haystack. I tried to pick his brain without tipping him about the bar or my plans; however, after several minutes of impatiently getting nowhere, I reluctantly told him about the bar and invited him into my cell to see for himself. He said that the cylindrical bar was probably a roller bar (a bar designed to roll whenever grinded by a saw), and suggested that I find a way to jam it and prevent it from rolling. Or else, he said, I would have to apply enough pressure to bend and snap it.

I first tried to prevent the bar from rolling whenever I sawed by jamming paper between it and the rectangular bar. When that didn't work, I cut the middle and both ends of the rectangular bar to loosen it; then I tied a sheet around the middle and started yanking on it in hopes of bending the roller bar inside. The roller bar bent slightly, but my 195 pounds wasn't enough to break it or bend it sufficiently for me to squeeze through. I had Haystack help, but he and I weren't enough either. Figuring that it would take at least three prisoners to bend the bar to its breaking point, I removed the sheet and sought help.

Finding a third party proved to be difficult. I had to weave through a unit filled with snitches and find the right person. Unfortunately, B.G. had been moved to Max a few days earlier, so I was left with Haystack, Amad, and Lorro, neither of whom had the desire to escape. And although they were willing to assist me, neither was willing to do so in the presence of the other. They trusted me, but they didn't trust the other. And that lack of trust prevented us from coming together and conquering an obstacle so trivial as a three-inch cylindrical bar.

Out of all of the prisoners in the unit, there was one whom Amad was willing to trust. At 6'2" 240 lbs., John was a big, corn-fed, white dude who seemed like the perfect help. He was a seasoned criminal who'd been in and out of prison for violent crimes, and now he was facing a lengthy sentence for being an armed career criminal. A week earlier, he and Amad had been quarantined in the minimum security section of the jail due to an outbreak of suspicious-looking bumps during a time when the jail was plagued with staph. While in quarantine, John discovered an easy escape route and planned to take advantage of it, but he was moved back to the unit before he could execute such plans.

Back in the unit, John constantly talked about trying to return to quarantine so that he could escape. He constantly talked about escaping; he even made a comment about sawing through the bar in his cell window. I didn't really take him seriously because it was common for prisoners to talk about breaking out, but very few had the courage and wit to actually do so. But according to Amad, John wasn't the average prisoner; he was seriously interested in breaking out. Therefore, Amad suggested that I take John as a partner.

The three of us met inside my cell to discuss the plan. I suggested that we tie sheets around the bar, break it, and then have Amad create a distraction while John and I exit the window, climb onto the roof, crawl to the front of the jail

43

where there was no fence, hop down, and walk away. John, on the other hand, wanted to exit the window, scale down the wall, hop the razor wired fence, and run through the woods where he'd have his friend, guns, and a get-away car waiting for us. With the guns, he suggested we go rob people. However, I didn't want any guns or robberies; I simply wanted to disappear quietly without disturbance. I also worried about sensors being around the fence, cameras aiming downward, and potential harm hidden in the woods—particularly deer. The only things I knew about deer were that they senselessly ran headlong into moving vehicles and pulled Santa Claus's sleigh. If they were capable of doing anything else—like attacking and capturing escaping prisoners—I didn't want to learn about it first-hand. Thus, I disagreed with John's plans.

After wasting several minutes haggling and debating whether or not guns and a get-away ride were necessary, we finally got down to business. We tied sheets around the middle of the bar and vigorously yanked and tugged. But disappointingly our 670 pounds of body weight wasn't enough to snap the bar. It was only enough to warp it. And although this might've created sufficient space for me, it didn't for John, who instantly became discouraged and defeated, and pleaded for a break.

During the break, John was behaving strangely. He wandered back and forth from the phone to the Plexiglas window in the dayroom, and when the nurse came to pass out the medication and forgot his, he yelled a slew of profanities at her, even calling her a "black bitch," which ignited the indignation of many prisoners including the snitches. With half the unit contemplating kicking John's ass, he roamed around the unit apologizing and claiming that his friends were black. To prevent things from getting out of hand and jeopardizing my escape, I went to John's rescue. Amad and I pulled him into the cell and told him to chill out because he was jeopardizing the escape. At that moment, John explained that he was frustrated because he was unable to reach his friend with the get-away ride. He asked that we postpone the escape until the following day and allow him time to secure a get-away. He also pleaded that I not leave without him.

Initially Amad was in total agreement with John—as far as having a get-away ride and designated place to go—but after witnessing John's bizarre behavior in the dayroom, he began to suspect that John was either scared or full of shit, and suggested that I leave without him. Not only did we have another prisoner willing to help break the bar, but also the bar was so warped that I probably could've squeezed my slender frame through the gap between it and the windowsill.

Instead of attempting to leave that night, though, I decided to wait until the following evening. After all, it was Sunday night, and I was confident that the guards wouldn't search the unit on a busy Monday. And with a little camouflage and adjustments to the window, I was confident that the warped bar and damaged window would go unnoticed until the following evening. So Amad and I readjusted the warped bar, and I camouflaged it by placing items in the windowsill. On that note, I called it a night and promised to leave immediately after dusk the following day—with or without John.

CHAPTER 6

SOMETHING ABOUT THE EYES

Monday morning, I was awakened by the sound of the cell doors buzzing open, signifying the end of what had been a miserable night of tossing and turning. My anxious mind had been burdened all night with unwanted thoughts of the warped bar being discovered. Every time the guards made their rounds I prayed that they wouldn't shine their flashlights on the back window and ask me to remove the camouflaging items on the windowsill. So when I awoke to dawn peeping through the window, I was relieved to have made it through the night.

With 12 hours till dusk, and very little chance of a shakedown, I climbed down to the bottom bunk and went back to sleep. It had been a weary night, and I had another one ahead of me. With incessant thoughts of escaping overwhelming my mind, I dreamt that I had escaped and jumped a freight train traveling West. I hopped off the train somewhere in a small mid-western town, wearing nothing but a white t-shirt and boxers. I mysteriously found myself conspicuously standing in front of a Wal-Mart contemplating my next move. Suddenly, three collegiate girls exited the store and flirtatiously offered me clothes and a ride. I accepted and hopped in the back seat of their blue Chevy Lumina.

Unexpectedly, the setting changed, and I found myself pacing dingy carpet in a cheap, two-bed motel room in Albuquerque, New Mexico. One of the girls was there, lying fully dressed on one of the beds. She pleaded for me to relax and join her, but I couldn't—I had neither time nor composure for cuddling with her. I was anxious and buzzing with paranoia and excitement. It wasn't until after pacing holes into the carpet that I reluctantly sat at the edge of the bed and looked into the girl's eyes. They were blue and empty—

just like John's—and she had prominent crow's feet as if she had eerily aged several decades in just several seconds. She smiled, revealing an exorbitant number of teeth, and then I heard someone on a bullhorn shout: "We have the place surrounded, so come out with your hands up!" It sounded like a scene in a 1970s cop movie, long before the War on Drugs⬚ militarization of police forces, and back when they knocked before entering.

I jumped from the bed and ran to the window and saw a circus of policemen surrounding the motel. Moronically, I ran back to the bed and hid under the blanket while the lady continued to smile and gaze at me through a set of vacant, blue eyes. "Get dressed!" she commanded, as if I were naked. I tried to respond, but the words wouldn't come out. "Get dressed!" she repeated. Suddenly, I awoke. It was all a terrible dream, but there was an old, blue-eyed guard standing in my doorway. "Did you hear me?" he asked. "Get up and get dressed. The maintenance guys are coming to the unit to do some work."

The guard's words resonated, and I immediately thought about the window and began to panic. There was absolutely nothing I could do but pray that the workers wouldn't look inside my cell and notice the damaged window. I prayed, but I had a bad vibe that something was wrong. I couldn't wrap my mind around it, but there was something eerily disturbing about that nightmare and those empty blue eyes. It was almost ominous.

Everyone was evacuated from the unit and ushered down to the gym. As we filed out of the unit, I noticed that John was absent. Downstairs in the gym, I learned that he had been called for an attorney visit shortly before the evacuation. Amad found the timing of John's visit suspicious, and after giving it some thought, so did I. Everything had been working fine in the unit, so the guard's claim that the workers were coming to do repairs didn't sit well with me and Amad. While the rest of the prisoners played basketball, Amad and

I wandered around, suspecting that John had snitched on us.

After several laps around the basketball court, Amad tried to ease my worries by suggesting that John might have not snitched on us and that he probably really did have an attorney visit. Amad was often confident and optimistic; in fact, he was the same guy who believed that an old, white judge would go against a white cop and rule that the cop illegally detained Amad and searched his car. But I knew that he really didn't believe John was visiting his attorney. I was almost certain that John had snitched, and so was Amad. So when a guard came to the gym and told us that we too had attorney visits, we already knew what was going on.

Before leaving the gym, I walked to the toilet and flushed my saw. We walked upstairs and were escorted up the corridor to the front of the jail where we were greeted by two U.S. Marshal deputies and an African American detective who had a fresh cold sore on his lip. As anticipated, the detective did all of the talking, using the typical wannabe-hip-negro-cop approach. He told the guard to lock me inside a holding cell while they took Amad upstairs to be interrogated. Apparently, Amad didn't have much to say, because they came for me five minutes later.

Initially, I was hesitant about going into an interrogation room without a lawyer, but since I knew my way around the tricks and traps, and was aware that everything would be recorded, I went along. I was certain that no cop could trick me into saying something incriminating, especially this textbook, negro cop. While being questioned I feigned to be naive and innocent, I even shed a tear when the detective pretended to be concerned about me as a person as opposed to me as a criminal. My purpose in agreeing to the interrogation was to see what I could learn about the investigation. I wanted to subtly counter-interrogate the detective, so to speak. The more he talked, the more I was able to infer what happened.

The night before, when John realized that we couldn't

bend the bar sufficiently to accommodate his 240-pound frame, he devised another plan to escape the unit and the lengthy sentence he was facing: He decided to snitch. He stayed awake into the wee hours of the morning and passed the guards a note stating that Amad and I were trying to escape and that he needed to be moved down to the quarantine cell for his safety. He demonized me as a potential armed and dangerous escapist and portrayed himself as a redeemed criminal who was simply trying to save society from me and my atrocities. Truthfully, though, he wasn't concerned for public safety; he was concerned for self–helping himself. As a result, he was moved to the quarantine cell (where he later tried to execute an escape, but failed) and gained the favor of the prosecutor for his upcoming sentence. Obviously, John had outwitted all of us—me, Amad, the guards, the detective, and the government. Now I knew what it was about those vacant, blue eyes.

CHAPTER 7

THE CAN

Instead of returning to the unit, Amad and I were assigned to Max, the jail's administrative segregation unit. Max was merely two symmetrical hallways connected by a perpendicular passageway. Each hallway had a secure shower room and eight single-man cells on one side, and a tiled cinder-block wall on the other side. It had the eerie ambiance of a dungeon, completely devoid of sunlight, with very dim lights on the passageway. Paradoxically, the place was both noisy and quiet, with sound resonating throughout the unit even when there wasn't much noise.

The cells gave true meaning to the saying: Locked inside the can. Everything was metal—the walls, the ceiling, the sink/toilet, and the bunk, which was merely a slab of metal welded to the wall. And, as if the excessive metal weren't enough to wear down a prisoner's psyche, each cell was double secured with, both, a heavy, steel door and a set of bars four feet inside the cell.

Amad was placed in cell #4, and I was assigned to cell #8. When I entered the cell, I felt an eerie vibe. I felt like I was stepping into a trap with a huge, steel door and a set of bars. Once I was beyond the bars, the guard stepped into the cell and secured the barred gate behind me; then, he exited the cell and secured the heavy, steel door, emphasizing the fact that I was trapped.

I stood in the middle of the cell with my back to the bars and my hands behind my back. Subconsciously, I was reluctant to touch anything without first cleaning up. The cell was not only ghastly but also filthy. It appeared to be contaminated with the staph bacteria spreading throughout the jail. The stainless-steel toilet had slimy, green sewage caked around the inside of the bowl, and the mat that I was expected to sleep on was extremely thin and filthy.

My psyche was in a state of ambivalence and somewhat indescribable. The best I could do was say that I was sad, dismayed, worried, and relieved. I was sad about my defeat, dismayed by my hopelessness, worried about what might come of me, and relieved to have no choice. I also wondered how long I'd have to endure such conditions. The more I thought about it, the more I realized that my life had been reduced to a mere degree above death. I felt like I'd been released and immediately rearrested. Just hours earlier, I had been so close to freedom that it was palpable.

I had been able to see people, cars, trains, birds, deer, and sunshine. I had watched as the weather changed from winter to spring; from snow-topped lawns, streets, and pavements to green grass, trees, and shrubs. I had seen streets occupied by wandering people—the epitome of life and freedom. Now that was gone. My world was now engulfed by metal walls and bars, and I was able to hear nothing but raucous prisoners and clinking metal. So much metal.

Max quickly sucked the hope out of me. I was so depressed that I lay on the bare steel, using a roll of toilet paper for a pillow, and tried to sleep away the misery. I managed to escape life for about an hour before awakening to more depression and resentment. I was hurt and disappointed by John and many more betraying people, people I only tried to help. I was frustrated and tired, and unable to do anything about it but stare at the walls and worry, and that seemed to make me feel even more hopeless and dejected. After all, this was my life. A waste.

Later in the afternoon, as I still awaited cleaning supplies and a bedroll, I heard the sound of hard bottoms treading the passageway outside the cells. Apparently, the detective was well aware of the effects Max quickly had on prisoners, because when the hard-bottoms stopped clacking, he was standing outside my bars. During the interrogation earlier, he offered to transfer me to a better jail if I revealed the whereabouts of the saw. He was now stopping by to see if I changed my mind. "Have you reconsidered what we talked about?" he audaciously asked, in a hushed tone that was actually loud enough for everyone in Max to hear.

"I don't know nothing," I replied loud enough to ensure that everyone heard. "Ask your snitch—he seems to know everything else."

Still, the detective pressed on, pretending that he wasn't concerned with the "cuts on the bar," and only concerned with the saw being used to hurt one of the guards. He essentially tried to dupe me into providing him with evidence that could be used against me. Apparently my youthful, schoolboy looks had misled him into thinking that I was not only soft but also stupid.

While the detective was walking away from my cell, an unknown prisoner with a raspy, yet boisterous, voice yelled out:

"Sir, I know where the hacksaw blade is." The detective paused for a second, then resumed walking out of the unit. The detective must've known that the prisoner was playing games and simply trying to waste his time. That same prisoner had been running his mouth ever since I entered the unit that morning. It seemed that he found solace in harassing and taunting people. He was flagrantly nosey, antagonistic, and cynical, and had a bad habit of invading the conversations of others and inciting arguments without even introducing himself. For example, when he learned that Amad had a bedroll and I didn't, he alluded that Amad might've snitched on me.

"Fuck you—whoever you are!" Amad responded with anger.

"I'm Qusai," the antagonizing prisoner replied. "I kick ass and chew bubble gum."

Qusai—who actually did kick ass and chew bubble gum—was a federal detainee for the Eastern District of Missouri. He'd been in Max for nearly two years because of kicking ass without the bubble gum, including the ass of the Assistant U.S. Attorney who had successfully prosecuted his case. He had already been convicted and sentenced to 54 years for possession with intent to distribute heroin and assault on a government witness; now he was awaiting trial for assaulting the prosecutor. He was labeled as being extremely violent and, therefore, isolated in Max without physical contact with anyone.

He'd been isolated so long that talking, debating, and quarreling with others was his only source of entertainment. Quite naturally, all of the experience had allowed him to master the art of provocation, and he enjoyed putting his skills to use.

While Qusai and Amad quarreled, two more prisoners joined in, teaming up on Qusai. As everyone attacked him, he buzzed with excitement and laughter, encouraging and welcoming all contenders. He enjoyed every second of it, and the more people he had to quarrel with, the more companions he had to entertain him.

Oddly, when the dinner trays arrived, he gave his tray to one of the prisoners he'd been quarreling with; then, he sent Amad and the fourth party coffee and cookies and asked me what type of commissary I like to eat. Ironically, the violent, antagonistic Qusai was also benevolent, and whenever he wanted to be, he was smart. Overall, Qusai wasn't a bad dude.

The prisoner to whom Qusai gave his tray was in the cell next to me. At 6'4" and 240 pounds of solid muscle, he was an imposing figure. Nevertheless, the War on Drugs had reduced him to a puddle of tears. At 39 years old, he had just recently finished serving 21 consecutive years in prison, and now he was facing another 20 for possessing an ounce of heroin. The prospect of spending another 20 years of his already wasted life behind bars was enough to turn his eyes into perpetual watery and puffy sockets.

Most of his tears stemmed from his falling in love with

53

a woman during his short period of freedom. He couldn't fathom how a measly ounce of heroin could provide the government with the authority to tear his girlfriend away from him for two decades. Qusai teased that his love for the woman would lead to his betrayal of every drug dealer he'd ever dealt with. It was either snitch or lose the chick. Torn between the two, he could do nothing but cry and pray all night, and tote a pocket-size Bible all day.

Despite Qusai's suspicion of everyone in Max, it appeared that the can had a good share of non-snitching men. They certainly seemed more trustworthy than the prisoners in the fed block. This was probably true because Max was occupied mostly by state prisoners who were facing murder charges and, therefore, had no incentive to snitch. B.G., who was in the cell next to Qusai, preferred Max over the fed block because he didn't have to worry about federal prisoners such as the Rat Pack "hopping on his case." In fact, he had been moved to Max after several members of the Rat Pack falsely stated that he'd confessed details of his case to them.

If I had been surrounded by prisoners like those in Max while I was in the fed block, I would have been free. Instead, I had been surrounded by the Rat Pack and prisoners like John.

It had been more than a decade since I'd actually hated anyone, but as I sat in the can moping over my fiasco, I couldn't help but hate John with a passion. It has been said that hate comes from a lack of understanding, and at the moment, I couldn't understand how a captive could have the audacity to help the captors keep other captives captive. I wanted to kill John. He not only foiled my escape, but also lied. He even said that Amad was planning to escape with me, although Amad was confidently waiting to be released. John was the quintessential crud– a creep, snitch, and liar– and, unfortunately, it worked out in his favor for the moment.

Amid the misery, there soon came news to rejoice about. After just one week in the can, Amad received the good news he'd been optimistically awaiting. The Honorable Reagan bucked the trend of injustice and granted Amad's motion to suppress the evidence in his case due to a 4th Amendment violation. Amad had been arrested after he and his friend were pulled over by a person whom I like to refer to as a "Pirate of the Interstate" (a financially motivated cop who patrols the Interstate hunting for money and property to seize, or contraband that could lead to money and property being seized and divvied up by law enforcement officers). The "pirate" alleged that Amad had been driving recklessly, but this was just a pretext. Truthfully, he detained Amad and his partner because they fit his profile of drug couriers—minorities with out-of-state license plates. And just like a pirate on the high seas, the cop ransacked the car in search of valuables and discovered heroin concealed in a stash spot.

Fortunately, the pirate's lies weren't good enough to dupe the Honorable Reagan, who concluded that the seizure and search were unconstitutional and, therefore, the evidence resulting from the seizure could not be used at trial. Unable to present the drugs or any testimony of them, the government had no case. The funny thing, though, Amad's co-defendant had already cooperated and pled guilty; consequently, he couldn't benefit from the ruling. He ended up going to prison while Amad went home.

CHAPTER 8

SOUNDS OF FREEDOM

My first week in the can was long, dreary, and weary. The excessive steel, the turquoise walls, the tan ceiling, and the pavement splattered with an infinitive number of black, brown, tan, and gray specks which, at times, appeared to be crawling insects seemed to galvanize my misery. It was almost like that was the primary purpose of the cell—misery. Sleeping and dreaming seemed to be my only form of relief, and fortunately, that came naturally and abundantly as if the dreams were a defense to my reality, a reality that lacked both mental and emotional stimulation. I basically slept the entire week away. It was either that or I stayed awake and counted the specks on the floor.

After a week of feeling sick and tired, I quickly grew tired of feeling sick and tired. I steeled myself and faced reality. I started working out, and on several occasions I attempted to count the specks on the floor, only to lose count after one thousand. Some mornings when others were still asleep I'd lie on the bunk and enjoy the peace and quiet.

One quiet Saturday morning, as I lay on the bunk thinking, I heard a familiar, nostalgic sound resonating through the metal walls. I paused and held my breath, unable to believe that I was hearing what I was hearing. I had heard stories—and even witnessed them—of prisoners becoming delirious from excessive solitary confinement, so when I heard the sound, I began to wonder whether I too had gone delirious. (Perhaps that would've explained the times when the specks on the floor appeared to be crawling insects.) However, as the sound persisted, I became convinced that it was real.

I quietly rose from the bunk and crawled to the 12 by 12-inch exhaust vent at the back of the cell. I placed my ear to the vent and listened. The sound was now louder, clearer, and intriguingly, free. It was the wailing tunes and jingles of an ice cream truck making rounds through the neighborhood around the jail. The sound was reminiscent of my childhood days in L.A. where ice cream trucks, blaring music, and police helicopters were daily sounds. Hearing such a sound in solitary confinement was like seeing a rose sprout from concrete.

After the sound faded away, I yelled down to Qusai and asked if he'd heard it. He replied that he'd heard it several times before and that he'd heard sounds much more fascinating than an ice cream truck. He said that, at times, he'd heard cars, motorcycles, sirens, and people. He spoke of the sounds as though they were no big deal. Apparently, he didn't perceive them as I did—as an oasis in the desert. It never dawned on him that the unrestricted crisp sounds were a clear indication that freedom was much closer than expected. To him, they were merely sounds, but to me, they were sounds of freedom.

Ever since that morning, lying on the floor by the vent and listening for sounds of freedom became my favorite pastime. I would stay awake during the wee hours of the morning, listening. What intrigued me most about the sounds was that, despite them sounding like faint whispers from afar, they were right outside the building and seemed to be entering through some type of opening. And the mere thought of there being an opening not far beyond the metal walls opened a mental floodgate of many more thoughts and curiosities. Soon I found myself analyzing the entire structure of Max and the jail at large.

Max was two symmetrically identical units (E-unit and F-unit) parallel to each other inside of one wing. For example, the shower room on the F-side was directly behind the shower room on the E-side, and the same symmetry was true for the cells. The only thing that separated the two units was a narrow utility passageway that allowed access to the back of the cells and showers. The passageway also served as an escape for the cell's ductless exhaust vents, which were merely slabs of riddled sheet metal covered with sloping lids welded to the back wall to prevent us from seeing into the passageway. The vent cover made me wonder whether there was something inside the passageway that the authorities didn't want us to see– something like an exit.

Certainly, there had to be some type of opening for the sounds of freedom to enter, I assumed. The more I thought about it, the more I was convinced. Granted, I didn't know anything about roofing, ventilation, architecture, or plumbing; nevertheless, I was able to use logic and common sense to infer that there had to be an exit beyond the back wall or the ceiling.

Convinced that I'd found a way out, I began to plot my next escape. I figured that, with a good saw blade, I could cut my way out of the psychedelic can in less than 48 hours. I planned to cut the two welds at the bottom corners of the vent cover and bend the cover upwards to break the upper welds; then, I would do the same with the riddled slab of sheet metal, and wriggle my slender body through the 12-by-12 hole. Whether there were other barriers beyond the wall remained to be discovered. Still, the plan seemed brilliant, and the fact that the guards were least expecting an escape from Max made the plan that much more impeccable.

My first step was to reach out to my cousin for another saw. I ordered it at the beginning of the week and expected it to arrive that upcoming Saturday, which happened to be two days before my scheduled trial date. When Saturday arrived, however, the package didn't. After doing a little querying, I learned that the guard didn't pass out any large pieces of mail that day. According to B.G., the regular guards were no longer allowed to pass out packages and large pieces of mail. Apparently, the administration was displeased with their manner of inspecting the large mail.

This changed everything. I had hoped to be gone by Monday, but now I was likely to be at court when the package was to arrive. More troubling was the fact that I could be at court Monday through Friday—the only days the regular mail lady worked.

Monday arrived, but my trial didn't. I awoke early that morning and waited, but around 10 a.m. it became apparent that my trial date had been postponed without my knowledge. Although I was upset because my attorney hadn't notified me, I was happy because I would be present when the package arrived. Also, I saw it as an allotment of time for me to execute the perfect escape.

Several hours after lunch, I heard the mail lady's cart enter the E-side. The sound of the rusty wheels churning made me nervous and excited. Although it was improbable that she'd find the thin, flimsy saw hidden in a two-inch-thick stack of papers, my worrisome mind incessantly reminded me that it was possible, especially given how thorough the mail lady was.

When I heard the cart come around the back hallway and stop in front of my cell, I took a deep breath and feigned to be surprised. The door was locked, but the small wicket was open, so she squatted and opened the package on top of the ajar wicket so that I could witness her open and inspect the package, which read: Confidential Legal Mail—Open Only in The Presence of Inmate. She flipped through the papers one page at a time as if she were expecting the saw too. At the rate she was going, I knew she'd find it, but there was absolutely nothing I could do about it. Had the door been open and she were standing by the bars, I could've reached through the bars and snatched the papers out of her hand. But with her being at the door—which was four feet away—I could do nothing but watch.

"What's this?" she asked, upon feeling a hard spot between two sheets of paper. "You trying to get over on me?"

I pretended to be ignorant and hoped she would overlook the lump and show a brother some love, but she eagerly tore the glued pieces of paper apart and gasped when she discovered the saw taped in the middle.

"You know you can't have this saw in here!" she said as if I didn't already know.

"What saw?" I asked, pretending to be ignorant and surprised.

"This!" she retorted, dangling the paper inside the wicket so that I could see the saw taped to it.

"Well, what about the papers?" I asked, unable to come up with any other response.

"No!" she snapped. "Trying to get over on me."

She tossed the papers on the cart and stormed out the unit, rusty wheels squeaking as they quickly churned. She really was angry, as if I really were trying to get over on her. It never once crossed her mind that perhaps I was trying to get over on the government, and, maybe, the guard who passed out mail on Saturday. She responded as if she had an interest in my continued incarceration as if there weren't more young black men lined up to occupy my cell after me.

As soon as the door slammed shut and I somberly flopped on the bunk, Qusai chimed in: "Bosco, you just don't give up, do you?" He was like an owl in a tree—nothing ever got passed him. When he was asleep, he still managed to hear everything occurring in the unit.

"Well, I got no choice but to give up now," I replied. The woman had killed the little hope that had been rekindled in me, and I had to laugh about it to not cry about it.

Wednesday morning, shortly after breakfast, a guard appeared at my cell with what appeared to be the same package that the mail lady had confiscated. I was baffled as to why this particular guard showed up at my cell doing the mail lady's job so early in the morning. I assumed that the mail lady had changed her mind and decided to let me have the package sans the saw, but the guard said that he found the package lying around the mail room and figured that the mail lady must have forgotten to give it to me. He didn't even look through the package; he just handed it to me and walked away.

Thinking nothing of it, I sat the envelope beside the bunk and lay back down. Suddenly, I remembered B.G. telling me that the mail lady was accustomed to leaving envelopes of contraband lying around her office without ever reporting it. I smiled at the notion of the saw still being inside the package and flipped through the papers in search of it. Yep, it was still there, taped to the sheet of paper. I nearly jumped through the ceiling with joy. The guard had just given me my key to freedom and didn't even know. How naive could he be? And what about the mail lady who had left the saw and package lying around her office or wherever she had left it? Two idiots, I assumed.

I jumped out of bed and started brushing my teeth and rethinking my escape plans. My spirits had been rekindled and I was floating on cloud nine until I tried to flush the toilet. It, just like the van filled with marijuana, wouldn't work. Now baffled and suspicious, I yelled down to Qusai and asked him to check his toilet. He responded by flushing it. It worked, and so did B.G.s and everybody else's. Something fishy was happening. First the timing of the mail; then the person passing out the mail; and now, the toilet. It seemed like a set up, but I couldn't understand the purpose or logic behind it. I couldn't fathom why the guards would provide me with a tool that could be used as a weapon or to implement an escape. Such conduct alone had to be a breach of security.

Although I was skeptical as to whether I was being set up, I, nonetheless, decided to remove the saw from the package and hide it. As soon as I removed the saw from the paper, I discovered a blue, powdery substance sprinkled all over it. It was the type of substance that only an inexperienced cop would put there. I dipped the saw into the toilet, and the water turned blue, thereby, confirming my suspicion–it was a setup. Still, I was willing to take my chance and go along with it in hopes of maintaining possession of the saw. I certainly didn't have anything to lose.

I quickly tied a string around the end of the saw and hid it in a crack behind the huge 48 by 8-inch fluorescent light fixture at the back of the cell. I tried several loops in the string, making it easier for me to later hook and fish out. I then pushed the string inside the crack so that it couldn't be seen. And to mislead the guards into thinking I'd tossed the saw down the toilet, I ripped up the paper on which the saw had been taped and tossed it into the toilet. Finally, giving the cops something disgusting to search through, I pissed in the toilet and tossed toilet paper into it.

As expected, within minutes, an army of Taser-gun-toting cops marched into the unit. As they passed Qusai's cell, I heard him ask: "What have you done now, Bosco?" They rushed into the cell, subdued me, restrained me, and escorted me out into the corridor where the negro detective stood with his arms folded across his chest and a smirk on his face. I couldn't help but wonder whether he would have been smiling had I sawed off one of his officer's head with the saw that he foolishly provided me with. He gazed at me for a few seconds and then ordered his officers to take me up to the front and strip-search me.

While I was upfront being strip-searched, the detective and several other cops were searching my cell. After unsuccessfully searching for nearly an hour, the detective came and tried to persuade me to reveal the whereabouts of the saw. I was tempted to ask if his offer to send me to a better jail still stood. But I refused to talk or answer any of his questions. My silence seemed to infuriate him and his officers. Ironically, they were mad because I wouldn't give them the saw that they themselves had given me. If they didn't want me to have it, they shouldn't have given it to me in the first place. Certainly, there were better ways to utilize police resources and manpower than to be searching a jail cell for contraband that they themselves had senselessly put there.

Later while plumbers were searching the pipes in the utility passageway, a nosey female guard entered and noticed the saw protruding from a crack in the wall behind the light fixture. The detective notified me of the discovery by strutting into the booking area and waving the saw in my face and happily exclaiming: "Bling bling!" I was upset, but ironically, I was somewhat happy for the detective. He was the only African American detective in the entire county, and had he not found the saw, he probably would have been reduced to issuing parking citations.

CHAPTER 9

A RAY OF SUNSHINE

After the senseless sting, I was returned to Max, but to a cell on the E-side. The detective posted on the outside of my door a written sign which read: EXTREMELY HIGH RISK INMATE–USE RESTRAINTS AND 2 OR MORE OFFICERS WHEN MOVING. The chance of such movement, though, was slim. Other than an occasional shower, I wasn't allowed out of my cell for anything. I was basically isolated from all forms of humanity, and fared not much better than a dead man. Eerily, the uncomfortable metal bunk was no bigger–and probably less comfortable–than a coffin. And just like the dead, I was quickly becoming irrelevant and unproductive to the world, and would soon rot and be forgotten by everyone except Mother.

To survive my deathlike ordeal, I was compelled to live through my dreams; without them, I probably would've been braindead. If there is any truth in the saying that freedom is a state of mind, I guess my dreams should have been enough to carry the day. But I wasn't content with that type of freedom–I wanted physical freedom. In my belief, such a saying was for the slave; it was a way for the oppressed to dupe themselves into being content with oppression. By the same token, it was a way for the oppressed to change their way of thinking as opposed to fighting to change their conditions. I wasn't content with dreaming–I wanted to change my environment.

In addition to increasing my level of security, the senseless sting enhanced my notoriety throughout the jail and erased any doubt from the minds of those who barely believed I was guilty of the previous escape attempt. I went from being perceived as the quiet, mysterious, innocent-looking prisoner who'd been accused of trying to escape to the quiet, sneaky, mysterious prisoner who would do anything to escape.

Some prisoners and guards wondered what my plans were for the saw. They didn't believe that a prisoner could use such a tool to escape from Max. In fact, one of the guards laughed and called me an idiot. He said that there was no way I could've used "that tiny saw" to escape. Most were so confident in the security of Max that they actually assumed the saw had been sent while I was still in general population and that it had simply arrived several weeks too late. However, while the guards were on the outside looking in, I was on the inside looking out; therefore, we had totally different points of view. Mine was much better because my desperate senses picked up on things that theirs overlooked, and their 8 hours didn't compare to the 24 that I had to think of ways to escape. So, contrary to their belief, I planned to do wonders with that saw.

Fortunately, as time elapsed, so did the memories of the guards and the extreme security measures taken by them. One afternoon when several prisoners were returning to their cells from rec, a prisoner who went by the name of Rooster looked at me through a small square window on my door, nodded, and slyly removed the "HIGH–RISK" sign from my door. Soon thereafter, the guards seemed to forget that I was one of their high-risk prisoners. With no warning sign posted on my door, and my quiet, humble demeanor, the guards seemed to forget why I was even in Max.

Qusai was right, I wasn't one to give up easily, no matter the odds or failures. As soon as it seemed that my last incident had faded to the back of the guards᳠memories, I began to plot my next move. This time, I had Qusai as a partner. He kept his eyes and ears open—as always—listening to the sounds of freedom and observing the guards from his end, and I did the same on my end. I even went as far as browsing local newspapers for pertinent data, and reading the *Home* section in hopes of learning about roofing, air conditioning, and ventilation systems. And to ensure secrecy, I created a coded language and coded alphabets so that

Quasi and I could clandestinely communicate through the vent and hidden messages in books.

In addition to listening to my surroundings and browsing newspapers, I did a lot of thinking. My mind worked incessantly. I often asked myself: *"Why?"* Why metal walls instead of cinder-block? Why cover the exhaust vent? Why have bars inside the cell? Why? I tried to logically answer each *why* by relying on common sense and the limited information available to me. In doing so, I realized that the cells weren't as secure as they appeared. They were simply designed that way to drain us of our energy, to depress our spirits, to warp our way of thinking, and to make us feel trapped and hopeless. In sum, the excessive sense of security was merely a facade, one that I was able to see right through.

One night, I overheard two prisoners talking through the vent. One of them was telling the other about the time he'd witnessed the female guard's finding of the saw in the utility passageway. Curious as to how he was able to witness something that occurred in the utility passageway, I butted in and asked if he had X-ray vision. He replied that he'd witnessed the entire event through a tiny hole in the rear wall of his cell. He was in cell #8 on the E-side; therefore, he was able to peek through the hole and see the back of my old cell.

Hearing him describe the hole aroused my interest and curiosity. I immediately tried to figure out a way to swap cells with him. I wanted to see the hole for myself. More importantly, I wanted to see the utility passageway and possibly locate the open space that allowed the sounds of freedom to enter the building.

A little more than a month later, on a Friday, the prisoner in cell #8 was released to general population, leaving the cell vacant and available for me to occupy. Instead of conspicuously asking the guards to move me into the cell, I waited until Saturday, when the plumbers and maintenance workers were off duty. Shortly after lunch, I smashed an empty peanut butter jar, and jammed it so far down the toilet that the plumbers would later have to take the toilet apart to unclog it. For added effect, I defecated in the toilet and left the excrement floating around inside the bowl, causing the cell to stink.

When the guard made his round, I griped about the toilet being stopped up, and requested a plunger. He walked away and returned minutes later with the plunger. While he stood at the bars watching, I used the plunger to no avail. I then asked for a snake, knowing that that wouldn't help either, but the guard had a better idea: He told me to pack my property and moved me to cell #8.

Cell #8 was much more ghastly than the others, much tackier, and dimly lit. Rather than having a huge light-fixture with bright florescent bulbs like the other cells, there was just a small, square light-fixture with two small bulbs, one of which was blown out. Two feet to the right of the light, there was a small coin size hole in the rear wall, and there was an identical hole two feet to the left of the light. Both holes sparkled with light shining from somewhere inside the utility passageway. When I stepped to the back of the cell and looked up, I saw that there were two more corresponding holes in the ceiling. It appeared that the four holes were remnants of where a large light-fixture—like those in the other cells—had once been affixed. Apparently, the original light-fixture had been removed—or perhaps ripped out of the wall by an abnormally strong prisoner— and replaced with the smaller one.

There was writing all over the walls, on which someone had used a permanent black marker to write the words *Freedom*, *Rasta*, and *Black Redemption*. I traced my finger over the writing and wondered how long it had been there. I also wondered whether the word *Freedom* augured well with my cause. The ink seemed to be years old, and the inscriber (probably the same guy who ripped the light-fixture from the wall) seemed to have had a lot of rage pent up. The writing made the cell appear tacky, but I didn't have the necessary

67

chemicals to remove it. And as time passed, I no longer wanted to remove it; I figured it would be a good diversion from the further damage I planned to do to the cell.

I stood on the sink and peeped out the hole on the left side of the light. The view wasn't broad, but it provided a view of the rear walls of the last three cells on the F-side, and the plumbing pipes and electrical wires running from them. I saw the 12 by 12-inch ductless exhaust vent on the rear wall of my old cell on the F-side, the same vent I'd spent many days and nights glued to listening to the sounds of freedom. On top of the cells, there were air ducts that supplied air to the cells via a riddled grate in the ceiling between the bars and the door of each cell.

Looking through the correlating hole in the ceiling, I saw the formidable roof made of concrete and reinforced steel beams. I spent the entire day looking through the holes in search for an exit. Although I didn't find one, I was just about certain that one was there. Having studied the attics of buildings inside the pages of magazines and newspapers, along with wondering why every cell had an exhaust vent in it, I concluded that every room and building must have some type of exhaust vent to release carbon dioxide and other gases, or else all living occupants would die from asphyxiation.

I believed that such a vent existed to the far left corner of the attic, beyond my peripheral vision. But, so far, the only potential exit I could see was the air ducts above the cells, and I had absolutely no idea where they began or ended. Nevertheless, if that were my only option, I was willing to wriggle through the ducts until I were either free or chopped to pieces by some unknown machinery.

Over the following months, I routinely looked through the holes every single day—as if something would change. Then, one afternoon I looked up and saw that the holes no longer sparkled. Someone had shut off the lights in the passageway. Naturally, I began to worry that I wouldn't be able to study the attic and the passageway anymore, but when I stood on the sink and peeped through the holes into the darkness, my worries immediately vanished. I'd found my exit. There were several rays of sunlight beaming from the northwest of my peripheral view. I followed the rays as if they were strands of a rainbow with a pot of gold at the end. I followed them until they disappeared beyond my peripheral and hid somewhere in the far left corner of the attic. I didn't see the exit, but I did see the light, and knew that it would lead me to freedom. Seeing the light was by no means a triumph; however, it was certainly inspiring.

CHAPTER 10

GOTTA GET AWAY

My daughter's birth was quickly approaching and I was still trapped inside the metal tomb. No amount of sun rays could've changed that. What I needed was another saw, and getting that was proving to be a difficult task. So until then, I could do nothing but sit still and dream about escaping.

Fantasizing about escaping was my only pastime. I didn't read books, didn't write letters, didn't do much socializing, and didn't think about my case. I only lay in my bunk, paced the floor, exercised, and thought of ways to escape. Nothing else seemed to matter. The thoughts came naturally and continuously, as though they were my only means of hope. They were also my only means of coping with the conditions of Max, including the ruckus, the thin mats, the 6-foot bunk which was too small for my 6'4" frame, the unhealthy food, and the lack of stimulation and productivity. Such conditions only exacerbated my desire to get away. Every night I went to sleep, I thought about getting away, and every morning I awoke with aching joints, I wanted to get away.

I actually felt victimized to be locked up like an animal for simply committing a victimless crime that caused no harm or threat to humanity. The only victim was I. I was the one confined to a 6 by 8-foot can without the ability to support my family or fulfill my responsibilities as a man. I couldn't even enjoy the companionship of a woman—and that is a God-given right. Even Adam, in the book of Genesis, couldn't cope without the companionship of a woman; he went so far as to sacrifice his rib for one. So for the government to deprive me of such a right was tantamount to a crime against humanity and universal law. For the sake of my own sanity, I had to get away.

With time quickly ticking away, Qusai desperately suggested that I have a couple of saws sent through the mail to a prisoner named Ray Ray, a prisoner who had no qualms about breaking the rules and sacrificing himself for the cause. Ray Ray was a self-admitted fool who often boasted of being a "Straight-up, Stomp-down, Black-nigga gangsta." He joked about carrying a bag of guns and a bag of bullets at all times, and claimed to shoot 3 guns at one time—two in one hand and one in the other. He also adored children and hated snitches. Since he was already serving multiple life-sentences for multiple murders across the bridge, in Missouri, he had absolutely nothing to lose and was willing to risk anything for the right price.

Ray Ray was from the south side of St. Louis, Missouri, but he was being held at St. Clair County jail because of a murder he committed in Illinois. Unlike most prisoners, he didn't deny committing the murder. He was so much a fool that he actually confessed to every crime he'd been implicated in, and others that he hadn't been implicated in. "That's... that's what I do— robbery homicide," he boasted when the detective questioned him. Although he told on himself, he would never tell on anyone else—he was too good and loyal of a friend for that. In fact, most, if not all of his crimes, were committed on behalf of friends.

Ray Ray was clearly psychologically disturbed, and that was apparent from the moment I first saw him. He spoke with an unnecessary stutter that was more so habitual than innate. The most conspicuous sign, though, was his head; the back was flat as a board, just like most crazy dudes. In fact, he looked exactly like the lizard in the Geico Insurance commercial. In a side profile, they could have easily passed for twins, their only distinction being the lizard's tail. Another indication of his insanity was his habit of ordering sales magazines and newspapers in which he'd circle cars and houses as if he were actually getting out some day to purchase them. He was so much of a disturbed and loyal fool that when I offered him $300 to receive the saws, he said that $300 was too much money. He said that he wouldn't even charge that much for a murder hit. Although he laughed, his eyes indicated that he was dead serious.

The plan was for Ray Ray to snatch the package out of the lady's hand without allowing her the chance to inspect it, and then hide the saw and pretend that there had been a cigarette inside. However, when the package arrived, the mail lady opened it while standing at a distance from his bars, thereby, preventing him from reaching out and grabbing it. Consequently, she thoroughly searched the package and discovered the saws. Instead of reporting it to the overzealous detective, though, she simply tossed the saws into the trash. Ray Ray suffered no repercussions. But I worried that it would attract more attention to me, and possible more security to Max.

At the time I had a nagging fear that Max would soon change for the worse and become difficult to escape. As it stood there were several flaws in the security, and it seemed that several prisoners were unwittingly taking advantage of them for frivolous reasons. I particularly worried about Ray Ray because he was always causing a disturbance, such as tossing urine on the guards, breaking free from the guards while being escorted in shackles, spitting in the face of a 70-year-old disciplinary staffer, using a makeshift knife to stab another prisoner in the visiting booth while the prisoner's family looked on and pounded on the Plexiglas window, and the list goes on.

Coincidentally, I was in the visiting booth next to Ray Ray during the stabbing incident. The victim was a guy who'd snitched on Ray Ray in general population and had Ray Ray sent to Max for attempting to extort him and other prisoners. Unfortunately for him, the guards had accidently placed Ray Ray in the same visiting room as him. When Ray Ray saw the guy, he winked at me and pulled out his knife and started stabbing the guy. While Ray Ray and the guy were tussling, and the guy's visitors were pounding on the Plexiglas window, I stood on top of the counter, removed one of the ceiling tiles, and searched for a way out. I was hoping that I could climb over to the other side of the booth where the visitors were, but there was a cinderblock barrier preventing me from doing so.

Ray Ray's most brazen stunt came when he robbed the commissary officer. The young, white, naive, wannabe-hipster entered Max alone to pass out commissary. The outer door to each cell was open, as they usually were during the day, so when he stepped into Ray Ray's cell to pass his commissary items through the tray slot, Ray Ray reached through the bars and grabbed him by the neck. Ray Ray began to ramble a psychotic stutter, feigning to be on the verge of a homicidal suicide and threatening to take the commissary officer with him. The commissary officer pleaded with Ray Ray, but Ray Ray tightened his grip around the man's neck and started complaining about his displeasure with his life and destitution—particularly his lack of commissary.

"Commissary—you need more commissary?" the man asked, with a sense of relief, as though he'd found an escape. Little did he know, he was walking right into Ray Ray's trap.

"Ain't...ain't no motha fuckin question," Ray Ray stuttered. "You...you already...already know I'm doing bad."

"If it'll cheer you up, I'll give you extra commissary," the officer said. "Why, you should've been told me—there's always extra bags in my office."

Ray Ray released the man, but first warned: "Don't—don't try no bullshit." Surprisingly, the officer returned with extra bags of commissary that had been unclaimed by prisoners who were released from the jail. Apparently, the officer was too ashamed to reveal that he'd been robbed by a prisoner secured on the opposite side of a set of bars, because he didn't report the incident. However, an unknown prisoner who overheard the incident snitched, and the commissary officers were no longer allowed to enter Max without another guard.

These acts were Ray Ray's way of passing time, but to me, they were worrisome. What worried me the most about Ray Ray was his manifest desire to take over Max and hold the guards hostage in exchange for a cheeseburger and curly fries combo he'd seen in a newspaper ad. Whether he was serious or not, I worried that the mere manifestation of such desire was enough to bring heat on Max. If there were going to be any changes in Max, I wanted my pursuit of freedom to be the reason for them, not Ray Ray's buffoonery.

I was eager to get away while the time was right. As it stood, I was surrounded by trustworthy prisoners. BG, Qusai, and I were the only federal prisoners, and the other thirteen were state prisoners, nine of which were charged with murder. In the cell next to me was Rayford, a brother from East St. Louis, who'd recently returned from prison after having his 60-year sentence and murder conviction vacated on appeal. And in the other cells, there were Ray Ray, Rooster, The Bull, The Bully, Black Mike, Flip and a few transient prisoners who often didn't stay in Max long.

The most frequent and annoying transient prisoner was old man Steve. At 55, Steve had been arrested at least 55 times for a slew of petty offenses; he'd been arrested at least half a dozen times during my stay in Max. He was often heard before seen—his voice was loud, deep and unmistaken—and once seen, there was no forgetting him. He was short, extremely dark, and rugged-looking with a short, kinky, salt-n-pepper afro. He walked with a slow, grinding swagger that is reminiscent of, both, George Jefferson's stroll and a sidewinder snake twisting and slithering about the ground all jumbled in one unique stroll.

His stroll could've easily been confused for an old man "pop-locking" and walking at the same time. He was by far one of the ugliest creatures on earth. Once locked inside the cell, Steve would pace the floor, dragging his crusty feet and talking to himself all day and night. He never slept—if he did, it had to be in ten-minute spurts— instead, he stayed awake, kicking and banging on walls and blurting out insignificant numbers that not even he knew the significance of. In his scruffy, boisterous voice, he was often heard shouting numbers such as "twenty-two thirty-nine," "Fourteen seventy-six," and so on. Whenever the crazy man wasn't yelling out numbers, talking to himself, or kicking on the walls, he was lashing out at the guards, threatening to burn them alive and put a "billion dollars" on their heads. He hated the guards so much that one day upon being released; he walked around to the front lobby and threw a brick through the glass window, and was returned to Max. With Steve around, it was the perfect time to get away.

One day while I was peeking through the holes in my cell, the guards came to get me for a visit. When I arrived in the interview room, I was disappointed to find my attorney already seated; I was hoping to see her when she walked in, as well as when she walked out. She'd come to try to convince me into cooperating and pleading guilty. Yeyo and Angel had already signed cooperating plea agreements; in fact, Yeyo had already pleaded guilty. Accordingly, in the eyes of my attorney, I had no choice but to do the same. When I refused, she called me an arrogant, confused puppy.

"Everyone else is snitching—so why and the hell won't you?" she snapped at me.

"Just because everybody else is doing it doesn't make it right," I replied. "Just because somebody hits me in my head doesn't mean that it is okay for me to go around hitting other people in the head."

"You're one confused puppy," she said, shaking her head.

"If I don't like something being done to me. Why should I do it to somebody else?"

"Uh...to save yourself and not spend the rest of your life in prison," she replied.

"If you really want to help me get out, bring me a saw," I was tempted to say, but instead, I fired her. I did so hesitantly because my mother wouldn't be refunded the retainer fee, but I really had no choice. Attorneys are good for nothing in the feds. A hacksaw was much more valuable than a lawyer any day. That was the last time I saw my attorney, and I can honestly say: She looked much better going than she did coming. I just wish I could've gone with her. I had to get away.

On September 19, 2004, my daughter was born. I was happy, but also sad because I was still trapped inside the can, feeling like an irresponsible sperm donor. I had wanted so badly to be present for my daughter's birth—even as a fugitive—and start our relationship off on the right note. But I failed. And that failure was one of the most dismal experiences of my life. To be confined to a cell while one's first and only child is brought into this world is enough to make anyone feel like a worthless parent. I beat myself up for a few days and decided that the only thing I could do to compensate for my absence was to hurry and get out before she became wise enough to notice my absence. What more could I do? I had to get away.

CHAPTER 11

GOING BACK TO CALI

Two weeks after my daughter's birth, I received beautiful pictures of her and good news. A new guard had recently started working at the jail, and he and B.G. became partners. After a couple of weeks of frivolous chitchat, B.G. asked the guard to bring him some cigarettes (which were prohibited inside the jail), and the guard agreed. Knowing my desperation for a saw, B.G. informed me, and I suggested that he offer the guard $500 to smuggle in a pack of cigarettes and a few candy bars. When the guard agreed, I had the $500 sent to Qusai's people, who in turn met up with the guard and did the transaction. Three days later, B.G. sang B.I.G.'s "Going Back To Cali" through the vent, clandestinely notifying me that the guard had brought the candy bars. This was good news.

There was nothing spectacular about the brand of candy bars; in fact, they were no better than the candy bars sold in the commissary. What made them worth $500, though, were the two 7-inch reciprocating saws concealed inside them. I kept one of the saws for myself, and stashed the other one in the TV room for Qusai.

Once we got the saws, we didn't hesitate to put them to use. Knowing that my ultimate destination was somewhere above the front left corner of my cell, I abandoned my earlier plans of sawing through the vent. Instead, I decided to cut a hole in the corner of the ceiling above the sink. The left corner of the ceiling was not only closer to what I believed to be an exhaust vent in the attic, but also easier and more convenient to start sawing. Instead of wasting precious time and energy scraping and grinding just to create a perforation in the metal, I was able to simply stick my saw through the peephole in the ceiling and start sawing.

Another advantage in cutting a hole in the ceiling was the fact that most guards never looked up. They were like trained soldiers, always looking down or straight ahead. They rarely looked at the ceiling. On the down side, though, sawing through the quarter-inch-thick ceiling was extremely loud. When the teeth of the saw grinded against the quasi-flimsy metal, it sounded like I was trying to saw a tank in half. The metal vibrated, and the thin metal walls caused the sound to resonate through both sides of Max. Luckily, most prisoners had no idea what the noise was, and the fact that Max was the noisiest place on earth at times, it was sometimes difficult to distinguish the sawing when prisoners were rattling the barred gates, kicking, pounding, and drumming the walls and bunks, and yelling back and forth at each other.

At a time like this, I appreciated having old man Steve around. In addition to Steve kicking on the walls all day and night, Ray Ray happened to be in the midst of a 3-day wall fight with his neighbor. They beat and kicked on the flimsy wall separating their cells all day and night to take their frustration out on each other. In all actuality, though, they were disturbing not only each other but also everyone else in Max. It was during these noisy moments when I made the most progress. It was also during these moments when I had to be extra careful because it was often difficult to hear when the guards entered the unit.

Whenever opportunity permitted, Rayford and B.G. would go up to the shower room and keep lookout for me. Also, Qusai (who was now directly behind me in cell #8 on the F-side) and I established a clandestine way of alerting each other whenever the guards entered the unit. Whenever the water buttons in our sinks were pressed, they made a loud clack followed by a buzz, so whenever the guards entered on the F-side, Qusai would press his button twice, and whenever they entered on the E-side, I would press mine twice. Often, a guard would enter on one side and walk around the back hallway to exit on the other side; therefore, we would knock on the back wall to notify each other of the guard's exit.

We sawed on and off all day and night. Surprisingly, it was

more arduous than we had anticipated. Trying to quickly and discreetly saw through the quarter-inch thick steel with a reciprocating saw blade wasn't as easy as it sounds. It was the hardest work I'd ever done. The small, grip-less blades are designed to be attached to machines, not hands. The task is tantamount to communicating by means of hieroglyphics and etched stones during the era of emails and text messages. It was that strenuous and time consuming. Despite the difficulties, I was able to make tremendous progress. But then we ran into trouble.

As if the normal conditions of Max weren't enough to frustrate my progress, I was slowed by the suicide of an 18-year-old black kid who'd only been in Max for one day. According to the prisoners on the F-side, where the suicide occurred, the kid had forewarned a white guard of his suicidal intentions and the guard allegedly replied: "Kill yourself!"

Half an hour later that same guard found the kid hanging from the bars with a pair of underwear around his neck and his eyes bulging from the sockets. Enraged by the guard's alleged apathy, the prisoners on both sides of Max went into an uproar. Ray Ray, taking things a step further, went up to the phone in the shower room and related the story to a local journalist. The journalist jumped all over the story and caused Max to be placed under the spotlight for a few days. Consequently, it was nearly impossible for me to get any work done.

The following Friday, my progress was stunted again by another unexpected event. Early that morning, as I lay in the bunk trying to steal a few Zs after an exhausting night of sawing, I was awakened by the sound of a chain falling to the pavement, shoes screeching, a prisoner shouting "God damn!" and a guard pleading with Qusai to calm down. It sounded like the guards had mistakenly opened Qusai's cell without first cuffing and shackling him, and he ended up doing something stupid.

I instantly thought about The Bull, an older prisoner who referred to Qusai and me as "Pinky and the Brain." The Bull hated Qusai so much that he and Ray Ray planned to disarm a guard of keys and enter Qusai's cell and kill him. The Bull had a history of murders and prison violence, but Qusai had no respect for him. In fact, Qusai viewed him as an old, fat cow instead of a bull. The Bull had once told me: "I don't know what you and that little pink, half-bred negro are up to, but whatever it is, be careful; he'll end up being more of a liability than an asset." Whatever Qusai had just done had me worried that The Bull had prophesied correctly.

"Bosco!" the prisoner in the cell next to Qusai shouted through the vent. "Your boy just killed a cop. There's blood everywhere!"

"Yep. The Bull was right—Qusai ruined the perfect escape," I said to myself, as the other prisoner tried to explain what occurred.

"It was this big, tall, bald, white pig, about 6'5" 270. Qusai hit 'em wit' a death blow...," the hysterical prisoner carried on.

Damn! was all I could say, and all I could do was worry that they'd discover Qusai's saw and the cuts in his ceiling and then make their way around to my cell. I worried and paced the cell for about 10 minutes before I heard Qusai's barred gate slam shut. Seconds later, he was at the vent relating the episode.

His trial was scheduled to begin Monday, so the marshals ordered that he be transferred to a jail closer to the court building. Two officers and a guard unexpectedly showed up at his cell and told him to gather his personal property and back up to the bars to be shackled and cuffed. When they walked him out onto the walkway to place a belly chain around his waist, the tall, bald cop playfully wrapped the chain around Qusai's neck. Qusai really didn't want to leave behind his rare opportunity to escape, so the cop's slavery-like gesture not only offended Qusai, but also gave him a reason to stall the transfer.

When the tall cop leaned forward and unsecured one of Qusai's cuffs, he hit the cop with a quick uppercut that sent him toppling unconsciously to the pavement. The cop's fall was interrupted by an open metal wicket protruding from a cell door, on which he split his head causing blood to splatter everywhere. The cop didn't die, as the hysterical prisoner believed, but he was busted up pretty bad and rushed to the emergency room.

We spent the rest of the morning awaiting the marshal's response. The worst that could've happened for me would've been the cops entering Qusai's cell and discovering the cuts in the ceiling. For Qusai, anything short of staying in Max would've been disastrous. But if the transfer was still in the Marshals' plan, there was absolutely nothing we could've done to prevent it. By the same token, if that's what they had in mind, they needed to send more officers because the two they'd sent were now reduced to one. And certainly one officer wasn't sufficient manpower to transport the little 5'6" 140-pound Qusai. Apparently, neither were two.

It wasn't until the top of the evening when we finally heard something. Qusai's standby attorney came to break the news, both good and bad. The good news was that Qusai would remain in max for the weekend. The bad news was that there was no guarantee he'd return from court Monday. Therefore, we had less than 60 hours to escape.

CHAPTER 12

MINUTES TO ESCAPE

Racing against time, I sawed unremittingly with little regard for the noise factor. Fortunately, I had only 4 inches to saw and I was done by 7 o'clock that night. Altogether, it took me several weeks of sawing my ceiling, and now I was rewarded with a hole in it resembling a huge slice of pizza—90 degrees of a circle. I pushed up on the detached slab of metal and quietly moved it to the side of the hole, then slowly inched my head through the hole. The first place I looked was to my left, where I instantly saw the exhaust vent, and was overcome with a surge of joy and anticipation. I was now only five feet and a little damage away from freedom.

Having seen all that I needed to see, I withdrew my head from the hole and positioned the huge slice of metal pizza back over it. To prevent the guards from seeing the cuts in the ceiling during their walk-by, I stuffed miscellaneous items in the upper left gaps of the bars, thereby, obstructing their view of the entire left corner of the ceiling. Next, I made a dummy by stuffing my jumpsuit with toilet paper, newspaper, and empty Cup of Noodles cups. After the guard made his round, I put the dummy in the bed and told Rayford to keep lookout while I climbed into the attic.

I crawled over to the exhaust vent, which was actually a louver with adjustable slats. I pushed open one of the slats and was displeases to see two steel bars between the louver and the outer vent cover, which was merely thin, nonadjustable slats. The bar was formidable, appearing to require arduous work. Before attempting to saw through the bars, I crawled to the other end of the attic in search for other potential exits, but there were none. As I quietly crawled across the ceilings of the cells, I was amazed at how well I could hear the prisoners below. The metal walls and ceilings amplified every sound, including the sound of Qusai's saw grating the metal ceiling.

Qusai had no idea that I'd made it into the attic, so I decided to pull a prank on him. I crawled over to his ceiling and grabbed his saw as it was reciprocated through a cut in his ceiling. "Is that you, Bosco?" he asked. I knocked twice on the ceiling confirming his suspicion. While he peeked through the cut, I pulled a pencil and piece of paper from my sock and wrote him a short note briefing him on the attic. I also expressed concern about the hole he was cutting appearing to be too small. I passed the note through the cut, and he replied that he'd measured the hole and that it was the perfect size. He did need help finishing the hole, though. He had made little progress and had a lot of sawing to go.

Before helping Qusai, I crawled back over to the exhaust vent, removed the slats from the louver, pried apart the meshed wire, and tried to saw through one of the bars. But they were alloy and therefore likely impossible to cut with the saw. I leaned forward, positioning my shoulder against the louver to apply more pressure, and shockingly the entire louver moved. It wasn't even mounted to anything. I pulled the louver out, leaving nothing but a couple of bars and the outer vent-cover standing between me and freedom. I pressed my face to the bars to inhale the fresh air and peek through the exterior slats, and, surprisingly, my entire head slipped right through the gap between the bars. It seemed that every barrier I encountered turned out to not be a barrier at all. First the louver and now the bars.

As easily as my head slipped through the bars, I saw no reason why my frail body couldn't follow. I slowly shifted and slipped my shoulders through the bars and felt a tingle of excitement as my face pressed against the vent cover, which happened to be the only thing between me and freedom. One kick would have sent the slats, as well as my foot, flying out into the free air. I was tempted to pull my head back, spin around, kick out the cover, and wriggle through the bars, but

I had to wait on Qusai. Also it was too early in the mission to be damaging the vent cover, especially since it was in plain view of everyone walking and driving by the jail.

With my face pressed to the slats, I stared out at the world. Freedom! I looked down and saw a small parking lot right below. I raised my head and looked through the gaps between the upper slats and was greeted by an inspiring view of a two-lane street running along the side of the jail. I now knew where the sounds of freedom were coming from. Across the street were houses with Neighborhood Watch signs in the windows. My face pressed against the slats for several minutes, gazing into the darkness of the night as headlights and taillights twinkled from passing vehicles. What an experience to suddenly, after so much time in a steel box, to see the night sky and hear sounds of engines roaring, horns blowing, and tires treading the tarred pavement. I was so stoked that I could literally taste freedom.

In the midst of my trance, a transit bus roared by, emitting the nostalgic odor of gas and engine exhaust. Shortly after the bus faded from my senses, I was aroused by the faint sound of high heels seductively treading the sidewalk. My heart fluttered at the prospect of seeing a member of the better sex. My eyes darted back and forth, from left to right, in search of the producer of the song the high-heels were singing. As the sound grew louder and nearer, I glimpsed a voluptuous woman wearing heels, slacks, and a trench coat. I felt like a pathetic stalker as I gazed at the woman, literally smelling her perfume, as she walked by. On the flip side, I felt very much alive because she symbolized freedom and showed me how so close I was to it.

I spent the following two days, Saturday and Sunday, lying on the top of Qusai's ceiling, sawing and finishing the hole he'd started, while he either helped or stood in the shower singing "Fire and Desire" by Rick James and Tina Marie. His singing was not only an attempt to distract the other prisoners from paying attention to the noise I was making, but also a clandestine way of notifying me whenever the guards entered the unit. Whenever they entered, he'd stop singing and I'd stop sawing.

There were a couple of occasions when we had to stop due to unexpected events. On one occasion a guard entered the utility closet at the front of the utility passageway between the showers, and stood there smoking a cigarette. He was in violation of jail rules. I lay on my stomach and spied on the mischievous guard, and felt a strange sense of authority in secretly watching the very guard who was supposed to be watching me, especially while he was breaking the rules like I. Then, on Saturday evening, Ray Ray went up to the shower cell, tossed water on a guard, and refused to come out. Consequently, the guards shot him with a Taser gun, rushed into the shower cell and restrained him, and carried him back to his cell.

When the guards tossed him back into his cell, he still had attached to his shirt the pronged wires that were ejected from the Taser gun. When Ray Ray discovered the wire, he used it as an antenna for his Walkman. He was so impressed with the reception the wire provided that he returned to the shower the following day, hoping to get shot again and obtain more wire. Both times interfered with our work and set us back several hours.

It was moments like this when Ray Ray got on my nerves. But ironically, after Ray Ray unwittingly slowed our escape and had been willing to help The Bull kill Qusai, Qusai suggested that we bring him along. Why? I didn't know, but I was quickly realizing that Qusai was as much of a psychopath as Ray Ray. Ray Ray had already said that if he were to escape he'd return to the south side of St. Louis and hold court in the streets, so for the sake of public safety, he had no desire to escape. Even if he'd changed his mind, I wasn't willing to wait for him—we'd already lost time.

It was past midnight Monday morning when we finished the hole in Qusai's ceiling, and just as I'd predicted: It was disastrous. The hole was not only square, but also several inches away from the corner of the ceiling; therefore, we couldn't use the ninety-degree angle at the corner of the ceiling to support the detached square piece of metal and prevent it from falling through the hole. That wouldn't have been a problem had we been able to just pull Qusai through the hole and immediately escape. However, we couldn't do that because the hole was too small.

Exhausted, discouraged, yet desperate, we resumed sawing in futile hope of expanding the hole before the marshals arrived to take Qusai to court. Dawn was quickly approaching, and we knew that we wouldn't make it in time. Nevertheless, Qusai was determined to keep going just for the sake of not giving up. It wasn't until the jail began to stir with distant sounds of doors opening and shutting, and food carts rolling around in the kitchen, when Qusai accepted the reality of the matter—we couldn't make it.

I understood Qusai's passion—hell, 54 years was enough to compel any man—however, I felt that the sense of urgency wasn't necessary. I had a strong feeling that he would return after court.

I was still on top of Qusai's ceiling when the marshals arrived. I had to stay there, holding the detached slab of metal in place so that it wouldn't fall through the hole when they slammed the bars shut. When they left, I quickly jimmy-rigged the hole and fitted the slab of sheet metal into it. Although I did the best I could, considering the circumstances, there was still the possibility of guards entering the cell and discovering the damaged ceiling.

I returned to my cell with intent on sleeping the rest of the morning and returning to finish the hole later. However, I awoke at noon to the sound of unusual activity and strange voices coming from the F side. It took a moment for the voices to register, and when they did, I began to worry. The voices were that of proper speaking white men, which was troubling because there were only two white prisoners in

Max, and they never spoke—certainly not proper English. The voices had to belong to either janitors or cops, only there were no hammers pounding or drills humming, which meant they were cops.

Fearing the worst—that one of the guards had entered Qusai's cell and discovered his ceiling—I pulled myself out of bed and peeped through my favorite hole. I didn't notice anything out of place; everything was exactly as I'd left it. However, that didn't mean that the worst hadn't happened. I went to the vent and asked Qusai's neighbor what was going on. "The detectives are investigating," he vaguely replied. What they were investigating seemed irrelevant; in my mind there were only two things to be investigated—the assault and the hole in the ceiling—and either one would eventually lead to the hole in my ceiling. And that notion was enough reason for me to worry and anxiously await the unknown.

It was approximately 2 p.m. when a lone detective appeared at my cell. I stood nervously at the bars as he pulled open the outer cell-door. Moments earlier, I learned that he was investigating allegations surrounding the suicide that recently occurred. Therefore, I didn't have much to worry about. But to be on the safe side, I had the detached piece of metal in my ceiling tightly propped in the hole, white toothpaste concealing the cuts, and miscellaneous items stuffed in the gaps of the bars to obstruct his view of the ceiling. Before the detective could step one foot inside my cell, I said: "I don't know nothing." I wanted the cop gone as quickly as possible, but he remained in the unit interviewing until around 4 o'clock.

As I expected, Qusai returned from court that evening. He was happy to return, but slightly disappointed that the investigation had prevented me from working all day. That night and the following night and days were monotonous. They involved me being on top of Qusai's cell vigorously sawing while he was either in court representing himself or in the shower singing "Fire and Desire" and bragging about the pro se defense he put on before the jury.

Monday and Tuesday there was a lack of urgency from Qusai. But that changed when he returned from court Wednesday evening. Closing arguments had concluded that day, and the case was now in the hands of the jury. He believed that a verdict, whether guilty or not guilty, would compel the marshals to expedite him to the nearest federal prison to await sentencing and finishing out the 54 years he'd already began serving. I highly doubted that, but Qusai, not wanting to chance it, was adamant on leaving that night.

Qusai's goal was possible because we had approximately 6 to 8 hours of work to go, but considering how abnormally quiet Max was that night, such a task was extremely risky. Every scratch, scrape, and bang seemed to resonate through Max and out into the corridor where the guards sat. By 10 o'clock, the guards were making rounds incessantly, and my hands were swollen and stiff from gripping the tiny saw. My intuition warned me that it wasn't a good night and that we should wait until the following day, which would allow me time to have everything ready for us. Following such intuition, I called it a night.

Exhausted, mentally and physically, I crawled back into my hole, snatched the dummy out of the bed, knocked on the wall and told Rayford that I was done for the night, washed up, and went to sleep to faint sounds of Qusai lightly, yet desperately, grating his saw against his ceiling.

Around 3 a.m. I was aroused by the sound of Qusai whispering my name. "My brotha, I need your assistance," he said with a sense of urgency. I reluctantly got up and peeked through my favorite peephole and was instantly alarmed and amused by what I saw. Qusai had grown impatient and tried to bend upward one of the unfinished sides of metal he'd been sawing, but instead of breaking, the metal was sticking straight in the air like an open hatchway. Furthermore, the hole was still too small, and when he tried to squeeze through, he ended up getting stuck. I had to grab hold of his arms and help pull him through. Ironically though, once out of the hole, he couldn't fit back in.

Now we were faced with a serious problem. There was no dummy in his bed, a plastic property bin—which he'd been using as a stool—on his sink, and a huge conspicuous hole in his ceiling, a hole that was illuminated with light from the attic. Worst of all, the guard was expected to make a round in less than 20 minutes. We were left with no choice but to leave, and we had less than 20 minutes to do so.

"Damn!" Qusai said. "I need to get my *Art of War* and *Bloody Moon* books." At that moment I was convinced that he was crazy.

With less than 18 minutes to go, we didn't have time to cut out the slats on the exterior vent cover, so we were forced to kick them out, on an unusually quiet night. But first, Qusai went to awake B.G., Rayford, and Ray Ray so that they could make a little noise to help drown out some of the noise we were making. Meanwhile, I rushed to my cell and gathered the pictures of my daughter and flushed the rest.

With less than 10 minutes on our clock, Max began to stir with toilets flushing, water running, bunks squeaking, and prisoners talking. Qusai and I were at the vent in the attic preparing to leave. As I pulled the louver out, I felt a surge of excitement and Qusai smiled like a kid at a birthday party. We were one kick away from freedom, one kick away from cheating the government out of 54 years in Qusai's case and a potential life sentence in mine. One kick.

I pressed my foot against the slats, cocked it back, and kicked. A loud, crashing sound of twisting metal echoed through the attic—and likely through the quiet residential neighborhood abroad—causing the prisoners down below to gasp in suspense. The slats were now dangling like limp tree branches after a powerful storm, and for a fleeting moment my right foot was actually free for the first time in nine months. I pulled my foot back in and tied a sheet around one of the bars to help aid my short drop to freedom. I clutched the sheet, stuck my head through the bars, and proceeded to squeeze my upper torso through. It felt like the bars were crushing my ribs, but not enough to stop me or change my mind. It was certainly a tight fit; however, I was limber and contortionistic enough to wiggle through. My head was free, allowing me to see the night sky and the red bricks on the outside of the building. One more second and more wriggle, and my torso would've been free.

But before I could wriggle free, I was stopped by a vision. On the side of the building, down below in the parking lot, there was movement. A body, a person. I quickly retreated, nearly ripping my ears off as I withdrew my head from between the bars.

"What are you doing?" Qusai asked.

"Somebody's out there," I whispered.

"Who?"

"I don't know," I said, attempting to stick my head back through the bars to see.

"No!" Qusai grabbed me. "They might see you. Just fix the vent and wait."

I cautiously pulled the twisted and dangling slats in and tried to stabilize them as best as I could. Suddenly, a bright light flashed on the louver, startling us like cockroaches. Instinctively, I moved my head to the side of the louver. When the light disappeared, I peeped from the side of the louver and saw a baffled cop standing in the parking lot and looking up at the louver. Apparently, he hadn't the slightest idea what was happening.

While the confused cop stood there figuratively scratching his head, we quietly crawled to our cell. Ironically, Qusai was now able to squeeze back into the hole. With no time to jimmy-rig the detached pieces of metal back into his ceiling, I simply covered the hole with a towel, and raced back to my cell. I dismantled the dummy and scattered the body parts underneath the bunk; then I lay in the bunk and pretended to be asleep.

Moments later I heard a couple of redneck guards inside the utility passageway searching for what they naively believed to be a trapped bird or rodent. I lay there, listening, worrying and praying that they stick with the trapped-animal assumption, and leave with the assumption that it escaped. However, when one of them climbed onto Qusai's ceiling to inspect the louver, he accidentally stumbled upon the towel covering the hole. He kicked it away and said: "Holy shit, Bubba, looka here."

All of the lights came on in Max, and an army of cops swarmed in. They pulled Qusai out of his cell; then, several minutes later, they made their way around to my cell. When they stepped to my bars and ordered me to cuff up, I noticed their eyes looking up at the ceiling for the first time since I'd been in Max. Impressed with my cleverness, some smiled and other stared with awe. Never before had anyone tried to escape from Max. In fact, such thoughts had never even crossed the minds of neither prisoners nor guards. Even when confronted with blatant hints and clues, they refused to believe. They didn't believe because they didn't believe it was possible. I changed all of that. The guard who once criticized me for attempting to smuggle the saw into Max was now choking on his words; he now knew exactly what could be done with a "tiny saw."

PART TWO: RUNAWAY SLAVE

CHAPTER 13

IT GETS WORSE

Once again, I found myself trapped in a cell asking myself that same question: Why? Was it stupidity, misfortune, or divine intervention? It was a damn cigarette—that's why! As luck (or divine intervention, or whatever you want to call it) would have it, there was a cop standing out in front of the jail smoking a cigarette when I kicked out the vent slats. He heard the loud crashing sound and thought there had been some sort of accident on the side of the building. When he walked around to the side of the building to investigate, he noticed that the slats in the louver were moving. Assuming that a bird or a rodent was trapped inside and trying to break free, the cop radioed for assistance. Dumbfounded, the two cops stared up at the vent expecting to see a bird or rodent come scurrying out, but little did they know that what they assumed to be a bird was actually a jail bird desperately trying to break free.

Whether I blamed Qusai, myself, the cop, or misfortune, deep down inside I sensed that it was something more profound than retardation and bad luck. No man could be so cursed as to be perpetually followed through life by a black cloud. By the same token, no man should be so foolish as to keep making the same mistakes over and over again. But there I was, doing just that.

Immediately upon learning about the escape attempt, the sheriff rounded up a posse of officers and flipped Max upside down. They moved us from our cells and locked us in various cells throughout the jail while they inspected every square inch of Max. They searched for saws and tools, cuts and scratches on the walls and ceilings, and anything else that could be associated with escaping. After the shakedown, we were all taken back to Max, including me—to a different cell, of course. As for Qusai, he went to court that morning and never returned. I later heard that he was found guilty and tossed a water pitcher at the jurors.

I went on to spend many dismal days inside my cell, kicking myself and being haunted by thoughts of being a worthless dad. There was no escaping my dejection. I was confined to my cell 24 hours a day, coming out only for a shower in leg shackles. And they made sure to place me in a cell up at the front of the unit, as far away from the louver as possible. The sounds of freedom were impossible to hear, and only those of the other prisoners talking, shouting, arguing, stressing, and banging on walls were heard. Occasionally, whenever the unit door was opened, I'd hear a sad song like John Legend's "Ordinary People" blaring from the TV in the corridor. Every song seemed to be a sad one, probably because I was sad.

I was so sad that I, like many other prisoners of the War on Drugs, hated everything about America. It was because of some clandestine racism that Reagan's War on Drugs was escalated and targeted toward African American men. And it was because of law enforcement, judicial jurisprudence, and congressional intent that I was facing a life sentence while Yeyo was sentenced to 46 months. And it was because of this ridiculous War on Drugs that I wouldn't be able to be a father to my daughter. I was so sad that I now understood the psychosis of hopelessness that could make a man sacrifice his life for the hope of a better afterlife. I was dejected to the point that a promise of 10 virgins and a blessing from God could've enticed me to do something crazy.

As if the psychedelic can and the agonizing concern of failing in my paternal obligations weren't enough of a psychological burden, my newly appointed attorney showed up one morning with more bad news. While my trial date had repeatedly been postponed, the government had been building a stronger case against me.

Investigating a trail of suspicious money orders purchased in St. Louis and cashed in California, the feds stumbled upon

Nicole, a white woman who'd transported marijuana from L.A. to St. Louis two times on my behalf. While in St. Louis, Nicole purchased postal money orders and cashed them when she returned to California. There was nothing criminal about purchasing and cashing money orders across state lines. But when federal agents questioned her about the money orders, she foolishly told them about the times she'd transported marijuana for me. And although I had never seen an ecstasy tablet before, she lied and said that I'd once strapped ecstasy and marijuana around her. She basically turned simple money order transactions into a money laundering charge.

The money order trail didn't end with Nicole, I had once mailed out a package of money orders using the return name and address of my friend and former girlfriend, Audrey, who was also white, and heartbroken, and scorned. I had no ill intent when mailing the money orders, nor did I intend to implicate Audrey in my business; I only used her name because I knew that I could trust her with the money orders if they were to be returned to sender or if I didn't make it back home safely. When the feds showed up at her door, though, she was terrified, and when they lied and told her that I had a slew of white women and that Nicole was living with me, she became indignant. All of this came on the heels of her learning that I fathered a child with a woman other than her.

Certainly, Audrey didn't know any details about my marijuana dealings; in fact, we'd broken up long before I started dealing marijuana. We were still good friends, though, and I still deposited thousands of dollars into her account every month for her to pay bills. But she didn't know where the money derived from. Still, Audrey stated that she was aware of my having white women who transported marijuana for me, even though she really didn't because the women the agents were talking about didn't really exist.

The money order trail also led to several others, but they didn't cave in and say anything incriminating about me. Instead, they tried to protect me by saying that the money orders were sent to them because I purchased cars and other legitimate materials from them. The agents even showed up at my mother's house, only to be cursed out and yelled at.

November 23, 2004, ten months after my arrest, and twenty-six days after Qusai and I were caught trying to escape, I was taken before a magistrate and arraigned on a superseding indictment charging me with three additional counts. Count 3 charged me with conspiracy to commit money laundering, and counts 4 and 5 charged me with attempting to escape from custody.

As expected, Nicole was charged as a co-conspirator to the money laundering; however, she was not charged with the drugs she confessed to knowingly and intentionally distributing. I couldn't help but wonder whether her skin color prevented the prosecutor from charging her with the more serious offense. I had heard tales of federal prosecutors being lenient in charging white drug-offenders, but I hadn't paid much attention to it until now.

Now that I had Angel, Yeyo, and two white women scheduled to testify against me, and the evidence was mounting, it was the perfect time to reconsider the cooperating plea my previous attorney had tried to convince me to agree to. As she had said, I could be out for my 40's, still a young, healthy, handsome man with vast opportunity for employment.

Yeah right! Young and handsome perhaps. But good health wasn't guaranteed to any man, especially one confined to a concrete and steel jungle of violence, stress, poor medical treatment, and terrible food. And decent employment seemed more like a fairytale than reality for a 40-year-old black who'd spent decades behind bars washing dishes, buffing floors, and counting bricks in solitary confinement. Quite frankly, a 40-year-old snitch couldn't even get a job in a criminal syndicate, let alone a corporation.

In my opinion, the only thing worse than a 40-year-old snitch is a 20year-old snitch because that means he'll be a snitch for a long time. Other than getting home before my daughter's graduation, there wasn't anything good to come from snitching. At the end of the day, there would've been more brothers imprisoned and separated from their family and community.

By the same token, the flow of drugs wouldn't have been disturbed one bit. If Pablo Escobar, Arellono Felix, and El Chapo can be taken off the streets and not slow the illicit drug trade, what good is there in taking a few small-time negroes off the streets? One more dude who can't vote, who can't get a decent job, who can't possess a weapon, and who can't be there to raise his children. I didn't want to be the 40-year-old snitch responsible for that decimation.

The prosecutor was so confident in his case that he called me and my attorney to the court building to offer me a deal. I was unexpectedly taken to the court building where my attorney, the prosecutor, and two federal agents (one of them who looked like the cartoon character Buzz Light-Year, with an enormous neck) greeted me in a private room. Suddenly, my attorney and the prosecutor excused themselves, leaving me alone with the agents. They sparked frivolous conversation, and I responded congenial, thereby, inadvertently giving them the impression that I'd be willing to cooperate. Apparently, they took my kindness for weakness, because they pulled out their ink pens and note pads when my attorney and the prosecutor returned. The prosecutor laid all of his evidence on the table, including actual statements for me to read, and said that he wanted to offer me a deal.

I flipped through the statements and proffers. Steve Carraway had proffered, Leandro Brooks, and many more people, including Derrick "Heavy D" Burton, a 400-pound member of the Rat Pack who didn't know me from a can of paint. Still, that didn't stop him from lying and saying that he'd purchased cocaine and marijuana from me during the summer of 2003. Yeyo's proffer claimed that I was "The Man" and that he was just a peasant who had been paid to keep an eye on me. I didn't know what to make of Angel's proffer; in one of them, he stated that I knew about the marijuana, and in the other, he was vague about it.

After I finished reading through the documents, the prosecutor said that if I were to cooperate, he'd recommend a sentence in the range of 15 years. Needless to say, I declined, causing the disgruntled agents to put their ink pens back into their pockets. While escorting me down to the basement, Buzz Lightyears aggressively bumped into me a few times, and the other agent said that I was making a big mistake. He went on to say: "You'd be amazed at how many prisoners still write me to this day, thanking me for the reduced sentences I've gotten them."

I didn't doubt that, because there are plenty of suckers who thank the devil for purchasing their soul. Many of them get out of the feds and return to dealing drugs. Unfortunately for the agents, my soul and dignity wasn't for sale.

As the government's case grew, and my discovery documents increased from 60 pages to 600 pages, I grew more stubborn and rebellious. It was now clear to me that my incarceration and the War on Drugs wasn't as much about suppressing the abuse of illicit drugs (which can be done only by suppressing the demand) as it was about suppressing certain groups and classes of people– particularly the black, brown, and the poor–to the benefit of other groups of people. Certainly the government was smarter than I, and even I knew that mass incarceration of African Americans wasn't the answer to America's drug problem. There was no doubt in my mind that the government had a hidden agenda.

Just the thought of the government's twisted agenda was enough to induce more thoughts of escaping. I was going to escape even if it meant dying in the process. I didn't care about the government, the judge, the prosecutor, or the cops. In my opinion, they all were supportive of a racist war–

the War on Drugs. Ever since my failed escape, the guards routinely inspected my cell every day, thereby, making it nearly impossible to cut another hole in the ceiling. Still, I came up with another way to escape the cell.

After noticing that the guards merely pounded on the vent cover when inspecting the cell, I devised a plan to convert the vent cover into a secret trap door. The plan involved my cutting around the welds that affixed the sloping vent-cover to the wall. With the welds still attached to the wall, I planned to carve deep grooves into them so that the pronged edges of the detached vent-cover could be jammed into them and hold the vent cover in place. I would then jimmy-rig the inner sides of the vent cover so that it would remain steady and undisturbed whenever the guards were to pound on it. I even made a paste out of toothpaste and crushed pencil lead to conceal the cuts around the rusty welds. The plan was brilliant.

B.G was able to persuade the same guard to bring him more candy bars, free of charge. By now, I was beginning to wonder whether the guard suspected something fishy behind the candy bars; after all, they were the same brand as those sold in the commissary at the jail, only bigger.

I wanted to believe that he assumed there were drugs inside, or perhaps he believed B.G. had a hell of a sweet tooth. Whatever his thoughts were, if he were thinking at all, I really appreciated him. And for the record, if he really did believe that the candy bars were merely that, I didn't intend to dupe him; I just believed that it was in our best interest that he didn't know what was inside. Thus, he wouldn't know about my escape plans, nor would he be a knowing and willing accomplice to them. If ever asked, he could've honestly said that he didn't know anything about hacksaws being smuggled into the jail.

With no local support, I paid Ray Ray to have his people prepare the candy bars, and I reached out to my friends Kacy and Courtney to meet with the guard and give him the candy bars and cigarettes. When I finally got the saws, I was slightly disappointed because they were extremely small. There were several of them, barely 3 inches long with a slew of tiny teeth. I spread them out in different hiding spots throughout the jail. I had one in the shower, the TV room, the law library, and my mouth, ready to be used at any given moment–there was no telling when opportunity would arise.

Every day, after cell inspection, I'd spit the tiny saw out and slowly grate the teeth against the metal around the welds on the vent cover. The task was very tedious, but surprisingly, the slew of teeth on the saw made it pretty efficient.

One evening while I was quickly sawing, my neighbor Dennis, the lone white prisoner, tapped on the wall and whispered: "You're too loud– you know what I mean?" Yes, I knew what he meant, but I pretended that I didn't. The old man was no fool though; he was probably one of the few prisoners in Max who knew what the faint grating sound was. He was around during my last failed escape, and according to him, he knew what I was up to then. He just didn't say anything.

"I can recognize that sound from a mile away," he said. "I've used 'em many times myself–know what I mean?"

"It's just a little piece of one I'd managed to hold on to," I lied to throw him off my trail. "I was testing to see if it'll work, but it won't, so I'm going to flush it." I flushed my toilet, adding a little color to my lie.

From that day on, Dennis would go out of his way to talk to me. Either he was trying to earn his way into my next escape, or he was trying to earn his name into my next stack of discovery documents as a government witness. I wasn't sure of which, so I was extremely cautious of what I said to him. Most of the time I just listened to what he had to say. "Listen to me, Bosco," he said, after a week of not hearing my sawing anymore. "If you're trying to go, you gotta go quietly."

"Yeah, I know," I replied, not really knowing what he was talking about. In fact, I hadn't done any sawing ever since the day he first tapped on my wall.

"Listen," he whispered. "S-U-L-F-U-R-I-C A-C-I-D. Did you hear that?"

"Yeah," I replied, still confused though.

"It's like magic," he said. "It'll eat through this (he tapped the wall) and this (he rattled his barred gate)."

Now he had my full attention. I had dreamed of an acid that could eat through metal, and now that he'd mentioned it, I reflected back to a scene in the movie *Bad Boys*, starring Sean Penn, where a nerdy juvenile prisoner smeared corrosive acid on a fence around the prison to escape.

"Don't take much for the both of us—know what I mean?"

The both of us? Just because he spoke anti-snitch jargon and had advised me of the so-called magic acid didn't make us partners. I had already told myself that my next escape would be a solo act starring myself. I certainly wasn't willing to take an old, strange guy along, especially one I'd met through a metal wall. After my bad experience with John and the two truck drivers, I was skeptical about trusting white men posing to be loyal criminals. I didn't express this to Dennis though. I just strung him along and told him whatever he wanted to hear—anything to keep him from snitching on me.

As time passed, Dennis began to sense that I was stringing him along. He spilled his heart to me, stating that he had a bad liver and a short life-expectancy. Escaping was his only chance at getting out of prison alive. He claimed to have too much dignity to cooperate with the government. He said that he would disregard his Christian values and commit the ultimate sin before he were to stoop so low and become a snitch. In fact, he'd already made a rope, and every night he lay in bed staring at the ceiling, he was tempted to use it.

I sympathized for him, but I still refused to involve him in my escape. I was slowly learning the hard way that altruism is a bad trait to have in prison and the life of crime. In order to secure my own success, I needed to develop a stone heart and a concrete mind. In other words, I had to be selfish and calculating just like everyone else, and although that was difficult for me, I had to learn to try. Another thing standing in the way of my bringing the old man along was his crimes. He had a murder charge hanging over his head in Missouri, and I didn't want the attention associated with a murderer on the I am.

Again, I never expressed this to the old man; instead I continued to entertain his fantasies and tales of hiding out in the Appalachians and being harbored by people he touted as being "good ol' boys." According to him, all I had to do was get us a ride to Tennessee, and he'd take it from there.

"But whoever it is, make sure they got soul, cuz I don't trust no white women," he said. He claimed to love his white women, but in the nearly 60 years he'd been dealing with them, he'd never met one who could keep her "pie hole" shut in the face of the law. "Even if they don't know anything, they'll lie, cry, and try, to keep from wearing cuffs," he said. "And trust me, Bosco, ain't nobody more dangerous in the court of law than a crying white woman."

Taking the old man's advice, I set out to find the sulfuric acid he'd spoken so highly about. It took several weeks, but I eventually located it and had it smuggled in through Rayford, who had it smuggled by the same guard B.G. had been dealing with. The guard had no idea what was inside the bottle, and I told Rayford to instruct him not to open the bottle under any circumstances. The guard followed the instructions and brought the acid directly to me at Rayford's request.

Wasting no time to test the acid, I poured some on the welds around the vent cover, and stared at them, expecting them to sizzle and incinerate before my eyes. However, the metal was impervious to the pungent, golden acid. A full hour passed without anything happening to the welds, so out of sheer frustration, I poured an excessive amount around the vent cover, allowing it to run down the sides and drip onto the pavement.

Surprisingly, the puddles on the pavement began to sizzle and produce small craters. Hopeful that it would do the same to the metal in due time, I poured more around the vent cover, a little on the bars, and a little on the sink, and let it soak overnight. The following morning I awoke to find that the acid wasn't as magical as Dennis touted it to be—either that, or I was doing something wrong. Dissatisfied with the acid, I poured it into a mouthwash bottle I'd purchased from commissary, and tossed it in the bottom of my plastic property bin with other items.

CHAPTER 14

MAX ON FIRE

I was awakened by what sounded like a squad of soldiers marching and shouting: "Orange Crush!" Whoever they were, they were either right outside the jail or somewhere inside, and they were getting closer with each stomp. As they neared, I heard a faint "One Two!" before thunderous "Orange Crush!" The "one two" sounded like a drill sergeant, and the "Orange Crush!" sounded like an entire platoon responding. I and several other prisoners were asking the same question: "Who in the hell is that?"

"That's Orange Crush!" Rayford warned everyone. "Get rid of all of your contraband!" The formidable marching and shouting stopped right outside Max, and the sound of barking dogs emerged. Suddenly, the front door opened, and at least two-dozen six-footers dressed in fatigue and ugly black boots with laces that seemed to never end rushed into the unit shouting for no reason. In groups of threes, they dispersed to each cell and ordered each prisoner to strip naked, open his mouth, lift his testicles, bend over and spread his butt cheeks, and back up to the bars to be cuffed.

We were pulled out of the cell, escorted out into the walkway, and forced to face the wall while two soldiers (or whatever they were) stood beside each one of us as the third soldier ransacked the cell. Ray Ray, being Ray Ray, refused to strip naked, so he was extracted from his cell, fully dressed and talking shit. Once out in the walkway, he looked down at the woofing dog and said: "What the fuck you makin' all that— all that god damn noise fo', mutt?" He then kicked the dog and spat on it before being dragged out of the unit by the toy soldiers.

Actually, they were a tactical team of correctional officers from the Illinois Department of Corrections. They were invited to the jail by the Sheriff to train the guards how to shakedown

Max. Since I was labeled as "the prisoner with rabbit in his blood," I was their primary focus, aside from the moment when Ray Ray stole the show. They threatened to take me to a prison where I'd never see the sun (as if I could see it in Max). They were basically a bunch of trained jerks who couldn't survive in Iraq, so they used their military gear and tactics on defenseless prisoners.

When all was said and done, the toy soldiers didn't find anything, not the acid in the mouthwash bottle, nor the tiny saw concealed in my mouth.

The relationship between Rayford and the guard had grown tremendously in a short period of time. The guard smuggled in tobacco, marijuana, and just about anything else Rayford asked for. Since the acid didn't work, Rayford and I were devising a plan to entice the guard to smuggle in more obvious escape paraphernalia, such as a small, electrical cutting-device and a crow bar. But first, Rayford wanted to rake in as much money as he could from his tobacco and marijuana business. He also wanted to make sure that the guard was open to supporting something like an escape

Meanwhile, Rayford's business was booming, and prisoners throughout the jail were having their friends and family deposit money into his commissary account. Before he ever got his hands on any marijuana or tobacco, Rayford had promised several other prisoners that he would supply them in due time. One of such prisoners was Rooster, who was also in Max at the time, but not indefinitely.

Rayford told Rooster to get out of Max and into general population and then he would supply him with enough tobacco to sustain his unit. Rooster, excited and full of hope, put on his best behavior and earned a bed in general population, where he stayed out of trouble and awaited Rayford's blessing. However, when the merchandise came through, Rayford blessed everybody but Rooster.

It was increasingly becoming known amongst the prisoners that the guard was doing personal favors. In fact, he was doing favors for a prisoner in just about every unit. Crazy thing, he wasn't even charging for his services; he was simply one of those cool dudes who couldn't say *No*. I wanted so desperately to pull him by his ear and warn him about his perilous behavior, but I could never encounter him without the prying ears and eyes of other prisoners or guards. Also I didn't want to meddle in the other prisoners' business.

While I patiently stood by waiting for the right opportunity to approach the guard, Rooster went behind Rayford's back and made his own proposition to the guard. Instead of using charisma, though, he tried to blackmail him. He caught the guard walking through the unit one night and passed him a note demanding a piece of the action, *or else*. When the guard refused to budge, Rooster filled out a complaint form alleging that the guard had smuggled contraband into the jail for the prisoners in Max, including the saw blades that were used in the attempted escape. Although he knew nothing about the guard's smuggling in the saws, he added that in hopes of pressuring the guard into reconsidering. He gave the complaint to the guard and told him to either cooperate or turn it in to his superior.

Rather than cooperating or taking it to his superior, the guard took the complaint to Rayford, who happened to be in the TV room at the time. Rayford read it and told the guard to bring it to me. At the time, I was in the shower-cell using a paper clip to pick the locks on my leg irons—just for practice. I read the complaint and didn't think it was such a big deal. After all, it was common for Rooster to bully and extort people—he was real gangster. Certainly, he was no snitch; he knew that the complaint wouldn't go any further than the guard. "Don't worry about it," I told the guard. "Throw it in the trash; I'll get at Rooster." I was sure I could clean up everything with a little diplomacy.

Instead of doing as I suggested, though, the guard heeded

the advice of another prisoner and wrote an incident report charging Rooster with attempting to blackmail a guard. The sergeant investigated the allegations and interviewed Rooster, who admitted that he knew nothing about the guard's smuggling in contraband, and that he was merely trying to extort him out of a cigarette or two. But what Rooster and the guard didn't know was that the black detective upstairs had gotten wind of cigarettes and reefer being dealt in the jail, and he knew about the money being deposited in Rayford's account. He knew that Rayford was dealing, and he suspected that a guard was supplying him. Now he had an idea who that guard might be. After all, there had to be something about the guard in order for Rooster to single him out from all the other guards at the jail.

While I pondered my approach to the guard, the detective was pondering his. Armed with a picture of the guard, he visited the family and friends of every prisoner whom he suspected of dealing with the guard, including Rayford's sister. Of course when he approached them, he pretended that the guard had already divulged everything. Once he duped the people out of enough information, he called the guard into his office for questioning. The guard, wanting to get everything off his chest and move forward with his life, confessed to everything—the cigarettes, the weed, and the bottle of liquid substance. He didn't know anything about the saws, but he did acknowledge bringing B.G. several candy bars.

On the day that the guard was scheduled to begin his work week, he arrived early, sans his uniform, sans his keys, and sans a radio. As prisoners were escorted to and from their visits, they saw the guard and quickly spread the word: The guard was locked in one of the small holding cells up front. Sadly, the guard learned the hard way that reticence is the best response when questioned by the cops.

The days following the guard's arrest were some of my most dismal. I was profoundly disturbed in many ways. I hate to see good people get in trouble, especially those who are only trying to help others. More disturbing was the fact that I played a role in the guard's fate. Also, on a more selfish note, I had missed out on a rare opportunity to get all of the tools and gadgets necessary to make a quick and quiet escape. I had a lot of hope invested in the guard, but all I had to show for that golden opportunity was a fist full of saws, a bottle of not-so-magical acid, somber days, and a burdened conscience.

The only good thing to happen in those days was that my privileges were reinstated and I was allowed to go to the TV room every day for an hour. The TV room was merely a barred cell right outside Max, in the corridor. Although it was called the TV/Rec room, there was nothing but a bench and a milk crate inside it. The TV was actually in the corridor, affixed to the wall. Most prisoners went to the TV room simply to watch the corridor and harass the guards and other prisoners as they walked by.

One afternoon, while standing at the bars watching a true crime story about a bank robber who had escaped from a federal detention center in North Las Vegas and was now hiding out in a cheap motel room with his wife and kids, I heard the captain of the jail walking up the corridor. There was no mistaking the sound of his shoes, a pair of hard-bottoms that sounded like high heels, but far from seductive. In fact, they sounded more like tap-dancing shoes, and they irked me every time I heard them.

It was extremely rare for the captain to come tap-dancing through this part of the jail, so when he stopped at the guard's desk in front of Max and asked for the keys, I began to worry. Just a couple of days earlier, I had resumed sawing around the welds on the vent cover, and although I'd done a good job of concealing the marks and cuts, I couldn't help but worry. He entered Max on the E-side, and came out ten minutes later on the F-side. He returned the keys to the guard, and tap danced down the corridor, leaving me puzzled as to why he'd walked through Max alone.

By now the fugitive on TV—whom I was fanatically rooting for—was barricaded in the motel room, surrounded by cops. It appeared that he had no choice but to come out either with his hands up or shooting. Having his wife and kids with him, I assumed he would do the former. However, he did something else: He killed his two daughters, then the wife, and then himself. And with that sad ending, the guards came and escorted me back to my metallic tomb.

As we passed the old man Steve's cell, he shouted, "Mistakes are to be paid for!" to no one in particular. He was just having one of his usual outbursts—a proverbial one, though. True indeed, I silently agreed. But some prices are much too steep. I thought about the amount of time I was facing for mine, and the price the fugitive on TV had paid for his. Steep. Too steep.

Later that evening while browsing through a stack of magazines that Rayford had given me the day before, I came across a porn magazine. I had never seen the magazine before, and although I had never thoroughly looked through the stack, I was almost certain that it hadn't been in there. To be sure, I yelled down to Rayford and asked him, and he replied that he had no knowledge of the magazine. After figuratively scratching my head for a while, I was left with no choice but to speculate that one of the guards had deliberately placed it there. A tacit solicitation from one of them, one in need of a few extra dollars.

To determine which guard, I searched through the magazine, hoping to find a message or clues. There was no message, but a quizzical mind will always find clues. The pages contained mostly black men and white women, so I excluded the white guards from my list. But then, in the back pages, I saw small clippings of black men and a white transgender, and suddenly the captain came to mind. He was white, egotistical, flamboyant, and overzealous. Like all overzealous men, his overzealous public persona was clearly a facade. Perhaps he was hiding his sexual orientation behind his facade, and perhaps he had a crush on me. That could've explained his narcissism and those shoes he wore.

Who better to help me escape than the captain? Certainly, he was the one who put the magazine there, but fortunately and unfortunately, he didn't have a crush on me—not that I'm aware of. He had placed the magazine in my cell to see if his guards would find it when they searched my cell. It was simply a test to see whether they were doing their job properly. When the guards found out, they became irate.

I had been in Max over a year now, and it had quickly changed for the worst. The Walkman's had been confiscated; the commissary had been reduced to garbage; the guards were now searching my cell every day; several prisoners had committed suicide; the captain was lurking behind the scene, trying to snare me and his guards, and he had several of the guards and nurses assisting him; and most of the long term prisoners had moved on, leaving me, B.G., and Rooster as the only remaining veterans of Max.

After having his murder conviction vacated because the verdict form failed to give the jury the option to find him not guilty, Rayford copped a plea which required him to serve only 6 more months in prison. He was sent to Menard State Prison to serve out that sentence.

The old man Dennis never did get a chance to put his improvised rope to use. One afternoon while I was in the TV room, two officers unexpectedly showed up at Max and transferred him across the river to a jail in Missouri, close to where his trial was scheduled to begin. The officers arrived so suddenly that he didn't have a chance to get rid of his rope. The guards later found it underneath his mat along with a bunch of pills he'd been saving up. I looked up and saw the old man being escorted down the corridor by two officers, one wearing a five-gallon cowboy hat and carrying the old man's property. "Good luck," the old man yelled at me. "Don't accept any wooden nickels." And that was the last I saw of him. Two weeks later I received a letter from him stating that his spirits were so much better. (Making me believe that it was Max that made prisoners so depressed.)

Even killer Ray Ray was now gone. Since Max had changed, he decided to take his show on the road. He quit delaying the trial and let it proceed so that he could hurry and get back across the river to the maximum security prison in Missouri to serve his multiple life-sentences. Although he went through with the trial, he was hoping to plead guilty and save the tax payers $100,000 in expenses. However, such a plea would have been contingent on him being paid $1,000. Anyone could've tendered the money, and he would've happily pled guilty and returned to Missouri. But since no one came forward with the money, he went to trial solely for the purpose of wasting the state's resources and tormenting the family of the deceased, who happened to be an officer.

Days before the trial, Ray Ray had the audacity to blame me for the changes in Max, as if he hadn't caused any disturbances. Apparently the administration concurred with Ray Ray. Violence and suicide had always been a part of Max, but nothing ever changed until my attempts to escape. So perhaps it was my fault that Max changed for the worse.

However, it wasn't my fault that escaping was deemed more of a threat than acts of violence. That has always been the law of the land. Indeed, the runaway slave had always been more of a concern to Master than the slave that beat other slaves. Violence upon each other is a form of submission; whereas, running away is a sign of rebellion. So in the eyes of the masters, I was just like Kunta Kinte. Had the law permitted in the twenty-first century; I would've been amputated at the foot just like Kunta.

CHAPTER 15

VICISSITUDES OF FORTUNE

Ever since my last escape attempt, I starved myself and quit doing pushups, and lost nearly 20 pounds of muscle mass. I referred to my new skeletal physique as my "escape weight." I was the perfect size for squeezing through the gap between the bars on the exhaust vent in the attic. Most of the guards and nurses who remembered me from when I first arrived at the jail, and use to hang shirtless from the rail of the top tier doing pull ups every morning, worried that I'd fallen ill. Many of the nurses tried to persuade me into getting tested. But I declined for fear of having my DNA stored in a federal lab to be later used against me in some type of Big brotherly way. Some nurses refused accept *No* for an answer. They practically tried everything they could, to persuade me, including flirtation.

Sometimes I wondered if "Massa" had put nurses on me out of concern that I might die on the plantation—he wasn't going to let me escape that easily. Every time I was in the TV room and a nurse walked by, she'd stop and ask me for blood. One particular nurse would go out of her way, even stopping at my cell whenever she passed out medication in the unit. She often arrived with moist lips, a seductive smile, and flirtatious eyes; as if she had a bet wagered that she'd get my blood before any of the other nurses. She was so outlandish and aggressive with her flirting that I half expected her canines to turn into fangs, and for her to pull me to the bars and suck the blood from me.

Ironically, this particular nurse wasn't even working at the jail when I was in general population and 20 pounds more muscular. She, like several other nurses, was judging my appearance in contrast to my mug shot and the rumors circulated by the guards and other nurses. "Looks are just looks," I told her. "Sometimes they can be misleading." I still felt strong, still could do 100 push-ups nonstop, and still had an erection every morning I awoke. "I'm perfectly healthy," I informed her. "I'm this skinny for a reason. Ain't no telling when I might have to squeeze through a small hole."

The nurse audaciously replied: "I have a hole you can squeeze into." At that moment, a secret liaison ensued between us, and she became the focus of my attention. I fantasized about her helping me escape and hiding inside her home while the feds searched the globe for me. She had me waking up early every morning with excitement and eager anticipation of what might come next. I made a point of requesting my hour in the TV room during the hours she'd be making her rounds through the corridor. During these moments, she'd stop at the TV room and slyly flirt with me, and pretend to check my blood pressure through the bars while we exchanged notes. She even surprised me by bringing me one of her cell phones.

Even through all of this, I still wouldn't give her any blood. In addition to the nurse's support, I became acquainted with another employee who, for the right price, was willing to smuggle anything into the jail. Between the two, I managed to obtain a cell phone, a battery-operated charger, and a multi-tool consisting of pliers, a saw, and a screwdriver. I kept the contraband concealed in my light fixture. I was also in the process of getting an electric saw, and a small crowbar.

Suddenly my luck changed. Before I could locate the right size electrical saw and have it smuggled into the jail, something happened with my anonymous source, causing me to miss my window of opportunity. I awoke one morning and the window was shut. Once again, my luck had gone bad.

I still had the nurse, but she had limits on what she would do. Although she claimed to want me, she obviously didn't want me badly enough to help me escape. She did, however, continue to charge my phone and do other favors for me. I can't say whether this was good luck, bad luck, or no luck.

Meanwhile I fired my attorney again and was appointed a lawyer who had once represented Qusai until Qusai punched him in his face as a way to force the court to remove him from his case. That was one of Qusai's trump cards. Whenever he grew tired of an attorney and the judge refused appoint another, he'd punch the lawyer in the face to create a conflict of interest.

The new lawyer visited me and informed me that in June, 2005, the government filed a second superseding indictment, adding a new co-defendant, John John, to the money laundering and marijuana conspiracy charges. It all stemmed from a drug bust in Alabama involving Twinky and John John. They'd been busted with cocaine, marijuana, ecstasy, and a myriad of firearms, and as soon as they arrived at the police station, they started snitching. Twinky implicated John John as a person who had rented cars and apartments for me to transport and store marijuana—in fact, the car that I was driving the night of my arrest was rented in John John's name—and John John stated that all of the contraband in the Alabama bust belonged to Twinky.

I learned all of this from my new stack of discovery documents. I also learned the real reason why Yeyo and Twinky were late in arriving to St. Louis. My intuition had been accurate that day. They lied about being in an accident; truthfully, they had been pulled over on Interstate 40 and arrested for carrying a gun, a large amount of currency, and a small amount of marijuana. Had I known that, I probably wouldn't have been at that truck stop that night. My luck was certainly in the bad luck phase.

Less than a month after I was arraigned on the superseding indictment, the guards came into the unit and surprisingly told everyone to pack his property. We were being moved to the F-side, and the prisoners on the F-side were being moved to the E-side. I was caught off guard by the move, and didn't have enough time to decide whether to grab the cell phone charger and tools I had hidden in the light fixture. I also feared the move might be a set up, so I left everything behind and hoped that B.G. or someone trustworthy would move into the cell. As luck would have it, though, B.G. moved into the cell next-door, and a strange dude who bragged of having victoriously fought his pit bulls against Qusai's years earlier moved into the cell. We contemplated having the stranger retrieve the items from the light fixture, but considering my luck, I chose to wait on somebody more trustworthy.

It didn't take long for the strange prisoner to be released to general population and for another prisoner to move into the cell. The new prisoner, Vaughn, was no stranger; he'd been in Max once before during my stay, and had been at the jail for quite some time, fighting drug and weapon charges. Vaughn seemed like the right man for the job; so, without telling him what was inside the light fixture, B.G. asked him to retrieve the items and take them up to the shower cell. Several minutes later, we heard Vaughn taking the light apart, and then go up to the shower. Ten minutes later, the sergeant and his cronies came into the unit and went straight to Vaughn's cell and searched the light. Fortunately, my cell phone had been with the nurse the day they moved us, because instead of removing the items from the light, Vaughn saw what they were and went up to the shower and snitched on B.G.

Yes, my luck had gone from sugar to shit. Nevertheless, since time was still moving forward, and it seemed like I would never get anymore tools, I started using the tiny saw in my mouth to cut around the welds on the vent cover in my new cell. I figured I'd better get it done before another unexpected cell move occurred. With a newfound sense of urgency, I worked at all hours of the day. Then, one day while I was in the midst of sawing, the sergeant and his cronies raided my cell, catching me completely off guard—I was still on my knees at the vent when they showed up at my cell. I tossed the saw into my mouth, metallic sawdust and all, but there was nothing I could do about the fresh cuts on the vent.

They cuffed me and shackled me, then locked me in the shower cell while they ransacked my cell. I heard them take the light fixture apart, and one of the cronies ask: "How would he get one of those in here?" Apparently, they were looking for the cell phone to go with the charger they found on the E-side. They knew that the contraband belonged to me because it was found in my old cell and my fingerprints were on it. What they didn't know, however, was that I'd been expecting them to come looking for the phone, so I told the nurse to keep it until things cooled down.

After 30 minutes of searching, the guards returned me to my cell. They had removed all of the screws from the light fixture, thereby, making it easy for the guards to inspect during their routine searches. They had done a thorough search, but not thorough enough. They, like many other guards and officers before them, had failed to detect the acid inside the mouthwash bottle. Most importantly, they failed to notice the exposed cuts around the vent cover, nor the metallic sawdust scattered on the ground beneath. Finally, it seemed that my luck had just changed for the better.

Anything that has been done once can be done twice, so B.G. began to search for another guard to corrupt. This time, he wanted in on the escape. He'd just been found guilty and was now facing a life sentence. Since he was like a little brother to me, I was willing to do anything to help him get out, even if that meant going on the lam with a convicted murderer. But first we needed better tools, specifically, an electric saw or a crowbar, because the tiny saws were essentially useless now that I was randomly being moved from cell to cell. Since he had successfully corrupted two guards in the past, B.G. was confident that he'd be able to do it again.

While B.G. was on the hunt, Rooster, who was in the cell next to me, had already caught. He and a new nurse (whom I'll refer to as Tee) had developed a personal relationship. Since Tee was willing to do anything for Rooster, and Rooster was looking to make money, he planned to have her smuggle in weed and tobacco, so that he could pick up where Rayford left off. Since I opposed any activity that could attract the attention of the black detective, and didn't want Rooster doing anything that would bring more heat on Max, I paid him to have Tee bring several cell phones.

Unbeknownst to me and my Godmother, who was sending the phones; Rooster had told Tee that the woman she'd be dealing with was his aunt from California. Tee had absolutely no idea that I knew about her relationship with Rooster, or that I was involved. Therefore, when she learned that the woman she'd been communicating with, and was receiving the phones from, happened to be my Godmother, she was shocked. Nevertheless, she still brought the phones and went on to recharge them for us. She never told Rooster that she knew the truth about his so-called aunt, but she'd smirk whenever she'd see me, thereby, subtly indicating that she was aware of my involvement.

Usually when the nurses came through Max, the outer cell-doors would already be unlocked, so the guards would simply open the front door and allow the nurses to enter the unit alone. Once inside Max, the nurses would walk up the walkway distributing medication through the bars. In order to do this, though, they had to step into the cells, out of the view of any guard who might be standing at the front of the walkway. As a way to get Tee to his cell, Rooster often pretended that his blood pressure was high. Since rooster was always complaining of his blood pressure and Tee was always the nurse to come, certain guards–particularly the "haters"–started walking to the cell with Tee.

By now, a couple of nurses had convinced the doctor to put me on a special diet that required more calories. So every night, the nurses would bring me a paper sack containing milk, fruit, and a peanut butter sandwich. Tee and another nurse often filled my bag with yogurt, grapes and other personal snacks. One day, I was shackled and escorted to the medical office for an exam, and while the guard focused on me, a nurse stood behind his back mocking him and filling my bag with food from her personal lunch box.

Since I was receiving nightly snacks, I became the go-through guy for exchanging notes, batteries, and cell phones between Rooster and Tee. Every night, before making her rounds, Tee would conceal the items inside my snack bag. Most of the times I'd be in the shower cell waiting for her to walk through the door; other times, I'd be standing at the bars in my cell. Sometimes I had her hide the contraband inside my sandwich, just to be on the safe side. And to be sure that we were on the same page, I sometimes called her ahead of time and planned our timing.

The more I interacted with Tee, the more she opened up and allowed me to see a side of her that most people at the jail had never seen before. She was really an adorable woman who simply wanted to do what her heart and years of nursing school had encouraged her to do; take care of people, and help those in need. Money wasn't anywhere in the equation, as far as her motive. She brought us the phones and charged them simply so that she could talk to Rooster and I could talk to my family without having to make expensive collect calls.

The more I talked to Tee, the more my heart grew fond of her, and the more Rooster became jealous. He became so insecure and paranoid that he began to accuse her of having a romantic relationship with me. He even went as far as to test her fidelity by having other prisoners attempt to court her. But she never fell for any of his traps—she really cared for him.

◇◇◇◇◇◇◇◇◇

Meanwhile, B.G.'s search for a corrupt guard had paid off. He called me on a cell phone I'd given him, and told me that he managed to allure a use-to-be-but-not-so-attractive-now guard named Gretchen. It was rumored that Gretchen had done personal favors for another prisoner who use to be at the jail. Now she seemed to be willing to do the same for B.G., only on a bigger scale. She said that she was willing to bring anything that could be concealed on her body, including a gun. I declined the firearm, and told B.G. to shoot for an electric saw and a crowbar.

Several days later B.G. said that Gretchen was ready to close the deal. Initially, she wanted B.G.'s mother to meet with her and hand over the cash and tools, but B.G.'s mom didn't want anything to do with it. Then, Gretchen gave B.G. the address to a P.O. Box in Fairview Heights (an odd place for someone like Gretchen to set up a P.O. Box) and told him to have the cash and tools sent there. But before I could fork over the $2,000, I needed her to do something to prove that she wouldn't screw us out of the money. I wanted her to give us something to hang over her head in the event she were to renege on her end of the bargain. I suggested that she bring some cigarettes to show good faith, but B.G. had a better idea; he asked her to bring a charger for the phone I'd given him. She had no idea that he had a phone, so when he told her, she was surprised and desperately wanted to know how he'd managed to smuggle a phone in but couldn't get tools.

Rooster's paranoia reached its zenith when I went behind his back and told Tee not to bring him any drugs or tobacco. This was done on the heels of his learning that she'd used her own money to buy me a new phone. She had told me not to tell him about the phone, but ironically, she ended up telling him herself.

So when she told him that I didn't want her to bring him any weed or tobacco, he had a green-eyed fit, threatening to blackmail her and some more. When I tried to dissuade him he told me: "Since you want to play Captain Save-a-Whore, you can pay the bitch's ransom."

The following morning as I lay in my bunk half asleep. I heard someone in the shower yell down the walkway: "There's a million cops fixing to come in here!" Using a string attached to my phone, specifically, for moments like this, I tied the phone around my penis and pretended to be asleep. The million cops rushed into the E-side and extracted the prisoners from their cells. Seconds later, they rushed into the F-side and did the same thing. When they reached my cell, I pretended to be startled and half asleep. They ordered me to get up and cuff up. I got up, staggering, stretching, and rubbing my eyes dramatically. I was wearing a pair of boxers with a tight pair of briefs underneath, so instead of searching me, they just cuffed and shackled me, and searched the waistband of my boxers before walking me out into the corridor and making me face the wall with all of the other prisoners.

The corridor was packed with myriad of law enforcement officers, including the FBI and the U.S. Marshals. It was certainly much more than a random shakedown. They were looking for something in particular, and I couldn't help but wonder if Rooster had made good on his threats.

Moments into the search, I overheard a group of cops huddled inside the shower cell whispering about something hidden above the roof of the shower. That "something" just so happened to be my extra cell phone and charger that I kept stashed up there. It was inside a sock and pushed to the back of the roof of the shower, by way of a small gap above the shower. It was pushed so far back that I used to have to fish it out to retrieve it. The cops were having difficulty retrieving it, so they called the maintenance workers to go inside the ceiling and retrieve it.

Apparently they found what they came for because after that we were returned to our cells. Everyone except B.G., who was transferred to another jail, leaving behind speculations and rumors. One rumor had it that he'd been caught with a cell phone, and another had him using that same phone to place a hit on one of his codefendants that testified against him. I myself didn't elaborate on the rumors; I just listened and kept an ear on Rooster.

Once the coast was clear, I removed the phone from my penis and called Tee to inform her of what happened. I also warned her that the feds would be questioning employees at the jail. I schooled her on what to say, and essentially told her the same thing the old man Dennis had told me: "Don't accept any wooden nickels." But the following day when she arrived to work, she did exactly what the old man said all white women would do in the face of the law. She accepted the wooden nickel and told everything, everything except the fact that I still had a phone.

CHAPTER 16

CAN'T GET RIGHT

B.G. was gone. My charger was gone. My nightly snacks were gone. Nurse Tee was gone, and the other nurses were no longer allowed to enter Max alone. My conditions were now much worse than they were before I started receiving personal favors. At least before, I still had the element of surprise. But now I had nothing but a slew of tiny saws, a dead cell phone tied to my penis—where it remained most of the day—and extreme anxiety. My nerves were so shot that the mere sound of the door opening was enough to make my heart flutter. Living in Max had now become tantamount to living inside a crack house, subject to being raided at any given moment.

Using the tiny saws to escape Max was now impossible, and considering the heightened security measures and the fact that I was the hottest prisoner in the jail (not to mention my involvement with two employees being fired), getting additional tools seemed unlikely. But like any man, having surmounted the nearly impossible before, I believed I could do it again. And with Gretchen still around, I had a hook to hang my hat of hope on.

I started going out to the TV room every morning in search of Gretchen. It was one late morning in early November when I caught up to her. She came strutting up the corridor on her way to the laundry room across from the TV room. She had her long mulatto hair pulled back into one long braid. From afar she appeared to be a young, sassy woman capable of stopping traffic on an interstate, but up close it was a different story. Her once pretty, caramel complexion and attractive features were quickly fading—a combination of age, stress, and probably hard drugs or booze. As she was entering the laundry room, I made my move. I had a small note for her tightly wrapped in plastic inside my mouth. I spat the note into my hand and called her name. She abruptly stopped, looked at me, rolled her neck back, pointed at herself, and asked, "Who me?"

"I have an important question for you," I said, stepping back away from the bars and holding up the note so that only she could see.

She sashayed over to the bars, still pointing at herself with a dubious expression and glassy eyes. I placed the note between the pages of a law book and gave it to her. Instead of taking the book into the laundry room, she moronically removed the note right there in the corridor and placed it in her breast pocket. She then went inside the laundry room and came out a few minutes later, looking around on the ground, and loudly asked: "What did I do with that note you gave me?" I patted my chest; she then reached into her breast pocket and pulled out the note for me and anyone else to see.

Bimbos. It was always the bimbos who were willing to help. Whatever happened to the courageous, smart, calculating female crime partners we see on TV? In the note, I informed Gretchen that B.G. and I were partners in the deal they had, and that I was still interested in the tools and the charger.

A couple of days later, I saw her again—this time she came looking for me. Her demeanor had changed drastically. She seemed more crisp and clear-headed; even her eyes were clear. I didn't know whether it was the money she was set to make or the sheer amazement that I still had a phone after the shakedowns, but she was enthusiastic, flirtatious, and extremely inquisitive. Although she was serious, she was also giddy and kept thrusting her breasts against the bars as if she wanted me to reach out and touch them. She even had the top two buttons of her shirt unfastened, and twirled her hair and toyed with a huge ink pen in her breast pocket. Throughout our conversation, she kept seductively asking me to speak up. Ultimately, she agreed to bring the charger. But after a week of hearing excuses about her being searched upon entering the jail, I asked another guard to bring me one, and he did.

Once I had the charger, there were two ways for me to use it. I used the power from either my light fixture or the power outlets in the law library. Since my access to the law library was limited, I mostly resorted to the simple, yet risky, task of taking my light fixture apart and connecting the charger to the wires behind the fluorescent bulbs. Taking the light apart and attaching the wires was the easy part. The risky part, however, was that at any moment a guard could've walked through while my cell was pitch dark and the huge Plexiglas light-cover and long fluorescent bulbs were lying on my bunk. Also, one wrong move with a live wire often resulted in the power being shut off in all 16 cells.

My first time blowing out the power was at night, and only the light in my cell went out. Fortunately, I was able to put the light fixture back together before the guard made his rounds. When he came through, I lay nonchalantly in my bunk as he flashed a light into my cell and asked about the light. "I don't know. You guys didn't shut off the lights?" I asked. However, I could sense that he didn't believe me. He knew that I'd been tampering with the light fixture, but he couldn't prove it.

The following morning they moved me back around to the E-side. Two days later, as I was jimmy-rigging the wires in the light fixture in my new cell, I accidentally rubbed the hot wire against some metal and blew out the power in all 16 cells. I quickly put the light fixture back together, and yelled for the guards to turn the lights back on, as if it were they who shut them off. Later that night when I was out in the TV room, one of the guards told me that the prisoner in the cell next to me had told them that he heard me tampering with the light fixture. So while I was feigning ignorant and innocent, they knew all along that I'd been tampering with the light fixture.

The following morning when the guards came to collect the breakfast trays, they took me up to the shower-cell, shut the gate behind me, removed my cuffs and shackles, and ordered me to strip naked. My heart dropped. I wasn't expecting this. The cell phone and charger were wrapped tightly inside a sock and stuffed in the crotch of my briefs. There was absolutely nothing I could do but hand the phone over to them; however, I wasn't going to do that. Instead, I stripped down to my boxers and briefs, hoping that they'd accept that as a strip search. But one of the guards told me to remove my underwear also. Now I became hostile.

For a moment I considered handing the phone over. I even began to feel a sense of relief, no more anxiety-ridden days and nights, no more taking my light fixture apart, no more worrying at the sound of the door opening. The peace of mind was alluring, but boredom was not. I couldn't just sit idly; I had to be doing something—either constructive or destructive. I reluctantly tugged at my waistband, and heard myself about to say, "I'm busted," when an idea suddenly popped up.

I turned my back to the guards, furtively reached for the phone with my right hand, and simultaneously pulled down my boxers and briefs with my left hand. With my underwear around my ankles, both hands and the phone pressed to my pelvic, and my bare buttocks exposed to the guards, I stepped out of my underwear and began performing the usual strip search routine. I squatted and coughed; while doing so, I picked up my underwear with my left hand, then stood up and quickly rotated my body 180 degrees to the left while simultaneously rotating my hand with the phone behind my back. I tossed the underwear through the bars while I simultaneously wedged the phone between my buttocks at the same time. I was now facing the guards with my hands in the air, buttocks clenched, and penis dangling before their eyes.

Surprisingly, the guards tossed my clothes back through the bars and proceeded to search my cell. I was exhilarated and flabbergasted. Either the guards were two dweebs or I was a magician. They didn't find the phone, but they did find loose wire in my light fixture, and, therefore, moved me to another cell. "Why do you keep messing with the lights?" one of the guards asked. There was no sense in denying it–that would've only aroused more suspicion–so I said, "Because I like to make sure y'all don't have any recording devices in there."

"Now, why in the world would you think we're putting recording devices inside your light?"

"Because every time y'all search my cell, y'all always go inside the light like y'all got something in there," I replied.

"Who in their right mind wanna record you?" the other guard joked.

"I don't know; probably the same guy who put the porn magazine in my cell–maybe he wants to record me while I'm jacking off."

Both guards laughed and walked off. As soon as I heard the front door shut, I took the light fixture apart in my new cell, and altered the wires so that I could later charge my phone.

Later that evening as I was charging the phone, I heard the front door open and the old man Steve being hustled into the unit. It had been a few months since he'd last been released, and he managed to stay out for so long that we began to speculate that he was dead. Unfortunately, though, he was still alive and placed in the cell next to me, and I found myself wishing that the speculations had been true.

Ironically, there had been a time when I enjoyed having Steve around, as long as he was a few cells away. But now that I was babysitting a cell phone and needed to hear whenever the guards entered, I couldn't afford to have him around kicking and banging on the walls all night, nor did I have enough commissary to pay off the ransom of "honey buns and cheese curls" he often demanded for his peace and quiet.

As soon as Steve entered the cell, he started knocking on the walls to see who was next to him. I didn't reply, hoping to trick him into thinking my cell was vacant, but the prisoner in the cell on the other side of him told him to quit knocking on the wall. Steve stopped knocking and started kicking.

"Get the fuck off my wall!" the other prisoner yelled, but Steve kept kicking.

"Mother fucker are you deaf?" he continued, but Steve ignored him and kept kicking

"Steve... Steve... Steve... Steve!"

"That ain't my name no more," Steve finally replied. "It's Stephan."

"Well, Stephan, quit banging on my damn wall," the other prisoner shouted.

"Send me something to snack on," Steve demanded.

"I got something you can *suck* on, you old bastard."

"I'll suck it for a honey bun," Steve shot back.

"Suck your own dick for a honey bun," the prisoner replied.

"I'll leave that up to ya mammy," Steve retorted.

"That's why I'm going to get out and fuck your daughter, Stephan."

"My daughter's really my son, and he probably wouldn't mind; however, ya mammy may have a word to say about both of her sons copulating with one another."

They went back and forth all night and the following night. I didn't mind the yelling so much, because as long as he was yelling, he wasn't kicking and banging on the wall. However, whenever he wasn't yelling, he was kicking and banging on the walls, demanding honey buns and cheese curls.

Fed up with the ruckus, a guard stormed into the unit and warned Steve to stop banging on the walls or else he'd be placed in the quiet-room. The quiet-rooms were three small, foul cells across the corridor from Max. They were used for suicidal prisoners, but whenever a prisoner behaved violently or disruptively, the guards were able to put him in the quiet-room under the guise of exhibiting self-harming behavior.

After the guard finished admonishing Steve and left the unit, I came up with a wicked plan to get rid of the annoying, old man for good. I began kicking and banging on the wall. The guard returned and sternly warned Steve one last time. Steve tried to plead his innocence but the guard refused to listen. Several minutes after I heard the guard exit the unit, I started kicking again. This time, the guard stormed into the unit, opened Steves door, and hauled him across to the quiet rooms. Steve tried to protest and plead his case, but his reputation of kicking and banging surpassed his pleas. Seeing that he had no win, he resorted to the language he spoke best: "You lousy son of a bitch!" "Ignorant bastard!" "Brainless turn-key!" "I got a billion dollars on yo head!" "I'm a burn you alive, you house nigga!"

That was the last I heard of the old man. The unit returned to normal, and I was able to charge my phone and hear when the guards entered. However, karma is real, and she never forgets. Several days later, after a guard found loose wire protruding from my light fixture, Steve was released from the quiet-room to make room for me.

It happened minutes after I returned from the shower; an entourage of guards came to my cell and ordered me to cuff up. They had just finished searching my cell and placed me back inside it, so I wasn't expecting them to return minutes later. The phone and charger were in the crotch pocket of my thermal pants, which were rolled up on the bunk; consequently, It seemed there was absolutely nothing I could do. I didn't have time to grab the phone, and even if I could've there wasn't anything I could've done with it. I certainly couldn't take it to the quiet room with me. So I reluctantly left it rolled up in the thermal pants on the bunk, and submitted to restraints.

The quiet-room smelled like years of accumulated feces and urine. Up until recently, there had been no running water or toilets inside the cells, so the prisoners in the past were forced to bang on the door and request to use the bathroom, or relieve themselves on the floors. Since most of them had mental issues, they often settled for the latter. The concrete pavement and cinder-block walls were, thus, permanently soiled with decades of bodily waste. In the corners and crevices of the cell, cockroaches brazenly huddled and went about their business as if the lights were off and I weren't present. The cell was by far the most disgusting I'd ever been in.

Upon entering the cell, I was stripped of all my clothing, and given a suicide smock. I wasn't allowed to have anything else in the cell but a mat and a roll of toilet paper—no sheets, no blanket, no towel, no soap, no toothbrush. Nothing. All I had were the roaches. I stared at them and they stared at me.

The other two cells were occupied by two prisoners who really were crazy and suicidal. Derrick was the typical African American prisoner: young, raised in the ghetto, and now headed to prison for a typical crime. The other prisoner, Jason, was a different story: young white kid from a rural farm town who'd murdered his girlfriend and toddler with a shotgun. Simply talking to them behind closed doors, they both seemed normal. But when the guard passed out dinner, Derrick thanked him by tossing a turd out onto the walkway; and as for Jason's state of mind, his crime spoke for that. They both were as crazy as the cockroaches huddled in the corners.

The fact that the roaches could've left at any moment but did not said a lot about their sanity. They were definitely crazy, and also brazen. When I became tired of facing reality, and tried to sleep, they moved in on me as if I were food. Seconds into REM, I was rudely awakened by nearly a dozen of them audaciously crawling all over me. I jumped up in a panicked frenzy and started brushing and shaking them off while simultaneously ripping off my smock and tossing it to the ground. The roaches scattered, some underneath the door, some under the sink, and some to the corners of the cell, leaving me standing in the middle of the cell naked and agitated.

I stood there, tired, cold, and irritated, cursing every

ground-crawler I could think of, from roaches to rats, snakes to crabs, and snitches to more snitches. They all were the same to me, and they all seemed to be a part of my misery. I cursed and vented until fatigue and cold chills forced me to put the smock back on and try the sleep thing again. But between the cockroaches and the cold air blowing from the vent above me, sleep was nearly impossible.

I had to throw wet toilet paper over the vent, tear a slit in the top of the mat, and crawl inside the mat like a sleeping bag. And I constructed parameters of wet toilet paper around the mat, hoping to slow or hinder the cockroaches' advancement. Even still, I had to get up every half hour to shoo them away. That was the most miserable night of my life. And when I got up for breakfast, Derrick's turd was still sitting out on the walkway like a piece of furniture.

Needless to say, the quiet-room was not my habitat. And every time a guard walked by and saw me living in such foul conditions, they griped more than I. In their eyes, I was too humane and cool to be treated so awfully. I had never exhibited any rude or disrespectful behavior toward any of them or anyone else. I just wanted freedom and was willing to take any step short of sacrificing others to attain it. And as a result of chasing freedom, I landed myself into a much worse state of confinement. But it wasn't about me and my conditions; it was about that little girl who didn't ask to come into this world. I had moral and paternal obligations, and I would stop at no cost in trying to fulfill them.

Ironically, although the quiet-room wasn't my habitat, as the days passed I found reason to endure. In fact, just like the cockroaches huddled in the corners, I began to like the quiet room. The guards never came in to search the cell; the light-fixture was in the corner, the perfect location to discretely charge a cell phone; the ceiling was sheet metal, just like those in Max; and I didn't have to worry about anyone listening in on me. Sure I had Jason and Derrick, but they weren't present even when they were present—they were in another world.

Furthermore, the administration confidently believed that they had finally secured Kunta Quawntay for good. Little did they know, they had placed me inside the perfect cell to escape from. And for these reasons, I began to appreciate the quiet-room. I was so determined to stay in that cell that not even a John Deere could've pulled me out without resistance.

CHAPTER 17

LEAVING ST. CLAIR

Shortly after breakfast one morning, a guard showed up at my cell with an orange jumpsuit, a pair of shoes, and shackles. After 10 grueling days in the quiet room, something more powerful than a John Deere came to pull me out: The United States Marshals Service. They were transferring me to another jail, and contrary to my previous position, I put up no resistance.

Physically and mentally, I was relieved to be leaving the ghastly quiet-room and going someplace I could perhaps sleep better and bathe more frequently. Emotionally, however, I was in distress because I had invested so much into escaping St. Clair County Jail, and now that I was in a cell in which that goal seemed likely, I hated to leave such opportunity behind. Adding to my distress was the fact that I had no idea where I was going, and feared it would be some place inescapable, a place where opportunity is nonexistent, and dreams are merely expired fantasies.

I reluctantly got dressed and was shackled and escorted up the corridor to the booking area. I passed several concerned-looking guards, including Gretchen, who acknowledged me with a subtle gaze and pursed lips. I replied with raised eyebrows and a subtle nod. Everyone appeared concerned with my leaving, yet happy for me as if I were going someplace better. It was December, 2005, nearly 23 months since my arrival at the jail, and now I was finally leaving, leaving behind an impression that will never be forgotten.

I was processed out of the jail and secured in the back seat of a police cruiser. When the wheels started rolling, so did my thoughts. It was a bright autumn day, and the sun reflected off the snowy ground, thereby, making the day appear brighter and the world more visible as we sped through it. I twisted my neck like an owl and allowed my eyes to lawlessly shift as I tried to absorb every bit of the panorama. Seeing the sun, the trees, and normal people was a rare, heartwarming moment, and I didn't want to miss any of it, especially the women.

There was something exciting and inspiring about being parallel to a car driven by an attractive woman. The mere presence of a woman was enough to arouse my heart and induce fantasies of being rescued and harbored by her. Especially if she looked at me and smiled. I didn't know if it was me or the windows, but from the back seat of that police cruiser, all women appeared to be attractive and the world more appreciable.

We detoured through the ghetto streets of East St. Louis, Illinois, a place where I'd sold marijuana. The streets looked no better than I'd left them; in fact, they were worse. The people appeared to be more jaded and lost. Apparently, my incarceration hadn't made the streets any safer. Thugs and potential snitches still wandered the hood, standing on corners in flamboyant colors, and patrolling the streets on big, worthless, chrome wheels. The flow of marijuana hadn't been disturbed; if anything, the people's appetite had changed. Heroin had saturated the streets, and that high was more fulfilling than any other escape the people were seeking.

Instead of going directly to my destination, I was taken to the federal courthouse, where I found myself pacing one of the bullpens in the basement and wondering what life would be like at the Super Max in Florence, Colorado. I was certain I'd spend the remainder of my days locked in a cell governed by compassionless beings, a place from which I'd never be able to touch my daughter or a woman, which were god given rights in which man had given a rib for. Just the thought of such manmade evil was enough to make my heart ache. And the realization that there might be no escape made it ache even more.

For the sake of sanity, I contemplated insanity. I steeled my heart and mind, prepared for the worst. The only way to survive such draconian environment is by giving up on all hope and dreams, and ripping the heart from the chest, burying it someplace it could never be touched again. Basically, one must become insane, cold blooded, and animalistic—abandoning the innate instincts of humanity—just to cope. Either that or awake to soggy pillows for the rest of your life.

After anxiously pacing the bullpen for an hour or so, my ride arrived. Two cops entered the basement carrying chains and shackles, just like two slave masters coming to collect chattel. According to the writing on their shirts, they were from the Alton Jail. It wasn't as secure as the Super Max in Colorado, but I'd heard that it was a newly built, high-tech, high security facility. Rumor had it that the prisoners were confined to their cells all day. I also heard that B.G. was there. I shut off my feelings and tried to ignore my incessant thoughts as I prepared for hell.

After riding in the back of a van for more than a half hour, I spotted the jail less than a quarter mile ahead; an erect U.S. flag and a parking lot filled with police cruisers made that obvious. It was located at the corner of a busy intersection, and directly across from an equally busy service station. As we approached the intersection, the van was snagged by a red light, so I seized the moment and scoured the landscape and real estate around the jail. I also studied the structure of the jail and searched for cameras, windows, and doors. And just as the light turned green and the wheels on the van began to roll forward, I looked up at the attic in search for louvers.

The van came to a halt at an unintimidating razor wired fence that only surrounded the garage and back parking area. The cop in the driver seat rolled down the window and pressed the button on an intercom affixed to the gate. Seconds later the gate slid open and the van rolled forward and stopped at a garage door. When the garage door opened, the van rolled forward and parked parallel to a secure door which led inside the jail to another door leading into the booking area, where a young, white guard with a spiky-topped buzz cut cuffed me to a stainless steel counter and proceeded to process me into the jail.

While I was sitting there answering basic questions and marveling at the jail's sophisticated technology, an obtrusive sergeant with a push-broom mustache, bald head, and flat, wide ass emerged from one of the sophisticated doors. His demeanor was offensive and revealing of his insecurities and egotism. He picked up my file, skimmed over it, then looked at me and rolled his eyes and proceeded to sell me death.

He sounded like Charlie Brown's school teacher to me, for I was intentionally not comprehending anything he was saying. Until he said that he would personally inspect all of my mail, going and coming, including legal mail; and that I would be confined to a cell with a camera monitoring me 24 hours a day; and that I would not come out that cell for anything but a shower. And before storming out of the booking area, he shouted: "You will not be escaping my jail!"

The jarhead guard was once again working alone, which was not unusual. Although he was alone, he had ample security devices watching over and assisting him. Not only were prisoners not allowed out of their cells without being chained and shackled, but also there were sophisticated cameras everywhere. Furthermore, every guard carried a Taser gun and a panic button that could lockdown the entire jail and prevent all doors from being opened without the assistance of a designated officer sitting in a control center downstairs. The jail was so secure that any hope of escaping was dying.

On the other hand, deep down in the core of my being, I wasn't completely sold on the jail's security. So, just in case that vibe was right, I contorted my face when the guard took my mug shot. Thanks to the quiet-room and the months of not shaving, the picture couldn't have come out any better.

When the spikey-topped guard finished booking me in, an older, quasi-liberal, cigarette smoking, Vietnam-veteran-looking guard escorted me to my cell. This is when I got a better layout of the housing area of the jail. It was merely a narrow hallway with cells on both sides—six on the left and seven on the right. Unlike Max at St. Clair County Jail, this place was well lit with cameras hovering above the passageway. In the first cell on the right, B.G. stood at the window grinning. At the end of the passageway, there was a huge, barred window that I would never get near alone or long enough to escape through.

My cell was second from the last on the left; the only things between my cell and the window were another cell, a shower and a narrow walkway. It was much larger and cleaner than the cells I'd lived in during the previous 23 months. There were two bunks running cattycorner to each other. The walls were white cinderblock, and the material of the ceiling was difficult to determine by sight. I could see only that it was white with a tiny vent in the center. The vent was similar to those in Max, a square slab of steel perforated with holes, only much smaller. And, hovering above the sink/toilet, peeking from a small hole in the ceiling, my worst nightmare stared at me: a small camera, watching me like a hawk.

CHAPTER 18

WASHED UP

For a facility in which prisoners were confined to cells all day, Alton Jail was rather placid. The prisoners here weren't as raucous as we were in Max. There was little shouting from cell to cell, probably because most prisoners had cellmates to talk to. There was no kicking or banging on the doors, and the cinder-block walls did a great job of insulating the sounds inside the cells. The walls were also easier on the eyes and the mind than those ugly turquoise walls in Max. The cells were spacious, and the mats were much thicker and fluffier. After ten days in the quiet-room, it seemed like I'd died and gone to heaven.

As soon as my body pressed the mat, I fell asleep. I slept for three days straight, awaking only to eat, brush my teeth, use the toilet, and shower. Other than the few moments I awoke swatting nonexistent cockroaches (which was really my mind playing tricks on me whenever I felt a slight breeze or sensation), my sleep was peaceful and undisturbed. I had no worries. Not even the sound of chains or the guards' footsteps aroused me. It was by far the best sleep I'd had in 23 months, and a part of me wanted it to last forever. On the other hand, I knew that sleep is the cousin of death and that nothing comes to a sleeper but dreams. Therefore, I quickly grew tired of sleeping and began to search for something to do, be it constructive or destructive.

Talking to B.G., I learned the real reason why the feds raided

Max, and then transferred me: Gretchen. She'd been wearing a wire and trying to entrap B.G., and perhaps me too. That explains the conspicuous ink pen in her breast pocket, the thrusting of her breasts to the bars, the myriad of questions, and her efforts to get me to speak louder. When she learned that B.G. had a cell phone, she told the information to the feds and they raided the following morning. Neither Gretchen nor the cops knew of my involvement. But my desperation and impatience compelled me to open a closed trap and step right into it. How stupid I was! I even told her how I planned to use the light fixture to charge my phone. That's why the guards always searched my cell after the lights were blown out; they knew all along—they just couldn't find the phone.

Several weeks after arriving at Alton Jail, my property arrived from St. Clair County. I wasn't allowed to have most of it, but I was allowed to have my legal documents and my clothing. Before giving me the clothing, the guards took it upon themselves to wash them. They later found the phone and charger floating in the washer. Surprisingly, the guards at St. Clair County Jail never found the phone. I have no idea what happened to the bottle of deadly mouthwash, but I hope no one tried to gargle any.

Sadly, not long after my phone was washed up, so was B.G. He was sentenced to spend the rest of his life behind bars. I was saddened by the news. He was just a teenager when he committed his crime. He was a good dude whose only flaws happened to be two of his greatest traits: loyalty and courage. Unfortunately, his traits were exploited by much older thugs who misled him. Ironically, those same older thugs were the first to testify against him for reduced sentences. So while B.G., the youngest of the bunch, will spend the rest of his life behind bars, the older thugs, who were old enough to be his father, will be released to society to lead more kids astray. And this is what the feds call justice.

Just thinking about the country's twisted concept of justice was enough to warm the blood of Kunta Quawntay.

CHAPTER 19

I SMELL FREEDOM

It was a cold rainy night when the spirit of Kunta Kente was once again revived inside me. I was lying on my bunk reading a boring hardback when I smelled rain. It was extremely unusual to smell rain while confined to a cell that was designed for a man to smell nothing but anguish and misery. Intrigued by the acrid odor, my eyes averted from the book, and my nose inadvertently sniffed at the recycled air. The last time I'd smelled rain was when I was in the attic above Max, staring out at the world through the slats of the louver. Thinking back on that experience triggered an epiphany of my staring at the world from a vent in the attic of the Alton Jail.

I put the book aside, rose from the bunk, and walked to the small exhaust vent on the wall above the sink. With little regard for the camera above, I stepped onto the toilet and sniffed at the exhaust vent. I was instantly overcome by the inspiring aroma of the universe cleansing and rehydrating the earth. The experience was intoxicating and nostalgic, reminiscent of cool, rainy nights in Southern California. The unrestricted odor of freedom inspired me to heed the advice of Toucan Sam and follow my nose. I started planning my next escape.

Escaping Alton seemed improbable but not impossible. By now, I was confident that any prison could be escaped with proper planning and support. I didn't have support, but I had a quiet cell which provided me with the peace of mind necessary to mastermind the perfect escape. When I'm in escape mode, all I do is observe, think, and workout; thus, I changed my routine accordingly. I exercised in the morning, observed during the day, and pondered at night. By now I knew that the ceiling was sheet metal, just like those in Max. A saw and a way around the camera was all I needed.

As with any other mission in life, success was contingent

on determination, information, courage, and application. In my quest for pertinent information, I observed and analyzed everything. I even counted the cinderblocks in the cell and the hallway, and the footsteps of the guards to estimate the dimensions of certain areas of the jail. Such trivial information proved to be valuable when analyzed with common sense. By far, the most difficult task I figured, would be getting around the camera. Nevertheless, I came up with a plan, a quite simple one.

The two cells at the front of the hallway were different than the others. They were single-bunk cells; whereas, the rest were double-bunks. They also had different structures; specifically, they were designed to accommodate paraplegic prisoners. Since there were no paraplegics at the jail, the sergeant used the cells to isolate prisoners whom he deemed unfit or undeserving of a cellmate. For example, there was only one white prisoner at the jail, and since he couldn't bunk with blacks, he occupied one of the cells, and B.G. had been occupying the other. These two cells were perfect for my plan.

When B.G. left, there were only two other prisoners likely to be moved into that cell: me and Sam "The Bully." The Bully was one of those prisoners who enjoyed attention and trouble. He and I were the only two prisoners living alone in double-bunk cells. And since we were refusing to live with another man, and the jail made huge profits by filling the bunks with federal detainees, it was just a matter of time before one of us was moved into the single-bunk cell. Knowing this, I came up with a plan.

I knew The Bully well. He'd spent a lot of time at St. Clair County Jail, and had been in Max when Qusai and I tried to escape. He was another Zip-ass-fool, emulating the likes of Ray Ray, Qusai, and B.G.; therefore, he was willing to go along with any plan that I put before him. So, without explanation, I asked him to refuse to move into the cell if the guard tried to move him there.

"You up to something, Bosco," was his only response.

As anticipated, the sergeant tried to move The Bully into the cell, but he refused. After a few minutes of fussing and squabbling with The Bully, the guards asked me and I happily obliged. The cell was much smaller than the others. It was neither square nor rectangular, but shaped more like the letter *L*. Upon entering the cell, there was a phone and intercom built into the wall left of the doorway. On my right, there was a paraplegic handrail running from the door frame to the front right corner of the cell.

On that right wall, 3 feet away from the handrail, there was a stainless-steel sink. Midway into the cell, the right wall made a ninety degree turn and expanded the back of the cell several feet to the right, thereby, forming the L-shape. In the corner of the expanded area, there was a toilet sitting high off the ground, designed specifically for paraplegics. In the back of the cell, the bunk was affixed parallel to the back wall. And protruding from the quarter-inch-thick sheet-metal ceiling, right at the ninety-degree angle of the L, there existed the reason I desperately wanted to move into the cell: the camera. The camera, unlike those in the other cells, was positioned to capture the entire back of the cell, thereby, leaving a blind spot in the corner where the handrail and the sink met.

Now that I was in the ideal cell, it didn't take long for me to make my next move. I had already figured it out long before moving into the cell. The idea had been conceived on that rainy night I lay in my bunk smelling rain and reading the boring hardback urban novel. Without much pondering, I clandestinely wrote a coded letter which could be decoded only by using a series of numbers in a manner that had long been established with my cousin. Using an improvised fishing line, I sent the coded letter to The Bully and had him rewrite it in his handwriting and mail it to my people in his name.

Several days later, I covertly sent out the combination numbers to the code by inscribing them behind a postage stamp. Instead of sending the combination out in my name, I used the name of the white guy in the cell across from me. He rarely, if ever, wrote letters, so the guards couldn't distinguish the handwriting. Also, he spent most of his days medicated and asleep with ear plugs, so he never heard when I slid the letter in front of his door for the guards to pick up. Now all I had to do was wait.

The phones inside the cells stayed on 24 hours per day. They were never shut off, and at 50 cents a minute for prepaid calls, and $1.00 per minute for collect calls, the jail had good reason for leaving them on. Being locked inside the boring cells all day and night, it was nearly impossible for us not to use the phones excessively (financial-wise).

Ever since my arrival at the jail, I'd been trying to tap into the jail's direct line and bypass the ridiculous fees; I had spent many hours with my back to the camera, dialing myriad of numbers. Now that I was in a cell where the phone was partially out of view of the camera, I was able to take the phone apart and apply more time and effort to getting a direct line. Eventually, I was able to access an unrestricted dial tone.

All of my calls were now free and unlimited. I was able to call anywhere in the world, whenever I wanted. I was uncertain whether my calls were still subject to being monitored or recorded, so I was mindful of whom I called and what I said. Still, I used the phone all day and night, calling everywhere, including the party lines. I even called my niece to play music through the phone while I worked out. My phone would remain this way until the phone company and the jail noticed an exorbitant amount of unpaid calls.

During the beginning of spring, I received a postcard in the mail. There was a picture of San Diego on the front, no greeting or writing on the back, just my name and address. Although San Diego is one of my favorite U.S.

cities, the postcard symbolized much more than a nostalgic memorabilia. In the coded letter that The Bully sent out on my behalf, I requested that books be mailed to an unwitting prisoner a few cells down from mine. I ordered 3 books–2 urban novels and 1 hardback economics book. I also asked that a postcard of San Diego be sent directly to me several days ahead to forewarn me that they were on the way.

Now that I received the postcard, I anxiously awaited the books. Mail was generally passed out with the dinner trays Monday through Friday. Since I was in the first cell and, therefore, the first to be fed every meal, I was certain to see all books that entered the hallway on the food cart. Every day, since receiving the postcard, I kept my eyes on the food cart whenever it stopped in front of my cell. It was there, on a Friday evening, where I spotted the books stacked on top of a couple of newspapers and magazines.

If anyone were watching me on camera, they certainly could've discerned that I was up to something, because instead of wolfing down dinner as usual, I sat the tray on the sink and resumed watching the guard push the cart down the hallway. When he stopped at my unwitting accomplice's cell, I held my breath and listened for his response. I smiled mischievously when the guard handed him the books. The prisoner had no idea who'd sent them, and he certainly didn't know that he would be assisting me in my next escape.

CUCKOO CAL

The other prisoners at the jail referred to me by several different names—Bosco, Sco, Cali, and Cuckoo Cal. They called me "Cuckoo Cal" because of my eccentric behavior—I rarely talked, and when I did, it was usually profound or humorous; I worked out excessively; and I didn't listen to the radio or read urban novels. In the eyes of most, I was weird, but in a groovy way.

Being that I was weird, and the only prisoner who didn't read urban novels, I knew that it was only a matter of time before the economics book made it to me. But how long could that take—a few days? Weeks? I wasn't willing to wait that long. I was anxious; I wanted the book immediately. As soon as the guard left the hallway, I was tempted to shout down the hallway and ask the unwitting prisoner if I could borrow the book, but I feared that such eager interest would raise suspicion.

I ate my dinner and paced the floor, pondering the best approach. Later that night, I sparked frivolous conversation with my blind accomplice and subtly inquired about the title of the books that I'd seen on the cart. And, as I expected, he said: "I got a weird book you might like." I got the book the following day; one of the guards brought it to me right after lunch. Instead of immediately tearing it open as I wanted so badly to do, I patiently set it on the ground beside the bunk and left it there until midnight.

When the lights were shut off and the cell was completely dark, I casually picked up the book and walked to the door, slowly flipping through the pages as if I were using the light from the hallway to read the book. With my back to the camera, I ripped the hardcover from the book, and discovered a white-coated, seven-inch reciprocating saw blade concealed inside. I ended up ripping the entire book to pieces, and flushed it down the toilet.

Now that I had the saw, I was back to being anxious Kunta Quawntay from Max. My ears were honed, and every footstep, buzzing door, and clanking key went straight to my amygdala. When I lay down to sleep that night, a jumble of thoughts incessantly flooded my mind, keeping me awake half the night pondering my next move.

When built, the Alton Jail wasn't designed to house federal detainees for long durations. That said, it wasn't really up to standard for the job. It lacked several different requirements to function as a detention facility under Department of Corrections guidelines.

There was no law library or law books to aid prisoners with legal Even the prisoners at Guantanamo Bay were allowed out of their cells for at least an hour a day. But at Alton Jail, other than coming out for a shower thrice per week, we were confined to our cells all day every day. issues; there was no medical department or staff, and, therefore, the untrained guards were forced to pass out medication and determine the sincerity of a prisoner's medical complaints; and the jail lacked recreation, the most significant issue, according to most prisoners.

It just so happened that during the time that my escape plans were coming to fruition, the jail was in the process of change. First, the bald guy was replaced with a much cooler sergeant; then, a metal screen was placed on the window at the end of the hallway, and a TV was affixed to the wall beside it. They were planning to let each of us out of our cells for an hour a day to watch TV, shower, and walk the hallway. While most prisoners applauded the change and couldn't wait for it to take effect, I didn't like it one bit. I deplored the prospect of prisoners walking the hallway while I'm in my cell trying to discretely saw a hole in the ceiling.

I also hated that the bald guy was no longer in charge; he was one of my sources of motivation. I had been dying to show him that his overzealous, oppressive tyranny wasn't enough to hinder me. I literally had dreams of his shouting and passing out upon learning of my escape. Now, however, I was forced to leave on the cool sergeant's watch. Not that it mattered—I wanted freedom no matter who was in charge—but it sure would've been sweet to do so on the bald guy's watch.

Breakfast at Alton Jail was always the same—cereal, milk, and pastries—and most of the time the guards would pass it out and leave the tray slots open afterward. The morning after receiving the saw, I stayed in bed with my head underneath the blanket, peeping through a tiny hole as the guard sat my breakfast on the ajar wicket and proceeded to the next cell. Instead of rising for breakfast, I remained motionless on my back, under the blanket, for about 45 minutes. I repeated this routine every morning after receiving the saw. In doing so, I was not only testing the guard's responses, but also getting them accustomed to mine. Minutes before the guard returned to shut my tray slot, I jumped up, grabbed the food, ate it, and began working out.

In the midst of my working out, I set up my chessboard on top of my property tub and sat it in plain view of the camera. In between sets of push-ups, I'd move a piece on the board and walk to the door, out of view of the camera, and yell out numbers as if I were playing chess with one of the other prisoners. While some of the other prisoners might've thought I'd gone crazy by yelling out insignificant numbers like old man Steve, it was really just a smoke screen intended for the guards.

While out of the view of the camera, whether one minute or three minutes, I was standing on the paraplegic handrail and the edge of the sink sawing a hole in the corner of the ceiling behind the camera. It was a tedious and noisy task, which required a lot of patience and slow strokes. Luckily, the cinder-block walls confined most of the noise. There were a couple of times, however, when I sawed fast and hard, and a couple of prisoners commented about the noise. But they weren't wise enough to know what the sound was or where it was coming from.

After just one week of sawing, I saw tremendous progress and couldn't help but think about the time my lawyer told me that I was stuck between a rock and a hard spot. I thought of the cinder-block wall as the rock, and the metal ceiling as the hard spot. I certainly had something for the hard spot.

One Sunday afternoon while I was standing on the sink vigorously sawing, I heard the door in the hallway buzz open. I immediately hopped down and stepped to the window to find the guard standing at my door with handcuffs and shackles in his hand. I was caught by surprise and didn't know what to do. I hadn't expected the guard to come search my cell while he was busy running visits. I honestly thought I was busted as I stood there clutching the saw with sprinkles of metallic sawdust on my hands. But to my relief, the guard said: "You got a visit."

"A visit?" I asked. I didn't know anyone nearby who cared to see me, nor did I have anyone on my visiting list. "Who is it?"

"It's a surprise," he replied.

"It might be ol' gurl," my neighbor, Old School, butted in.

"Ol' gurl" was Tonya, an older white woman whom Old School hooked me up with a couple of weeks earlier. Being that Old School was in the cell next to me, and the receiver-less phone was built into the cinder-block wall dividing our cells, he was able to hear all of my calls. Since my calls were free, I'd make calls for him from time to time and he'd try to speak to his people by screaming through his phone, which was right behind mine. One day, he gave me the number of a woman he'd met through the classified ads. He'd only talked to her once or twice and didn't want to spend any more money talking to a stranger whom he wasn't really getting anywhere with, so he gave the number to me.

When I first called Tonya, I was greeted by a ring tone of a rap song by Ludacris, which I found to be odd for a white woman who claimed to be late thirtyish. Initially, I wasn't expecting anything to come out of our communication but a little entertainment and information. But as time went on, Tonya began to feel butterflies in her stomach (perhaps that was a sign for her to run the other way). For her, it was now much more than entertaining conversations: She was falling head over heels.

Judging from our conversations, Tonya had qualities; she was slightly older, sexy, loyal, dependable, compassionate, understanding, and she didn't agree with the prospective punishment for my crime. Consequently, I too began to feel excited about a potential relationship. And now that she'd managed to finesse her way into the jail without being on my visiting list, and surprised me with a visit, there was no doubt that she was my type of woman.

"I'm refusing," I told the guard, shocking him and the other prisoners listening in.

"Are you for real?"

"Look at me," I said, running my fingers over my short, scraggly facial hairs, which I purposely hadn't shaved in months. "I can't go out there like this."

Although I really wanted to go out and see what Tonya looked like, I didn't want to go out there looking like a bum, and I really didn't want to go out there while I had visible cuts in my ceiling and sawdust scattered on the floor.

"Go get him some trimmers and let him shave," one of the other prisoners shouted.

"If I get you trimmers and give you a few minutes to shave, will you go?" the guard asked.

While I contemplated, the other prisoners shouted, "Go! Go! Go! Go! Go!" And I reluctantly agreed.

The guard raced off to get trimmers, and I quickly tied a string around the saw and concealed it inside the cut in the ceiling, leaving a trail of string sticking out so that I could later retrieve it. I then covered the cut and string with white paste I'd earlier made from toothpaste and soap. Finally, I used toilet paper to clean up the metallic sawdust. Ten minutes later, and looking ten years younger, I was cuffed, chained, shackled, and escorted to the visiting booths.

"So what does she look like?" I asked the guard.

"She's not your type," he replied with a wry face as if he'd just taken a bite into a lemon. How'd he know my type? My type was any woman with a hand to grip a steering wheel and a foot to mash the gas pedal. Yes, his opinion was disheartening, but I wasn't going to let his opinion determine my standards of beauty. After all, looks weren't important; and considering all the qualities Tonya exhibited over the phone, she couldn't be that bad.

When I entered the visiting booth and saw Tonya sitting on the other side of the glass partition, smiling and staring at me as if she were in a trance, I nearly turned around and ran back to my cell. The only thing that stopped me was the shackles around my ankles. *I've been duped*, I thought. Except for her hair and height, she looked nothing like the woman I was falling for over the phone. The woman sitting before me looked like a stoned hippie who was oblivious to, yet confident in, her physical appearance. Her skin was leathery and sun burnt, and the prominent lines around her eyes suggested that she was much older than the late thirtyish she had claimed to be. I'd been duped by not only her delusive description, but also her ring tone. She looked more like a fan of Big Joe Turner ("Shake Rattle and Roll") than Ludacris ("Shake Your Money Maker").

On the other hand, setting my shallowness—and her face—aside, Tonya wasn't that bad. She didn't meet America's shallow standards of beauty, but she seemed to possess that perpetual, universal type of beauty, the type that couldn't be destroyed by age or accident, or enhanced by scalpel and silicone. Above all, as evident by her willingness to drive fifty miles to surprise me with her smiling, albeit ugly, face, she certainly had a huge, compassionate heart that was capable of providing unconditional love and joy. What more could a man ask for, especially one in my position? It wasn't like Meagan Good, Alicia Keys, Viola Davis, Jennifer Hudson, or any other woman was willing to come see me.

I set my shallowness and selfishness aside and enjoyed my visit. I focused on and appreciated the good things about Tonya, including her stylish appearance. I took notice of her stylish hair, cute high heels, and sexy attire. Years of incarceration made me appreciative of the little things like that. At the end of the visit, she promised to come again.

As soon as I returned to the dorm, everyone wanted to know what she looked like. "Like John with a wig on," I said, causing the dorm to erupt with laughter. John was the older, baby-boomer guard who'd escorted me to my cell when I first arrived at the jail. Although I was being sarcastic, the two did have similarities. I didn't dare express such shallowness to Tonya, though. Instead, I told her that I liked her hair, her heart, her determination, her shoes, and her strut, and that I was tempted to run and jump out the window at the end of the hallway to join her— which was true. "If you ever decide to jump, let me know, so that I could be there to catch you," Tonya replied.

Now, she was talking my language. Did she mean that literally, or was she simply being romantic? She certainly had me thinking now. She didn't have any idea about my escape plans, so for her to say that, I began to wonder if God had sent me an angel to assist in my escape. Perhaps I was taking her comment out of context, but if she meant what I hoped she meant, then she was certainly my type of woman. If she were willing to mash the gas when I hop in the car and yell, "Step on it," I would have probably been willing to overlook her facial features and ride straight to the wedding chapel with her. We could've then gone to a plastic surgeon afterwards and both got face lifts. A pretty face can be bought, but a heart and courage can't.

"Okay now," I said. "If I call you and tell you to be there to catch me, don't leave me hanging."

"I won't," she promised. Little did she know, though, I really had plans on jumping, just not from the window.

The following Sunday, Tonya showed up again. This time I was ready. All week, I'd been thinking about her promise. I wasn't sure if we were on the same page or if she was able to discern my intentions. By the same token, I wasn't sure that I wanted her to. In fact, I wasn't even sure that I wanted her to be around when I jump. I was certain, however, that someone needed to be there. So to ensure that we were on the same page without actually being on the same page, I wrote her a note and concealed it behind an address label on a large legal envelope containing legal documents, and took it with me during the visit.

In the note, I stated that the court would be ordering my release on an undetermined date in the immediate future, and that I would need for her to be parked up the street waiting for me on that day. I further stated that the release would take place at any time between the hours of 10 p.m. and 2 a.m. and that I would notify her of the date by calling her earlier that day and saying a code word.

I justified the peculiar circumstances by stating that I had an outstanding warrant in California, and that the jail would hold me for up to 72 hours after the court's release order, thereby allowing the California authorities time to come get me. If they don't come within the 72 hours, I stated, the jail would have to release me at midnight, give or take a few hours. Finally, I stated that if the California authorities arrive after my release, they might come looking for me and, therefore, it would be best that she drive a car other than hers, so that they wouldn't know where I've gone.

The purpose of my falsehood was to shield my escape plans from   not only Tonya but also the guards, in the event they were to discover the note behind the label. Before going into the visiting booth, I asked the guard if he could give the documents to Tonya, claiming that I had a deadline in which the documents had to be filed with the court the following morning, and that I desperately needed for Tonya to take them to my lawyer. The guard agreed and gave the package to Tonya after thoroughly inspecting it. During the visit I silently instructed Tonya to look behind the label. She read my lips and nodded.

CHAPTER 21

SIGHTS OF FREEDOM

It was Friday evening April 28, 2006, when my saw performed its final stroke through the quarter-inch-thick ceiling. After several weeks of tedious work, I was finally done. I had managed to cut 90 degrees of a circle into the corner of the ceiling. The only thing preventing the carved plate of metal from falling to the floor was the caulk along the edges of the ceiling. I pushed up on the slab of metal, breaking the caulk, and slid the slab of metal to the side of the hole. The space above the ceiling was dark and discouraging.

There didn't appear to be any exit up there. I had been expecting to see some type of light shining up there, particularly rays of light beaming through the slats of a louver that I had predicted to be near. I stacked a few books onto the sink, for extra height, and stuck my head through the hole in search for the huge vent I'd seen on the side of the attic the day I arrived at the jail. Sadly, though, I saw nothing but darkness. I withdrew my head from the hole, climbed from the sink, and collapsed on my bunk.

Something wasn't adding up correctly. Either my analysis of the building had been wrong or I was missing something. According to my observations and estimations, the space above the ceiling was supposed to be more spacious, and there was supposed to be a huge exhaust vent somewhere above and not too far from my ceiling. My cell was on the side of the jail facing the gas station across the street, and on that side of the attic, there was supposed to be a huge exhaust vent. Not only had I seen it from the back of the van, but also Tonya had unwittingly confirmed it. But judging from the darkness, such vent wasn't above my cell. I lay on the bunk in deep thought, waiting for the guard to make his round so that I could climb above the ceiling and search for an exit.

On the sink, I had a cup of soapy water with many pieces of peppermint candies soaking in it. They'd been there for days and were now gooey and mushy. As soon as the guard finished his round, I went above the ceiling and searched for hope. I gave myself five minutes to get in and out. The enclosure was warm, stuffy, and almost airless. The little air that did circulate was extremely dusty, confirming my fear that there was no exhaust vent. I crawled along the side wall of the enclosure, searching for any sign of an exit. It was so dark that I had to use my left hand to navigate through the darkness, and my right hand to grope the wall for any sign of an exit.

As I quietly crawled across the ceiling of the cells, I had to fight off multiple urges to sneeze—it was that dusty. And sadly, that dust only suggested the worst: There was no exhaust vent. It now appeared that I was trapped and that my only way out was back inside my cell, inside my bed, under the covers, where I could sleep my dejection away and escape via my dreams. With beads of sweat dripping from my forehead, I begrudgingly made my way back to my hole. I moved with less care than I had before. I really didn't care whether or not the prisoners below could hear me. Halfway to my hole, I heard a door buzz open, and panicked. I began to rush back to my cell, stumbling on the way, and jammed my pinky toe on a piece of scrap metal somewhere above Old School's cell. Just as I was wriggling through the hole in my ceiling, I heard the hallway door next to my cell buzz open. The door shut at the same time my feet hit the ground, and I stepped to my window just as a guard walked by.

Luckily, he was in a rush and didn't look my way. Had he done so, he would have seen that I was completely covered in black dust. There was so much dust caked on my face that I could've passed for a negro minstrel. I stood at the mirror, laughing to the point of tears. I cracked up at the sight of the minstrel in the mirror, but truthfully, the sight was a sad indication that no exhaust vent existed in the enclosure above the cell. It appeared that I was trapped, and I had to laugh to not cry.

My only hope rested on the narrow air ducts above the cells. I knew that one had to lead to an air-conditioning machine, and the other to an exhaust vent. Nevertheless, I doubted that they'd lead to a hole big enough for me to squeeze through. Still, I summoned up the courage to wrap a towel around my face and a T-shirt over my head, and climbed back above the ceiling. I desperately followed the narrow air ducts, only to be sadly dropped off at a cinder-block partition where the narrow ducts continued without me.

Having lost all hope, I crawled back to my hole, consumed by discouraging thoughts of having to spend the next month or so trying to chip through the cinder-block partition. Duck-walking back to my hole, I jammed my toe again on a long, sturdy piece of scrap metal. This time, I stopped and picked it up with intentions of later using it to chisel through the cinder-block. But out of sheer frustration, I jabbed the metal into the concrete roof, and surprisingly, debris came raining down.

Intrigued by my discovery, I struck the roof again, and more debris fell. I curiously reached up to grope the roof and discovered that the roof wasn't even concrete; in fact, it wasn't even a roof. Since it was pitch dark, I couldn't tell what it was or what it was made of, but I knew that it was worthy of my time, attention, and more strikes from the scrap metal. I continued to strike it until I was rewarded with balls of Styrofoam spilling down on me.

Momentarily satisfied with my discovery, I rushed back to my cell to make an appearance before the camera and ponder my discovery. Before wriggling down into my hole, I disrobed my dusty linen and stashed it above the ceiling.

After appearing before the camera and figuring out my next move, I grabbed a pair of thermal pants, an extra shirt that had mistakenly been placed in my laundry bag, and the cup of peppermint candies, and set them above the ceiling. I then climbed into the hole and crawled over to the small crater I'd created. Using my hands and the scrap metal, I quickly expanded the hole sufficiently for my arm to fit through, and reached inside. After feeling nothing but insulation, Styrofoam balls, and air, I withdrew my arm and resumed expanding the hole until more Styrofoam balls rained on me.

Once the hole was big enough, I closed my eyes and cautiously inched my head through it. When my head safely cleared the mass of insulation and Styrofoam balls, I heard the sound of air conditioning machines humming. At that moment I knew I'd found my exit. I opened my eyes and was instantly consumed by a wave of joy and excitement. The huge louvers were glowing in the darkness of the attic. The bright lights outside the jail were shining through the slats, giving them an almost sacred-like glow. My hard work paid off, and I was finally able to see freedom.

I withdrew my head from heaven, grabbed the shirt and thermal pants, stuffed them with Styrofoam balls, and tied them together to form a headless dummy. For a head, I would later round out a cracker box, wrap it in a brown towel, and tie my do-rag around the crown. Before descending back into my cell, I removed the peppermint candies from the cup of water and stuck them around the upper edges of the detached plate of steel I carved from the ceiling, and left it beside the hole to dry.

The following morning, the sun was shining through the louvers, filling the entire attic with sunlight; I was now able to see that the barrier between the crawl space above the cells and the attic was actually plywood. I used my hands to break off chunks of the plywood and expand the hole sufficiently for my shoulders to fit through; then I pulled myself up into the attic and looked around. It was very spacious, and the roof was triangular like the roof of a house. There were several huge air conditioning machines and a maze of air ducts. There were four huge louvers, two approximately 15 feet to my left, and two more way on the other side of the attic. They were so huge that I could've walked through them had it not been for the slats and mesh screens on them.

With little contemplation, I decided to escape through the nearest louver. I quickly duck-walked to it, pried the screen apart, and started sawing the ends of the bottom three slats, which were thin strips of aluminum and, therefore, easy to saw through. After sawing the first slat, it dawned on me that the louver was much higher than the one I'd seen upon my arrival at the jail. This louver was approximately 40 feet from the ground and in plain view of the gas station and the busy intersection. Considering this, I began to wonder whether I'd chosen the wrong louver.

Disregarding my five-minute time limit, I gave myself ten and went to the other end of the attic to check out the view from the other louvers. On my way, I came across a flight of stairs descending down into the jail, and had the urge to descend them. Resisting the urge, I continued straight ahead, only to find that the other vents fared no better. Although they were closer to the ground and invisible to the busy intersection, they were right above a slew of police cars, cameras, and office windows. For that, I preferred to stick with my first choice, and chance being seen scaling down the building by one of the motorist traveling the busy intersection than a cop sitting in his office sipping coffee.

As I rushed back to my side of the attic, I couldn't resist the urge to explore my curiosity and descend the steps in the attic. I was less than two minutes away from my ten-minute time limit, and knew that I was taking a risk, but still I went down the steps, passing a box of police academy trophies on the way. The stairs led to a corridor containing more staircases, one leading down and one leading up into another attic. I chose the attic and discovered more louvers, much closer to the ground. They appeared to be the same louvers I'd seen upon my arrival at the jail. Leaving that attic,

I found more routes, which, if explored, probably would have allowed me to walk right out of the jail.

The thought was tempting, but I'd already found my exit and been in the attic beyond ten minutes. Any further searching would've been an unnecessary venture. Racing back to my cell, I was tempted again, this time by the trophies. I thought about stealing two of them and leaving one in my cell when I escaped; the other one would be my prize. I seriously contemplated it, but dismissed the arrogant thought for fear of jinxing myself. I quickly made it back to my cell and wriggled through the hole. Since I was done for the day, I covered the hole with the plate, and the peppermint candies, which were now dry and forming a ledge around the plate, prevented it from falling through.

I spent the rest of the day preparing for my escape. First, I ripped one of my blankets into long strips and made a rope out of them. Then, I used cardboard and scraps from an old gray thermal shirt to fashion a hat, which I planned to wear during my escape. And I stretched and twisted narrow strips of plastic sandwich bags into floss-like string, tying them together to improvise 150 feet of invisible string.

Immediately after the guard handed me my disposable lunch tray Sunday afternoon, I pulled the dummy from the ceiling and waited for the guard to reach The Bully's cell. When The Bully received his tray, he stuck his arm out of the tray slot and harassed the guard, inciting a quarrel sufficient to attract the attention of anyone up front monitoring the cameras. With all monitors likely on The Bully's cell, I squirted clear Maximum Security toothpaste over the eye of the camera and quickly placed the dummy in the bunk, under the blanket. I then stood on the sink, out of the view of the camera, and wiped the camera clean with one swift wipe.

Although I didn't expect anyone to be monitoring my cell while The Bully was causing such a disturbance, I remained in the blind spot for a moment, just to make sure. When The Bully calmed down and the guard finished passing out trays, I still remained in the blind spot, waiting. I waited several more minutes and when no one came to my cell or said anything over the intercom, I climbed into the ceiling.

Since it was Sunday, a day in which the guards were preoccupied with running visits, and I had the dummy in my bunk, I had ample time to spend in the attic. The first thing I did was finish sawing the slats. Then, I tested my rope by tying it to one of the legs on the air conditioning machine and yanking it. Satisfied with the results, I spread the rope across the floor of the attic, so that it wouldn't become tangled, and I tied one end of the floss-like string to the middle of it. Next, I grabbed the other end of the floss-like string, crawled 40 feet across the attic to another air conditioning machine, tied a topless and bottomless plastic soda bottle to the leg of the machine, ran the floss-like string through it, crawled back to the louver, and set the loose end of the string beside the loose end of the rope.

With all of my pieces in position, all I needed to do was call Tonya. But first, I killed time staring out the louver. The world looked beautiful out there. I watched as the traffic flowed through the intersection and myriad of people enjoyed the bright, sunny day. I watched as customers entered and exited the service station across the street, and smiled as an exiting man held the door open for an entering woman whom he ogled with a twisted neck. And I watched with envy as another man strolled by with a little girl who happily skipped along and snacked on potato chips.

The panoramic view of reality and freedom had me wondering if the people starring in my show ever took time to appreciate their freedom as much as I. I wondered if they really understood the significance of everything around them. I certainly did. Where many people saw automobiles cluttering the streets and polluting the atmosphere with expensive and harmful gas, I saw a bunch of people with the power to go wherever and whenever they pleased. I didn't see a man harassing an attractive woman; I saw a man simply experiencing the natural attraction between man and woman, and the ability to enjoy such God-given right.

In my eyes, the man and child weren't big brother and little sister, or uncle and niece, but father and daughter bonding during the most nurturing years of a child's life. I envied the man to the point of moist eyes. I was so close to not only freedom but also being a real father, and I couldn't wait.

CHAPTER 22

KUNTA QUAWNTAY

It had planned on leaving that Sunday night. Tonya proved to be reliable by parking her borrowed SUV across the street and up the street from the jail at 10 o'clock on the dot. She remained there for hours, anxiously awaiting my release. With the lights off in the cell and the dummy asleep in the bunk, I climbed up to the louver in the attic and waited for the right moment. However, that moment never came. Just as I pulled the slats from the louver and prepared to toss the rope out, a police cruiser zoomed out of the parking lot, and another cop hopped out of a car and ran toward Tonya's SUV.

Needless to say, I had chosen the wrong night, because the police were in a heated pursuit of a criminal suspect who ran right pass Tonya as she naively and conspicuously sat behind the wheel of the SUV. With all of the drama going on outside the jail that night, I reluctantly returned to my cell, called Tonya, and told her to go home for the night.

Monday night, though, I had my mind set on leaving regardless of the conditions outside the jail. Early that evening I practiced my timing and mechanics, I studied the flow of traffic at the intersection and tried to time the police cruisers as they patrolled Broadway and policed the traffic, which was much heavier than the night before. I was somewhat concerned about being seen by a motorist at the intersection, or a customer at the gas station; nevertheless, I was willing to take that chance. I resolved to not let anything but a hail of bullets stand in my way that night.

Several hours before 10 o'clock, I called Tonya to ensure that she was still willing to catch me when I jumped. I had everything figured out, except where I would go immediately after the escape. I had a long-term plan, but not a short term plan. I thought about calling Rayford, but figured I'd have time to decide on that afterward; after all, it all depended on Tonya's response. My heart hoped Tonya would hide me somewhere safe, but my mind knew better. This was a moment of strategic thinking, and a hopeful heart is for the fool at such a moment. Success, I admonished myself, would be contingent upon the mind, not the heart.

In the event that Tonya were to deem me too heavy to catch, I prepared an alternative. I groomed myself and put on my cleanest linen. I put on crisp white socks, fresh boxers, a brand new thermal shirt, and a pair of dark gray thermal pants that were stretched out so that they appeared to be sweats. Lastly, I dusted off the gray hat I'd made and tucked it underneath my shirt. And to ensure that my clothes wouldn't get dirty, I wore my prison jumpsuit over them. I was well groomed enough to walk to the casino and hitch a ride if necessary.

I hadn't drunk coffee in 13 years, but for this occasion, I drank a cup just in case I needed to stay awake for a couple of days. I stretched to loosen up my muscles, and brushed my teeth (brushing my teeth helps me think more clearly.) I was now energized, confident, excited, and humble. I felt like a baller minutes before a championship game. I was ready.

Around 10:30, the guard made a round and shut off the lights in the cells. After he exited the hallway, I shouted out my farewells to my fellow prisoners. "I'm going home," I joked. Nobody had a clue what I was talking about, not even The Bully. They all thought I was just being sarcastic. Little did they know that there was a hole in my ceiling, a dummy in the corner of my cell, a rope in the attic, a get-away ride parked up the street, and a tube of clear Maximum Security toothpaste in my hand, waiting for the right moment.

The right moment came approximately one hour later. I was standing at the door, seemingly conspicuous, when the guard made another round. He asked why I was up so late. "Waiting to go home," I sarcastically replied. As soon as he exited the hallway, I climbed onto the sink and squirted the toothpaste over the eye of the camera, thereby, blurring and obscuring whatever vision it had in the dark cell. Moving quickly enough to finish before the guard made it back to the monitors, I placed the dummy in the bed, in the very same position I myself had lain every night since receiving the saw.

With the dummy in the bunk, I was now free to take my time. Nevertheless, I quickly climbed into the attic, crawled over to the louver, disrobed my prison jumpsuit, put on my hat, tied the loose piece of floss like string around my right wrist, and grabbed the loose end of the rope. I was instantly overcome with excitement and that difficult to describe feeling of fear swallowed by courage. After 828 days of confinement, 749 days in solitary confinement, 10 in the quiet-room, 300 since my last court appearance, and 588 since the birth of my daughter, I was now finally on the verge of being free.

I looked out the louver and spotted Tonya's borrowed SUV conspicuously parked in the exact same spot it was in the night before. To my left, the traffic at the intersection was heavier than it had been the previous night, but lighter than expected. I scanned the service station and noticed a few customers, but neither seemed to be interested in looking at the jail, much less the louver. I removed the bottom two slats and prepared to crawl out, but I was startled by a light beaming right at my face. It shined from an alley directly across the street and perpendicular to the jail. I quickly moved my head out the line of view and held the slats steadily in place while the headlights of a pick-up slowly approached. The truck came to a stop at the tip of the alley, and remained there as if the driver were confused as to which way to turn. After what seemed like minutes, the truck turned right and made another right on Broadway, perhaps en route to the casino.

Just when it appeared that the coast was clear, and I began to remove the slats, a police cruiser pulled out of the parking lot and sped up Broadway. Once the coast was really clear,

I finished removing the slats and tossed the rope out the louver. It landed about four feet from the ground, exactly as I had estimated. I then tugged on it one last time to ensure that it would support my weight, and with both hands and legs tightly wrapped around it, I descended to freedom.

Halfway down the rope, I spotted what appeared to be the same police cruiser from earlier speeding into the parking lot as if the cop had been watching and waiting for me to crawl out the louver. If I had time to think, I would've thought that Tonya set me up. But I didn't have time to think, only time to panic. On the spur of the moment, I began sliding down the rope so fast that the wool cloth burned the flesh from my palms and fingers, forcing me to lose my grip and fall. Fortunately, I was only eight feet from the ground and landed on my butt. But unfortunately, I landed on a concrete walkway down by the basement door of the jail, and was, therefore, blinded in a valley between the building and a grassy slope.

I couldn't see the parking lot, where the police cruiser had gone, or the street, where Tonya was parked. I didn't know what awaited me at the top of the hill; perhaps that hail of bullets that would put an end to Kunta Quawntay for good. Still, I ducked down and ran up the hill in Tonya's direction with a huge smile on my face as the cool, crisp air of freedom washed over me. As I ran away from the jail, the rope, being pulled by the string tied to my wrist, retracted into the louver, exactly as it was contrived to do. Apparently the cop hadn't seen me, for I didn't hear any gun shots or feel any bullets pierce my back.

As I began to jog across the street, Tonya started the vehicle and began to pull away from the curb. When she pulled into the middle of the street, I ran to the passenger door and pulled on the latch, but the door wouldn't open—it was locked. I repeatedly pulled on the latch, but the door still wouldn't open. At that moment, it appeared that Tonya had reneged on her promise to catch me. However, she was trying to unlock the door, electronically, but the switch wouldn't work while the gear was in drive. Realizing this, she reached over to the passenger door and pulled the lock.

Apparently, Tonya really did believe that I was being released, because when I hopped into the passenger seat, she repeatedly said: "Oh...my...God." Nevertheless, she continued driving. Where to? I didn't know and didn't care, as long as it wasn't back to prison. When she drove onto the highway and crossed the Mississippi River, I began to experience the euphoric feeling of freedom, which intensified with each passing mile. It was definitely the best feeling I'd ever experienced. Freedom!

PART THREE: CAPTURED SLAVE

CHAPTER 23

REGRETS

I'm so stupid. So naive. So foolish. I must have some type of mental retardation, or some type of psychological disorder that hinders me from doing what's right. I knew better. How stupid could I be? I awoke in the middle of the night cursing myself. I had hoped that it was just a bad dream and that I would awake in the motel room—or even in my cell at Alton Jail—but the stinging pain in my hands and the hard concrete bunk proved that it was no nightmare. It was real. I had lost the championship game. Fumbled the ball. And that was the worst feeling I'd ever felt in my life. I was so damn stupid.

After my escape, Tonya drove me across the river into Wentzville, Missouri. According to her, she knew the perfect place for me to hide out for a couple of days. First, we stopped at an ATM so that she could withdraw some cash. When she exited the vehicle, and began to walk to the ATM, she abruptly stopped and returned to the vehicle. "This isn't my truck," she said as she withdrew the key from the ignition. I laughed because I had never even thought of stealing the truck. I don't steal, especially from people who are trying to help me. But now, I wish that I would have driven away in the truck and left her standing there in the cold.

She withdrew a few dollars from the ATM, then drove to a nearby Walmart where she intended to buy me clothes and a disposable cell phone. Once she parked in the deserted parking lot, though, I had a change of heart. I didn't feel comfortable sitting in a deserted parking lot seconds away from the ATM she just used. I preferred to be indoors, somewhere out of sight. A black man being chauffeured by a white woman in the outskirts of St. Louis was unacceptable, especially at that time of night. Such a daring act was essentially a plea to be pulled over. Having my seat reclined didn't make things any better; that only made it seem that she

167

was hiding me. I preferred to be at the hide-out.

The hide-out was a shabby two-bed motel room rented under an assumed name. Since Tonya was acquainted with the manager, she didn't have to show ID. She drove around to the back of the motel and snuck me through the fire escape.

Once inside the room, I began to feel a little better, but not yet completely relaxed. I was still anxious and excited, and unable to sit still. It seemed like I'd been in this scene before, but I couldn't remember where. I didn't try to remember; my mind was too preoccupied trying to figure out my next move. Tonya sat at the edge of one of the beds, still shaking her head in disbelief. Yet, she was supportive and expressed willingness to protect me. She didn't agree with the War on Drugs, and appeared to be a genuine rebel to such wicked scheme. She gave me the impression that we were on the verge of being the modern Bonnie and Clyde—the interracial version. The only question was: Could I trust her?

In the back of my mind, I knew that I shouldn't, but my heart and hope for a romantic ending believed otherwise. I hoped to believe that she wasn't the typical white woman Dennis had warned me about. After all, she was proving him wrong thus far. More importantly, she promised to hide me. And that's all I needed, just one day of protection, enough time to figure out and secure my next move. Shortly after arriving at the room, she went out and bought me clothes, food, and supplies to patch up my hands. She couldn't get the cell phone because that department was closed, so she bought me a calling card. She was doing all she could to uphold her promise—even though that made her a knowing and willing accomplice. Considering all of this, I saw no reason to believe that I couldn't trust her for one day.

Knowing that it was just a matter of time before the cops showed up at Tonya's house in search for me, we discussed ways to protect not only me but also her. She suggested that she stay at the motel room with me all day. She wanted to cuddle and have sex. That wasn't a bad idea for my sake, but it wasn't a good one for her. Being missing would have made her a prime suspect, and generated a media frenzy. A black escapee and a missing white lady would have certainly drawn national media coverage and a manhunt that I didn't want.

She then suggested that she shouldn't talk to the cops, but that too wasn't a good idea. A white woman refusing to talk to the cops is peculiar in itself. Things like that don't happen. I also didn't think that it was a good idea for her to lie and say that she hadn't heard from me, because earlier that night, she went inside the service station across from the jail and purchased a soft drink; therefore, the cameras there would've refuted such lie. More incriminating was her unusual ATM transactions that night. For her sake, I believed it was best that she keep her normal routine, and, when the cops question her, admit that she'd given me a ride.

She had a doctor's appointment scheduled for 8 o'clock that morning. So the plan was for her to fulfill that appointment, go to Wal-Mart to purchase a disposable phone, bring the phone to me, then go home to await the cops. When asked, she was supposed to acknowledge picking me up from the jail, but under the belief that I had honestly been released. To support that claim, she still had the misleading note I'd given her at the jail. As for my location, I told her to tell them that she dropped me off at my friend's house in East St. Louis, and that she had no idea where I went from there.

Before she left, I gave her a few pointers on counter-surveillance. I told her to make a lot of turns and U-turns, and to drive down one-way streets and deserted roads to ensure that she wasn't being tailed. I also asked her to keep her cell phone shut off while driving.

As she was walking out the door I stopped her and said, "Thanks! My life is in your hands; please don't let me down." Gazing at me through a pair of vacant eyes, she promised to protect me. She then stole a quick kiss from me before reluctantly departing. I really felt in my heart that I could trust her, but my mind wasn't so sure.

Alone in the cramped room, I had difficulty relaxing. Emotionally, I was excited to be free, but mentally, I was nervous and anxious. I knew that I wasn't really free yet, and was still in the line of danger. Something was bugging me and preventing me from enjoying the moment. I tried to lie down and rest, but I couldn't. I began to pace the floor, peeping out the windows and listening to every faint sound. Suddenly I remembered where I'd seen the scene. The two beds, the dingy carpet, the crows-feet around Tonya's vacant eyes, and the look she gave me as she was leaving were reminiscent of the dream I had the morning John snitched on me. Something creepy was going on, and I began to worry that I might be making a big mistake.

In attempts to ease the anxiety, I turned on the TV and turned to the news. My attention was immediately grabbed by an extremely attractive African American news reporter by the name of April, who was reporting live from outside the Alton Jail. In the background, I could see the damaged vent with a few feet of rope still dangling from it.

Apparently, my retraction device had jammed. And later a news blogger visiting the jail noticed the rope and damaged vent, and immediately notified the police inside the jail. Knowing that there was only one prisoner who could've pulled off such an escape, the police ran straight to my cell and started pounding on the door and yelling my name. Little did they know, the person in the bunk was actually a dummy, and I was long gone.

In the background, I could see that police had the jail surrounded, searching both the inside and the immediate vicinity. Since there was only a short piece of rope hanging from the vent, the cops assumed I dropped 30-plus feet and was, therefore, stranded somewhere near, severely injured. I smiled at the notion of the cops searching the vicinity. Then, when they flashed the ugly mug shot I'd taken upon my arrival at the jail—which didn't look anything like me—I began to think that I might have pulled off the perfect escape. Then suddenly my mood was dampened when they mentioned my ties to an unidentified woman in Warrington, Missouri.

They were moving fast. It was barely 8 o'clock and they were already on Tonya's trail. It was just a matter of time now, and I was now having a change of heart—or rather, my mind began to take over. I now wanted Tonya there with me, anywhere other than someplace they could question her. I now cared less about covering her tracks. I needed to cover mine.

My mind was immediately overwhelmed with thoughts of fleeing. I looked at the phone on the nightstand and contemplated using the calling card to call Rayford. I couldn't, though, because he was not only on house arrest but also on my phone list at the jail. I really had nobody else local to call. All of the time I'd spent in jail not communicating with anyone had now come to haunt me. The only local number I had that the feds didn't know about was my friend Amy's, but in the event I were to need to seek refuge at her house, I didn't want to call her from that phone; I preferred to call her from a more secure line.

I had planned to wait for Tonya to return with the phone before making any calls, but my intuition kept urging me to make plans outside of Tonya. So I called my cousin in California, and told him to call around and get some assistance nearby. And fearing that the feds might've known about Tonya's doctor appointment, and perhaps following her, I told my cousin to call her and tell her to not return to the room or her house. I wanted to keep her away from me and the cops until I could escape the room and get somewhere safe.

While my cousin was busy making calls, I resumed watching the lovely April. By now the big-wigs at the jail were addressing the public, and April was drilling them with questions. When one of the cops deemed me armed and dangerous, April went to bat for me. She questioned their logic and brought up the fact that I was charged only with possessing marijuana. She asked whether there was any evidence suggesting that I might be armed or violent, and the cop said, "No." I found myself wishing that I had April representing me in court; she was definitely going to bat for me. I also hoped that I would be able to say the same for Tonya.

As the morning slowly waned, the name Quawntay Adams and the ugly mug shot were rapidly gaining notoriety, and I was increasingly growing paranoid. Tonya wasn't answering her phone for my cousin, so I assumed that she was either still at the doctor's office or at Wal-Mart buying the phone. Her phone being shut off seemed to indicate that she was sticking to the script. Still I was ambivalent to whether I should stay in the room and wait for her or leave the room and wait for an alternative ride. I looked out the window at the gorgeous, sunny day and found my answer—I decided to step out and feel my first rays of sunshine in more than 27 months.

I worried that the color of my skin and the cuts on my hand might alarm the predominately-white community. But I was even more fearful of being trapped inside that room. I put on the clothes Tonya brought me, and left the room in search for some place to hide. Any place would have sufficed, but I particularly had my eye on a trash bin and the basement of a house in back of the motel.

As I walked to the back, a sassy, black woman walked in my direction. She wasn't fine like April, but she had alluring eyes with a hint of interest in them. Our eyes locked for a couple of seconds, and as we passed each other, she looked up and smiled. I wanted so badly to say something to her, but I couldn't summon the nerve.

When I made it to the back exit and pushed the door open, I was slightly startled to encounter a conspicuous-looking white man standing next to a parked car with the engine running. He seemed surprised to see me and stared as if

172

he were searching my face for a hint of recognition. Nearly panicking, I put my head down, reached into my pocket as though I'd forgotten something, and turned around. I took long strides back to the room, and peeked out the back window. The man was now sitting in the car with the door open, his feet on the pavement, and a beer in his lap. It turned out that the man was just a harmless wino, and I was a paranoid schizo.

Discouraged by the wino and my paranoia, I sat on the bed, never taking the time to realize how much more comfortable it was than the beds I'd been sleeping in for the last 27 months. I tried to convince myself that everything was okay and that I had ample time before the cops raid the room. On that note, I decided to stay in the room and wait for either Tonya or my alternative ride– whichever were to arrive first.

About an hour later my ride arrived. I looked out the window and saw a tall, white man wearing a wind breaker with *POLICE* on the back. He was looking inside the trash bin that I earlier had intentions on hiding in. The sight of this imposing figure alarmed me, and had me hoping that he was just a security guard making his rounds. Nevertheless, I had an eerie feeling that he was looking for me. I went to the front window to peep out, but I was stagnated by the sound of footsteps. Instead of peeking out the window, I peeked through the crack underneath the door (yea the room was that shabby). The feet began to multiply, and I found myself praying that they belonged to an army of room servants marching to clean up the rooms.

But as much as I prayed for the best, I knew what time it was. It was nearly two hours before noon—much too early for room servants and check out time—but there was nothing I could do about it. The inevitable happened: the cops kicked in the door, pressed their knees into my back and their cocked pistols to my head, and shouted, "Don't move or I'll blow your brains out!" As dejected and disappointed as I was, moving probably wouldn't have been a bad idea. Certainly, a bullet to the head would have put me out of my misery and set me free once and for all. But then again, considering my luck, I probably would have survived and spent the next 30 years as a quadriplegic prisoner.

While the cops were celebrating and giving each other high fives as though they'd won the Powerball lottery, I was sitting on the ground, shackled, fuming, and wishing that I'd done things differently. I should have tied her to the bed and stolen the SUV. I should have made her drive me to Chicago, then hopped out and left her sitting at a red light. I should have kept her in the room and cared less about covering her tracks. I should have had sex with her and given her a reason to protect me. I had a laundry list of things I could have done, but ultimately, I should have never had any compassion or trust for her from the start. As the old man would've said, I accepted the wooden nickel.

Indeed, it was Tonya's fault. Instead of going straight to Wal-Mart after her doctor's appointment, she stopped by her house, and the cops were there waiting for her. She lied at first and told them that she didn't know where I was, but after being pressured and told that I was out to kill women and children, she caved in. Unfortunately, she was still arrested and charged with harboring me, a felony offense that would result in probation.

Although I was disappointed in her, I was more disappointed in myself. I had known better than to be entrusting a strange, white woman with my freedom. I thought about what the old man, Dennis, had told me: There wasn't a white woman in the world that could keep her pie-hole shut in the face of the law. Audrey, Nicole, Nurse Tee, and now Tonya. How stupid could I be? I even thought about the white woman in Atlanta who'd turned in Brian Nichols (the black man who escaped from the court building in 2005) after fucking him and feeding him pancakes. At least he got pussy and pancakes.

As I was being escorted out of the room and hustled to a police car, the media were setting up around the motel, and a crowd of spectators were gathering. The sassy black woman I'd passed earlier was on the second tier staring at me with a hint of compassion and curiosity in her eyes. I couldn't help but wish that I had been up there with her. Perhaps eating pancakes and.

My pain and disappointment was unexplainable. I felt like an NFL player after fumbling the ball just inches before crossing the goal line with seconds on the clock, only a lot worse. I felt like I let down my daughter, myself, and all freedom-loving proponents who might have been rooting for me. And I hated myself for that. My self-hatred was one degree below suicide as I stared blindly at the formidable concrete ceiling, reliving the regrettable events that landed me in an escape-proof cell at the notorious federal penitentiary in Marion, Illinois. I wanted another chance, a chance to do it all over again. I swore that I would do it differently. But there were no more chances. History had already been written, and I'd forever have to live with the regrets.

CHAPTER 24

GLIMMERS OF HOPE & INSANITY

And that's how I ended up in Marion, a maximum security penitentiary that was built to replace Alcatraz as the country's most secure federal prison. It was once home to some of America's most notorious criminals, including John Gotti and Manuel Noriega. Marion housed the worst of the worst, and everyone confined there had already been convicted and sentenced; everyone except me. I had never even appeared before my judge, let alone been tried, convicted, and sentenced. But now that I was labeled an escape artist and southern Illinois' most high-risk detainee, there was no other place secure enough or willing to house me.

Considering the condition of my previous 27 months of confinement, Marion wasn't bad. I had a TV in my cell; the food was excellent, for prison standards; the commissary had a diverse selection of affordable items; the education staff made daily rounds, distributing legal and educational materials; and although I was in solitary confinement, I was allowed out of my cell every day for an hour of recreation, in either the gym or an outdoor courtyard.

Although I appreciated the amenities Marion provided, most of the other prisoners resented the deplorable solitary confinement. Looking at it from their perspective, I understood their gripe. Most were long-term prisoners who'd been isolated for many years. Many were lonely, depressed, miserable, and had no chance or hope of getting out of prison while they were still young.

For me, however, things were different. I still had a chance, and as long as I had that chance, I had reason for hope, and reason to look forward to the next day. One prisoner liked to analogize my situation to that of a boxer in the ring. The federal court system was the ring, and as long as I was still in it, I had a chance to win the fight. That gave me a glimmer of hope, but in the back of my mind lingered the question: What if I don't win the fight?

Half hopeful, half fearful, I began to study bits and pieces of the law. I mainly focused my studies on the Speedy Trial Act. The Act demanded that a defendant be tried within 70 days of his initial court appearance or indictment; however, reasonable periods of delay were excludable under the ends of justice. Many prisoners argued that I was simply wasting my time because no court—especially in the Seventh Circuit—would respect the Speedy Trial Act. They said that few federal judges respect law dictating how he or she should manage the court's calendar. But I refused to let a bunch of hopeless prisoners rain on my parade. I had been awaiting trial twelve times longer than that required by the law: therefore, I believed I had a chance.

Most prisoners believed I would be better off pleading guilty or playing crazy. To them, 30 years was better than a life sentence, but to me it was all the same. So most of their advice went through one ear and out the other, everything but the advice to play crazy. I figured playing crazy would help show the prejudice needed to support my speedy-trial claim. At the least, I assumed, it could help get me transferred to a less secure jail from which I could escape in the event my speedy-trial claim were to fail.

To prepare for such defense, I observed and learned a lot from the mentally and emotionally disturbed prisoners at Marion. There were many, and being that I was housed in a special unit above the medical department, I encountered a fair share of them.

The first lunatic to speak to me was really sane and manipulating. He often said that we must manipulate the system just like it manipulates us. And manipulating the system is exactly what he did! He had been on a hunger strike for months, thereby, forcing the captain to assemble a team of guards to extract him from his cell twice a day and force feed him. The administration had gotten so tired of   him and the inconvenience he was causing them that the warden came to his cell one morning and offered to transfer him to any penitentiary of his choice if he were to eat just one meal in his presence. The prisoner agreed, and two days later he was gone.

Then there was Tony G. Ricky A Hill (that's what he said his name was), the grand loony of them all. Tony G, aka "Fish," had landed himself in Marion by using a sharpened broomstick to kill his cellmate at another prison. He was charged with the murder, but deemed not guilty by reason of insanity. Fish had the loudest, deepest, melodious voice I'd ever heard in person; his tenor was in the range of Barry White and James Earl Jones. Many nights, he would have loud dialogues with himself and his alter egos, altering his voice to represent the many different imaginary characters participating in the dialogue. Often the conversations would end with him and one of his alter egos having a physical altercation. The funniest of his dialogues were those with his Jamaican alter ego. In the midst of the squabble, he would yell out his door: "A Bosco, this damn Jamaican won't shut the fuck up—he keep fucking with me. He 'bout to get his ass whipped."

Whenever Fish wasn't arguing with his alter egos or flooding his cell, he was drawing weird drawings. All of his drawings were pieces of psychotic art. With the exception of one of a gagged little boy sitting in a cell with a lot of eyeballs on the walls staring at him, all of the characters of his drawings were extraterrestrials. They were eerie-looking creatures with demonic auras. And his photo album wasn't any better; all of the pictures were of deceased people. If they weren't pictures of his deceased family members, they were newspaper and magazine clippings of deceased people, including pictures of Emmitt Till and Precious Doe (the unidentified deceased toddler whose remains were found near Kansas City in the 1990s).

Out of all the bizarre behavior Fish exhibited, there was only one that I was willing to emulate: The chicken bone. He thoroughly cleaned a chicken bone, inscribed the word *Life* on one side and *Death* on the other side, and fashioned himself a necklace with it. I planned to inscribe the word *Freedom* in my chicken bone.

I was humored and entertained by all of the lunatic prisoners, but I was not willing to emulate all of them. Particularly, there was one who would smear feces all over his body for no reason. Also, there was a midget who'd deliberately go on suicide watch so that he could be stripped naked, placed in a transparent cell, and masturbate in the presence of the guards assigned to watch him. Unfortunately for the guards, they had to sit outside the midget's cell and observe him for eight-hour shifts. The midget didn't mind that the guards were male; he'd still stand there at the transparent, Plexiglas door, masturbating and talking dirty to them.

I initiated my bizarre behavior with a letter to my judge, expressing a lack of trust for my lawyer—and any other lawyer. My judge responded by summoning me before him for the first time in the 29 months my case had been assigned to him.

Although he seemed genuinely concerned, I couldn't help but wonder whether my newfound notoriety was the real reason he showed interest in seeing me. After all, every other time he'd made a decision in my case, he did so without my presence. At the hearing, I subtly exhibited more bizarre behavior by stating that I felt as though someone—alluding to my attorney—would chop off my head and serve it to the court. "Well, we sure wouldn't want that to happen," the judge caustically replied.

I wasn't proud of feigning crazy before the court, but as the prisoner at Marion put it, they were manipulating me. In fact, the entire criminal justice system and War on Drugs is nothing but a huge scheme in which prisoners are manipulated for the political and financial benefit of judicial, legislative, and executive officials. How many of them actually admit when they're wrong? Point proven.

In any event, the judge appointed another lawyer to represent me. But I had no intentions on proceeding with him because Lorrie was in the process of retaining a big-shot lawyer by the name of N. Scott Rosenblum to represent me. For me to allow my daughter's mother to give an attorney $50,000, I must have had a newfound attitude on justice. For the first time in my life, I had a bit of faith that I might get a fair shake in court. Particularly, I was confident in my Speedy Trial Act claim. I was so confident that I no longer thought about escaping. Now that I felt as though I had a legitimate chance of walking out of prison, I quit hiding my daughter and had Lorrie bring her to Marion. This was our first visit; up until then, I had only seen her in pictures. Although we were separated by a glass partition, the moment was heartwarming and life altering.

It certainly justified the reason why I couldn't voluntarily go to prison for 30 years. Looking into her curious and humbling eyes was an indescribable moment. I had gazed into a set of eyes that seized control of my heart in a way that made me both powerless and powerful. Seeing her had given me strength and reason to endure. I didn't even want to feign crazy anymore; I just wanted to go home and be a father.

My stay at Marion didn't last as long as anticipated. The Federal Bureau of Prisons decided to close Marion and convert it into a medium security facility. As a result, on August 4, 2006, I was transferred to the Franklin County Jail in Benton, Illinois where, that following Monday, I was taken to the U.S. District Court in Benton and arraigned on a third superseding indictment which charged me with the escape from Alton. Then later that evening, I was surprised again with a transfer to the Jackson County Jail in Murphysboro, Illinois.

I was upset over leaving the Franklin County Jail because there was a sexy, flirtatious guard there whom I had been looking forward to getting close to. I was so upset that when

I arrived at the Jackson County Jail I refused to answer all questions except those about my health, and I answered those in the affirmative. When the officer was done, my booking profile stated that I didn't know my name or age and that I was suffering from every illness and infectious disease known to man.

I was housed in the jail's Administrative Segregation Unit, which was merely a small, square structure consisting of three cells, two tables, one phone, and one shower. I was placed in the cell with a prisoner who turned out to be the grandson of a black sergeant who worked at the jail.

The prisoner never told me that the sergeant was his grandfather—I found out through the grapevine after he was shipped off to prison. I was surprised when I found out. I couldn't fathom how a captor could entrust the captive into the hands of the captive's relative. I guess it was no different than entrusting slaves into the hands of other slaves. Had that been my grandfather, he would have been discreetly ushering me out the back door. But he was not my grandfather, and this was not Compton, California. This was Southern Illinois, and the people here were cut from a different cloth than my family.

The guards at Jackson County Jail were like no others. They were by far the coolest, classiest, and most professional I'd ever been around. Unlike most jails, although there were only two African-American guards (the sergeant and a younger dude), there was no racism exhibited by the guards or the Administration. They also knew how to draw a fine line between oppressive detention and secure detention. Even the cook was an amazingly sweet, professional woman. She went out of her way to accommodate my special diet of no beef, no pork, no processed meats, and no white breads. She prepared special meals for me, consisting of oatmeal, eggs, fish, chicken breast, and peanut butter. My meals were so exquisite that all of the other prisoners envied me. The guards at the Jackson County Jail were simply hard-working, good people who quickly disarmed me of that phony, snobby attitude I carried into the jail.

In the administrative unit, we were confined to our cells 23 hours a day, so most of my rec and entertainment was provided by my new cellmate whom I called James Brown. He was a 19year-old, nappy-head, brown-skinned dude with wide eyes and a huge, yellow, perpetual smile that clearly suggested he was mentally disturbed. When I asked why he'd been arrested, he just smiled and said: Driving.

I understood that to mean he'd been arrested for driving without a license, but after weeks passed and he still hadn't been released, I asked around and learned that he'd been driving alright; he'd been driving a stolen Corvette and led the police on a high-speed chase that ended with the Corvette being wrapped around a pole.

In addition to providing laughter and bizarre entertainment, James Brown provided me with higher learning in Psychology. He'd stand at the sink all day, looking in the mirror, smiling, singing, and talking to himself. Most of the time, his self-talk resulted in his bursting into hysterical laughter. His laughter was so contagious that I often followed suit with laughter of my own, which seemed to intensify his. Every week during commissary, he'd order a dozen 16-ounce, plastic tumblers and stack them in the corner of the cell, just for the hell of it. After a few weeks, he had about 30 of them stacked like a castle. He'd also buy several bars of soap, and while standing at the sink, looking in the mirror and talking to himself, he'd lather them in his hands until they were completely dissipated. One day he bought a 12-ounce bottle of shampoo, lathered its entire contents into his hair, and left it in for days. He roamed around the cell and dayroom for nearly a week with a flaky, bluish-white afro with a plastic fork sticking out the side as if it were an afro pick.

There were some days when James Brown didn't talk, laugh, sing, or smile at all; he'd just sit in the corner of the cell depressed. He wouldn't eat any of his food, and he'd gather all of his commissary and offer it to me. Initially, I declined to accept it, but after witnessing him throw it all in the trash, I started accepting it, and would return it to him whenever he came out of his slump.

On September 6, 2005, my new attorneys, Scott Rosenblum and Adam Fein, and I appeared before the court for a hearing on my motion to dismiss for violation of the Speedy Trial Act. Before arguments began, the judge asked that we bear with him because this was his first Speedy Trial Act hearing. This meant that I was the first defendant in his 12 years on the bench to put up such a fight. We argued that more than 70 non-excludable days had expired, but the court found that only 64 days had expired. In its finding, the court had erroneously started the clock from March 2, 2004, the day of my arraignment, rather than February 18th, the day of my indictment, as the law required. When I tried to convince my lawyers and the judge that they were wrong, they looked at me as though I were crazy. Ultimately, the judge crushed my heart and denied the motion.

During the ride back to the jail, I was stunned and dejected. The judge was wrong, and I was sure of that. While at Marion, I had read many case laws stating that whenever the defendant is arrested on a criminal complaint, as in my case, the Speedy Trial Act clock begins the day after the indictment is filed. So when the judge—who was much smarter and more informed than I—flat out denied my motion, I concluded that he didn't have any respect for me, or my rights. Ironically, I had suspected that all along.

I felt like a fool for even thinking that I'd get some justice simply because I had high-paid attorneys. After all, it was still a political system designed to fill prison cells with young black men, put money in the pockets of useless attorneys, provide jobs to rural white folks, and to militarize Black communities. The judge was simply doing what Congress and Ronald Reagan's War on Drugs demanded of him. It was the fear of such injustice that had motivated my attempts to escape in the past, and now that the judge had denied my motion, I was reminded that such attitude was not a bad one.

The day after the hearing, my attorney sent a gorgeous intern to visit me and try to persuade me into pleading guilty. She was cute, and I was a sucker for a woman, but I wasn't crazy–I was just playing crazy. No matter how cute she was, she had a better chance at water-boarding a whale into a confession than persuading me into voluntarily putting my life on ice for 30 years. "If you lose in trial, you can believe Herndon will sentence you to life," she said, trying to scare me. (Mind you, Herndon had never sentenced a drug dealer to life, if there were alternatives.) I was willing to take that chance, though. 20 years, 30 years, 40 years, and a life-sentence were all the same to me. Men in my family rarely lived to see 65, so 30 years was essentially a life sentence.

My trial was scheduled to begin September 11, 2006. On Friday, September 8th, the guards came and told me to pack my property because I was being transferred to a jail closer to the court. Also, the judge wanted me in court that morning for a hearing. During the hearing, despite my previously filing a motion to dismiss for violation of my rights to a speedy trial, the judge boldly postponed the trial date again. Unlike the previous continuances, he made sure I had input this time.

Also during the hearing, my attorney Adam provided the judge with case law supporting my position that the Speedy Trial Act clock begins on the day after the indictment is filed. Confronted with the case law, the judge reluctantly reopened my motion. However, instead of adding the additional 12 days onto the 64 he'd already determined, and dismissing the charges, he simply ordered my attorney and the government to file additional briefs on the matter. In any event, it was still good news, and had me thinking that perhaps the judge wasn't as bad as I thought.

Ironically, after the hearing I was taken back to the Alton Jail—the same jail I'd escaped from. I would have never guessed that I'd return to Alton. I was nervous and embarrassed about returning; I worried that the other prisoners would ridicule me for being so damn stupid and soft, but when I stepped into the dorm, I was greeted like an athlete bringing home a trophy. The prisoners whistled, shouted, chanted, and kicked on the door as though I were their hero. To them, I symbolized hope and the possibility of escaping hell—even if just for a day.

Just like an egotistical athlete, I basked in the glory. But when they brought up Tonya, my mood changed. It was like hearing the name of someone who'd murdered a loved-one. Her name will forever sting because it is a reminder of how stupid I was. And although the prisoners didn't say so, I couldn't help but suspect that they were tacitly criticizing me for such stupidity.

They each had a different version of how it would've turned out had it been him; nonetheless, they each had the same theme. Neither would have trusted Tonya; she would have been beaten, tied up, fucked, carjacked, and dumped in a Mexican desert. Everyone I'd encountered since my capture said the same thing—even guards and police. Even Fish and the midget at Marion knew better. The criticism had me questioning my own sanity. Perhaps I *was* crazy.

CHAPTER 25

ESCAPING ALTON AGAIN

The moment I was secured in the cell, I began to think of ways to get away from Alton for good. I was confined to my cell 24 hours a day, and had nothing but one shower per week to look forward to. I couldn't write or receive personal letters, and the only time I was permitted to use the phone was to talk to my attorneys. I complained to my attorneys and the judge, but after a couple of weeks passed without change I took matters into my own hands.

Using tricks, I learned from James Brown and the prisoners at Marion, I pretended to be insane. I paced the cell every day, scratching the same spot on my head and talking to myself. I quarreled with an invisible Jamaican man whom I pretended to be confined in the cell with me. I slept underneath the bunk, pretending that the Jamaican was sleeping *on* the bunk. I refused to eat, claiming that the guards were trying to poison me; instead, I would dump the food in the corner of the cell for my invisible dog to eat. I drafted several look-a-like fish out of pieces of Styrofoam, and put them inside a bowl filled with water as if it were a fishbowl. When the street deputies came to do their daily cell-search and saw the fish, they swore that I'd gone crazy.

After a week of feigning crazy, I started destructing the cell, and The Bully, who was in the cell across from me, followed suit. When I broke the metal bunk, the chief became fed up with me and had his deputies shackle me to a concrete bench inside a freezing holding cell at the front of the jail. Then, after I used a piece of metal to pick the locks on the shackles and used them to wreck and destruct the holding cell, I was placed in a restraining chair, strapped at the ankles, waist, wrist, and head. After several days I was weak, tired, and ready to give up. Then one morning two officers from the Jackson County Jail came and rescued me.

CHAPTER 26

JACKSON COUNTY JAIL

"**H**i! I'm Brian Lee Phelps, FBI," a scrawny, fortyish white guy said, stepping to me with his hand extended. When I failed to respond quickly enough, he grabbed my hand from my side and shook it without my concurring. His grip was tight like a pair of vice-grips, and he refused to let go. He just stood there staring at me, displaying a smile that not even a mother could love. His appearance was both comical and creepy. His hair was long, dark, and shaggy, but the crown of his head was a few strands away from being completely deserted. He had dark eyes, prominent laugh lines, and very few teeth. The few teeth that he did have seemed to be attached to his gums by strands of thread. He appeared to be two bites into an apple away from being toothless. It didn't take long for me to discern that the prisoner was crazy.

While I was away, the superintendent wisely opened the small segregation unit and now allowed the prisoners to mingle in the day-room where they could be better observed all day. Along with James Brown and the FBI agent, there were two other prisoners in the unit, and they too appeared to be mentally disturbed. As much as my four mates had me laughing, I'm sure that in the eyes of anyone on the outside looking in, I too appeared to be crazy.

The unit was a constant riot of laughter, with James Brown and Brian Lee Phelps leading the pack. They all were funny, but Brian Lee Phelps was the most comically annoying of the group. Any eye contact with him provoked a vacant smile, a nod, and an arrogant "yes sirrr" as if he were the handsomest man on the face of the earth. In support of his arrogance and vanity, he carried a small comb in his breast pocket all day, and every half-hour, he'd excessively comb the dissipating strands of hair hanging from his head. Apparently, his hair and teeth were his pride and joy, because in addition to excessively combing his hair, he excessively brushed and tried to salvage the few teeth reluctantly hanging from his gums.

Brian Lee Phelps was not only an FBI agent, but also a priest. Whenever he wasn't brushing his teeth or combing his hair, he was walking around the dayroom with a Bible and a cup of water—which he claimed to be Holy—sprinkling water everywhere. One night he held a Bible study with James Brown and another prisoner. As he was preaching the Gospel and explaining how Jesus sacrificed his life by dying on the cross for everybody, James Brown interjected, "For me too?"

"Yesss brother," Brian Lee grinned. "For you too."

A huge, yellow grin formed on James Brown's face; he licked his huge, chapped lips, paused for a few seconds, and said, "I don't even know the dude, but for him to give his life for me—a dude he ain't ever met—man... I got a lot of respect for that dude." I found this dialogue to be very funny. Later that night as we were being locked in our cells, James Brown called out to Brian Lee and asked: "What was the name of that dude who gave his life for me?" I literally fell to the floor in tears.

Between James Brown and the FBI agent, not an hour passed by without my laughing. Unfortunately, though, while in his depressed mode, James Brown punched a guard in the face, and was moved to a cell in the booking area. I haven't seen him since. Not long after that, Brian Lee Phelps smacked a guard upside the head with a Bible, and also disappeared, leaving me with a bug-eyed prisoner that drank a gallon of water an hour and complained that it was going someplace other than his stomach and bladder. He'd walk around the day-room asking everyone: "Do you know where my water is going?" When we had no answer for him, he'd ask the guards and medical staff. "Poke a bunch of holes in yourself and see if it squirts out," a facetious guard suggested. Fortunately, the bug-eyed prisoner wasn't that crazy.

My mood had greatly improved at the Jackson county

Jail, and believe it or not, breaking out of the jail had never once crossed my mind. You could say that the judge's reconsideration of my Speedy-Trial claim provided me with hope, and had me optimistically believing that justice was attainable. For that, my attitude exuded exuberance and confidence. I smiled a lot and laughed a lot. I spent my days exercising, studying law, and eating. Even my physical appearance was restored; I was back up to 200 pounds of chiseled muscle.

I was just about certain that the judge would rule in my favor. After all, he'd already determined that 64 days expired on the clock. If he were to add the 12 days from February 18th through March 2nd, I'd be 6 days over the 70-day limit. I was so confident that I began to make plans to take my daughter to Sea World.

Providing more hope, my Attorneys brought me a copy of every motion and order for continuance ever filed in my case, and most were in my favor. The Speedy Trial Act set limits on when a judge can postpone a trial, and requires that a continuance be absolutely necessary. Most of the continuances in my case were unnecessary.

For example, on one occasion my trial was delayed so that my co-defendant Nicole and the government could finalize a cooperating plea agreement they'd been working on for 7 months. Certainly, it wasn't necessary to delay my trial so that Nicole—who was out on bond—and the government could take their merry time to finalize a certain plea that could've been completed in an hour.

Another disturbing continuance occurred in October, 2005, when my attorney, unbeknownst to me, requested a continuance so that he could prepare for Nicole's cooperation and expected testimony against me. Mind you, Nicole had been cooperating and promising to testify against me ever since the feds first showed up at her job a year earlier. Thus, my lawyer should have long been prepared for Nicole's cooperation.

Then in March, 2006, the very same attorney, after being granted 3 consecutive continuances for a total of 6 months, asked that the trial be postponed again because he had another trial "likely" to begin a week "after" mine. More disturbing was the fact that I'd been incarcerated more than 2 years awaiting trial while the defendant in the other case was out on bail and hadn't been waiting half as long as I'd been waiting to be tried. What made the other guy's speedy trial rights more important than mine? If I weren't so naive, I'd probably say: Because he was a rich, white kid whose parents were connected. Ironically, after my trial was postponed, the other defendant's trial still didn't begin; he ended up pleading guilty, as anticipated.

After going over these bogus continuances and many more, I was confident in my claim. But my lawyers weren't sold. They opined the judge was reconsidering merely to clean up the record for the Court of Appeals. In fact, since my first hearing, the judge went through his entire docket and cleaned up all of the absent and vague continuance orders. To me, this was clear indication that he'd been making mistakes in the way he'd been freely issuing out continuances—what is right doesn't need to be corrected—and I was hoping he'd reward me for bringing such mistakes to his attention.

Sure as shit stinks, to my dismay, my lawyers and the miserable prisoners at Marion were right: The federal courts don't respect the Speedy Trial Act. The judge denied my motion again. I didn't learn about the judge's order until mid-January, 2007. After that, my lawyers filed a writ with the Seventh Circuit Court of Appeals, thereby, pacifying me for several months, but in June, 2007, that too was denied.

Quite naturally, at that moment Kunta Quawntay was again revitalized. Reality was: No judge was going to let my black ass out, even if the law required. I had to put my freedom into the hands of either myself or the jury, and lord knows how I felt about a jury in Southern Illinois. I preferred to be carried by 6 Blacks than judged by 12 closed-minded Whites.

The first thing Kunta Quawntay needed was time, and since my Judge had no problem handing out continuances, I decided to ask him for the 16th continuance in my case. All I had to do was tell him that I was interested in pleading guilty, and he granted me a continuance all the way up to March 3, 2008. That seemed to be ample time to execute an escape.

By now I'd been moved to a larger unit with 2 tiers, 6 cells, and 12 prisoners. There were long, narrow windows in the cells. They were too narrow for me to squeeze through, but they were wide enough for me to look out and see the better side of an unformidable barbed wire fence.

Whenever inside the cell, I stared out the window continuously, ogling the women visitors and staring at the parked cars in the parking lot. I wasn't really interested in the cars (as a matter of fact, I planned on fleeing to a country where donkey, camel, or elephant is the primary mode of transportation), but I liked to stare at them because they provided a reflection of the building. Depending on the position of the sun and the cars, I could see the roof and the side of the jail. I studied the reflections, in search for any sign of a louver or any other potential escape route.

I never saw a louver, but I did notice that the roof was much higher than the ceiling in the day-room and cells. Based on this, I was able to determine that there was a lot of crawl-space above the ceiling, which seemed to suggest that there was an exit up there.

How would I get up there? The ceilings in the cells were solid concrete, so, unless I were to smuggle in a sledge hammer and chisel, it was impossible for me to access the attic from the cells; therefore, it wasn't even worth my pondering. In the dayroom, however, there was a mysterious door inside the community bathroom, which was in the far corner and out of the view of the cameras. I suspected that the door would lead to a utility closet that might allow me to access the crawl-space above the ceiling. After several weeks of mulling, I decided to break into the room and see where it would lead me.

First I wanted to smuggle in a saw and have everything necessary to conquer any unforeseeable barriers. Smuggling a saw into Jackson County Jail was not easy; in fact, it proved to be a difficult and time-consuming task. We were not allowed to order hardbacks, so I had to try other ways. I tried for months to get a saw, but nothing ever panned out. My last resort was to recruit a reserved partner and have a saw sent to him through the legal mail, and since I was quickly running out of time, that's what I did.

I was so desperate for a saw that I went against my rule and brought on a white dude by the name of Suan. The crazy thing about my decision to bring on Suan was the fact that his eyes were identical to John's (the prisoner who snitched about my first escape). Coincidentally, not long before this, I received a copy of a letter that John had written to the prosecutor, demanding that he be transferred to the Clinton County Jail where he could "smoke cigarettes and order pizza," or else he would tell the truth and testify on my behalf rather than against me. Although Suan reminded me a lot of John (even their names rhymed), he seemed upright and rebellious. He boasted of beating up child molesters and snitches while in prison. Based on all of this, I disregarded his weak eyes, and had the saw sent to him.

The saw came. I broke into the room and was sadly disappointed to discover that it was nothing more than a concrete storage with absolutely no type of an exit, not even for an insect. While I racked my brain to figure out another route, Suan came up with what he naively believed to be another way out. Around the time that I broke into the storage room, my good friend and cellmate, Merve Butler, was preparing to start trial on a drug conspiracy charge.

One day while Merve was at court, the marshals surprisingly transferred Suan to the Franklin County Jail. The following day Merve went to court and returned with bad news: Suan was just like John—a lowdown rat. He showed up at Merve's trial and testified against him. Although he had never met Merve until the day he moved into the unit, he decided to lie for the government and testify that he knew all about Merve's alleged drug dealings. Merve's revelation hit me like a sledgehammer to the solar plexus. I was devastated and couldn't even think straight. How stupid could I actually be? I knew better than to be trusting that weak-eyed white dude. I felt like using the saw to cut my head off. Why was I so damn trusting? Never again, I swore on my daughter.

I anxiously dragged myself around the unit for the remainder of the week, waiting for the guards to come searching for the saw, but they never came. Apparently, the weak-eyed snitch wisely remained mum about my escape plans. After all, revealing such information would've only incriminated himself. Certainly he wouldn't have been rewarded a sentence reduction for providing information about a prisoner breaking into a storage room. Thanks to the weak eyed snitch, though, the week ended with Merve shockingly being acquitted (something unheard of for a black person tried in Benton, Illinois) and my escape intentions remaining a secret.

The shower in the unit was merely a small, secluded enclosure near the front of the day-room. We were allowed to use it whenever we desired. Most prisoners usually showered once a day for about 10 minutes, but with my March 3rd trial date quickly approaching, I started using the shower twice a day for an hour per session. Instead of showering, though, I was inside with my clothes hanging over the curtain, and the water running, while sawing a hole in the ceiling. When the hole was complete, I concealed it with a chessboard plastered in off-white paper the same color as the ceiling.

When the time was right, I returned to the shower, wiggled through the hole, and climbed up into the second floor of the attic in search for an exhaust vent or some other potential exit. But there wasn't one. The entire attic above the unit was enclosed with cinder block walls; the only potential exit was the air ducts running through them. I contemplated sawing through the one leading to the exhaust.

While blindly groping the roof, I discovered that it was merely corrugated steel, and that there was a plumbing pipe running through a small hole in it. I broke off a piece of a reinforcement bar protruding from a cinder block and poked it through the gap around the pipe. Amazingly, it went straight through with little resistance, thereby, indicating that there were no other barriers above the corrugated steel roof, nothing but rubber to prevent water from leaking through the cracks. When I withdrew the bar, it was cold and had traces of snow on the tip. I had found my exit.

Twice per day, while pretending to be showering, I'd climb up to the dark attic and vigorously saw the corrugated steel. Starting from the gap around the pipe, I sawed two parallel lines approximately 8 inches apart from each other, just enough space for me to wriggle my slender frame through. I sawed hard and fast with no regard for the noise I made. I was so far up above the ceiling that the raucous prisoners below in the day-room didn't stand a chance of hearing me, even though I heard them clearly. They had no idea what was going on; they simply thought I developed an obsession with showering excessively.

"It helps relieve stress," I'd say.

Wednesday, February 27th, while I was up in the attic sawing, my lawyer Adam surprised me with a visit. Fortunately, I heard the guard (a super cool, old, white dude everyone called Red) calling my name, so I was able to rush down to the hole in the shower and yell out, "I'll be out in a minute." Apparently, they'd been watching me on camera, because Red replied, "Hurry your ass up—you've been in there for nearly an hour. Save some of those babies for when you get out of jail." I quickly wriggled through the hole and covered it with the plastered chessboard. Since I was naked while in the attic, I was able to stand under the water for a few seconds and rinse off before putting on my clothes and being escorted to my visit. For a man who'd been in the shower for an hour, I sure did stink.

When I entered the interview room, I subtly scolded my lawyer for surprising me. I hated surprise visits, for there was no telling what I might be up to—or up in, for that matter. The purpose of the visit was to find out where I stood on the plea agreement. Although I knew that I wouldn't plead guilty, I told him that I needed more time to think about it. We both knew that the judge wouldn't postpone the trial date anymore. It had already been four years since my arrest, and the judge had had enough of my lingering around the detention facilities. But I figured it wouldn't hurt to try—a few extra days wouldn't disrupt anything.

In any event, whether or not the judge would continue the trial date was insignificant to my plans. At the rate I was going, I was certain to be done sawing by Friday night. And Sunday night, Merve would have a get-away ride parked up the street for me. Several hours before lock up, I'd climb into the attic, squeeze through the hole in the roof, crawl to the side of the jail, hop down, casually walk to the car, and drive to a nearby hide out Merve would have designated for me. I had it all figured out, and it was pretty much guaranteed. It was going to be better than the Alton escape. I had an adrenaline rush just thinking about it. I couldn't wait!

Friday morning, as I was preparing to go up to the attic and get some work done, a guard came to the unit and crushed my heart. He told me to pack my property. I was being transferred to another jail.

CHAPTER 27

PLAYING THE DOZEN

After 17 months in the Jackson County Jail, I was sadly leaving. Apparently, I was being transferred to a jail much closer to the court for my upcoming trial. I should have known that would happen, but I figured I wouldn't be accepted at any other jail. After the last stunt I pulled at Alton, the chief said that I was no longer welcome at his jail, and during my last lay over at St. Clair County Jail– which occurred when I was taken to court from Marion–the superintendent (who was now the former, flamboyant captain) griped about my being there for two nights. Therefore, I was almost certain that I'd never return to either of those two, especially considering the corrupt guards and the saws I still had scattered about St. Clair County Jail.

As I was leaving, several guards shook my hand commending me on my stellar behavior and respectful attitude, and wished me well. The adorable cook even prepared one last meal for me. Their respect and admiration for me nearly brought a tear to my eye and induced a bit of shame to go along with my dejection. Although I had shown them my true character, I couldn't help but feel like I'd duped them into believing that I was a saint.

In all actuality I really was a good dude, and trying to break out of jail didn't negate that. Being considered a bad boy by the terms of the law didn't take away from my good heart and manners. As the prisoner in Marion had said, I was just manipulating a system that was manipulating me. It had nothing to do with the cool people at Jackson County. It was about escaping the heartless justice system. To my surprise, I was taken back to the St. Clair County Jail. As soon as I stepped into the booking area, the black detective smiled and yelled out my name like we were old friends who hadn't seen each other in years. He inquired about my case and well-being, and reached out to shake my shackled hand. It didn't dawn on me until later that night that I actually shook hands with cops and guards for the first time in my life.

After I was strip-searched and scanned with a metal detector, I was taken straight to Max and placed in the same cell I nearly escaped from. Once inside the cell, I immediately started working on getting back to Jackson County Jail. I crawled under the bunk and stayed there the entire weekend. I refused to eat, refused to drink water, refused to talk to guards, and refused to come from under the bunk until Monday when I was taken to court. The guards pitied me, thinking that years in solitary confinement had finally taken its toll on me. Exacerbating their concern, when they inventoried my property, they discovered several bizarre drawings that I had forgot to return to Fish before leaving Marion. They also discovered a chicken bone inscribed with the word *Freedom* on one side and *Death* on the other side.

When I appeared before the judge that Monday morning, I appeared a mess. I was stinky, nappy-headed, hungry, dehydrated, and delirious. The jail officials had informed the marshals of the chicken bone, the drawings, and my bizarre behavior over the weekend, and the marshals informed the prosecutor, who in turn informed the judge. When the judge began to query me, I responded by putting on an Oscar-winning performance. I slowly began to tremble, and released an outburst of feigned insanity that sent my attorneys quickly rolling away from the table in their swivel chairs. I pounded on the table and griped about the court and the criminal justice system's lack of empathy and understanding for me and other young black men. And I stressed that I was doing absolutely fine until they took me away from Jackson County Jail.

The judge immediately stopped the proceedings and had me placed in the holding cell. My attorney Adam (the only one who didn't scurry away when I pounded on the table) followed behind me and tried to console me. Although

I sensed his ability to see right through my bullshitting, I told him that I'd been hearing voices and seeing imaginary creatures. I specifically told him that a dummy kept popping up out of nowhere chanting the word "abracadabra." I further explained that I didn't have such problems when I was at the Jackson County Jail. Adam went to report this to the judge, and later returned with good news and bad news. The good news was that I wasn't going back to St. Clair County Jail. The bad news, however, was that I wouldn't be returning to Jackson County either. Instead, I was going to the Clinton County Jail.

Before being locked in a cell at the Clinton County Jail, I was taken to the emergency room at a small hospital in the boondocks of southern Illinois. The doctor was a middle-aged white man who seemed to be awaiting my arrival. My two escorts and I stepped into his office, leaving the door open behind us. The doctor gazed at me, and I averted my eyes to the ground as if I were a bashful child.

"What's your name, young man?" Doc asked.

"Quawntay," I somberly replied, still gazing at the ground.

"Do you know what day it is, Quawntay?" he asked.

"No—not really."

"Do you have any idea?"

I gleefully looked up with wide eyes and said, "I know the month," as if such knowledge was worthy of a treat.

"Can you tell me?"

"February," I confidently said, although it was actually March.

"So what's bothering you?" Doc inquired, studying my face.

I fell silent, resumed gazing at the ground, and started fidgeting.

"It's okay. You can tell me," he said, soothingly. I remained mum, fidgeting.

"It's okay—I'm here to help," he urged.

I somberly looked up at Doc, then over at my escorts, and began to tremble.

"Nothing," I mumbled with a feigned hint of uncertainty and trepidation. Doc looked at my escorts, then asked them to step out for a moment. They were reluctant, but since I was shackled like a captured runaway slave, they obliged. Doc shut the door behind them and opened the blinds so that they could look in.

"Okay, now will you tell me what's bothering you?" he asked.

"I don't know," I hesitantly replied, with a tear running down my cheek. Although I was faking, the tear was real, just not for the matter at hand.

"It's okay. Tell me what's bothering you."

"I don't like talking about it because I'm afraid you'll think I'm crazy and I don't want people to think I'm a crazy man."

"Well trust me, young man, I don't think you're crazy. I just think that you're going through an unusually difficult time in your life right now. And I know that the right treatment will make things better, but you have to talk to me so that I can help you."

I told Doc about the dummy, about the voices, and about the years of solitary confinement. He replied that I was suffering from mild delusions due to years of solitary confinement, and that my upcoming trial seemed to be agitating my mental condition (he stopped short of using the word "crazy"). He went on to say that my condition was similar to that of many prisoners of war. Comparing me to a POW, he said that it's common for our minds to create imaginary companions to soothe the loneliness and depression caused by solitary confinement and extremely stressful conditions. He said that even after being freed, our minds may still call upon that old imaginary companion to help us get through difficult moments.

I totally understood what Doc was saying. Years of confinement to a prison cell can be as harmful to the human psyche as being held by enemy combatants. In fact, there isn't any difference– captivity is captivity. I was no soldier fighting for his country, but I was a prisoner of war—the War of Drugs.

The doctor finished consoling me; then, he opened the door and let my captors back in. He told them that he would be prescribing me some medication because I was suffering from anxiety and mental illness, and that I was not in my right mind to withstand trial. He suggested that I be further evaluated and treated.

As he explained the necessity of postponing the trial, I smiled inwardly, silently rejoicing and applauding myself for the stellar performance. Had the doctor's office been a Broadway stage, I would have walked away with the Tony award. I never knew that I had it in me. Man will be surprised by what desperation can bring out of him.

Clinton County Jail wasn't a bad place to be detained. Although the food wasn't as good as I had it at Jackson County Jail, it wasn't bad for a county jail. There were also plenty of gorgeous female guards there. It seemed that the sheriff had went out to a beauty pageant and hired a slew of models to work for him. Under normal circumstances, I would have loved to stay there and flirt with the ladies, and possibly woo one of them into helping me bust out. But considering the fact I'd already secured an exit at Jackson County Jail, I had no desire to stay.

The following day when I appeared in front of the judge, he surprisingly ordered that I be sent to the Federal Bureau of Prisons (FBOP) for a psychological evaluation. The court wouldn't accept the public doctor's word for it; federal courts relied upon government employed doctors, those that were likely to diagnose in the government's favor. It has widely been known that FBOP doctors are one-sided—after all, they do work for the Department of Justice. In any event, I didn't care about the diagnosis; I had only one agenda: to get back to Jackson County Jail.

Generally, it took 4 to 6 weeks to be transferred to the FBOP facilities. Meanwhile, I was expected to wait idly at Clinton County Jail, locked in a cell with a camera watching me, and not even allowed to have a toothbrush or reading book. I tried having my family and lawyers persuade the marshals into sending me back to Jackson County Jail, but that didn't work.

Since my civil approach wasn't working, I resorted to buffoonery, just as I'd done at Alton Jail. I started by flooding the cell, causing water to gush out into the hallway and into the officers' control center. When the guards shut off my water, I started destructing the cell, breaking anything that could be broken. To halt my destruction, they stripped me of my bedding and placed me in shackles. Defiantly, I hid in the corner of the cell where I couldn't be viewed via the camera or the door. They countered by shackling one of my ankles to the bunk. I countered by breaking out of the shackles and using them to destruct the window and the walls. They rushed in with Taser guns and restrained me with chains and heavy-duty padlocks; then, as if I were a dog, they connected a chain to the chain around my waist and secured it to the bunk, leaving just enough leeway for me to hobble to the toilet and to my food which they would sarcastically set on the floor by the door.

Unable to break out of the locks and chains, I was forced to endure the torture. The room was extremely cold, and the concrete floor was wearing on my body. After two agonizing, sleepless nights, I was weak, tired, angry, and ready to throw in the towel. But first, I had to try one more stunt. I peeled white paint from the wall and chewed it until it appeared that I was foaming at the mouth. I then began to quake and flop on the ground, pretending to be having a seizure. A couple of guards rushed to my door, but they were not allowed to enter. While one of them radioed for help, the other shouted: "Hang in there Quawntay!... Can you hear me?... If you can hear me, hang in there... Help is on the way." However, it was well after midnight on a Saturday, so help was slow to arrive.

Not wanting to overdo it, I stopped flopping, and just lay there with the white paint foaming from my mouth. By now a third jailer arrived and suggested that they enter the cell, but the other two didn't like that idea. The sheriff had given specific orders not to open my door unless one of the street deputies were present. After a couple of minutes, two deputies arrived and assisted the guards in removing the chain from around my waist.

Shortly thereafter, the paramedics arrived and I was dragged out of my cell and propped against the wall in the hallway. The medics asked the guards to remove the chain from around my wrist. They then placed me on the stretcher and began to check my vital signs and ask me a series of questions. I was silently rejoicing at the prospect of getting away from the jail and going to the hospital to be around pretty nurses, but apparently my answers and the tests didn't add up, because the medic lowered the stretcher and said: "You can put him back in his cell—he's faking."

"What about the foaming from the mouth?" one of the guards asked. "Was that fake too?"

The medic examined the residue on my white mouth and said, "Yeah, it's toothpaste or something."

Now the guards were baffled because they knew for certain that I didn't have any toothpaste in my cell; in fact, I didn't have anything in my cell but underwear and the chains wrapped around me.

Monday morning, the sheriff and his goons came to my cell to have a long talk with me. He said that as long as I continued to be disruptive, I would remain chained to the bunk like a dog. If I wanted to improve my condition, he lectured, then I needed to first improve my behavior. He said that he would reward me for every day of good behavior. Such rewards ranged from the chains being removed to a TV being placed in my cell.

Removing the chains sounded like a good reward, but the

TV was nothing, but a pacifier—that's why they have them in every prison. Nevertheless, I wanted to behave just long enough to get some rest and get the TV so that I could slam it against the wall.

I behaved the rest of the day, and was rewarded by having the chains removed. Tuesday he gave me the option of either a mat or a TV. Out of pure spite, I chose the TV, just so I could slam it against the wall when he returned the following day. But my plans were stifled Wednesday morning when a few guards arrived at my cell and told me that I was leaving. Right then was my chance to seek revenge and slam the TV, and perhaps knock over one of the computers in the booking area. Certainly the thought crossed my mind, but it quickly dissipated when the sweetest guard at the jail appeared. Conventionally, she was far from the most physically attractive, but she was older with a pair of soulful, hazel eyes that were pleasant enough to disarm me of all diabolical intentions. Like a blushing schoolboy, I obliged with all of her commands and departed the jail without incident. I was off to the feds for a psychological evaluation.

CHAPTER 28

IT JUST AIN'T MEANT TO BE

From a small airstrip near Scott's Air Force Base, I was boarded onto an airplane with approximately 150 shackled prisoners, and flown to the FBOP transit center in Oklahoma City. The transit center was built on a small airport, so the plane pulled up to an annex that allowed us to disembark and walk right into the prison. I didn't stay long at the transit center. Two days later me and another prisoner were boarded onto a small Cessna jet and flown to a federal correction center in Butner, North Carolina.

As I was waddling through the corridor of the collegiate-looking prison, I began to question whether I should continue playing the dozens or try to hurry back to Jackson County Jail before someone were to stumble upon my escape route. After pacing a small holding cell for a couple of hours, my question was answered when a tall, chocolate woman pulled me out for an interview. The moment I looked at her soft, full, juicy lips, and into her alluring eyes, I had neither the desire nor composure to continue playing crazy. As soon as I stepped out of the holding cell, she looked up at me and said, "Boy you know you ain't crazy." I busted out in laughter and silently agreed.

It was after 4 p.m. when I was finally processed in. By then, the captain had left without reviewing my file, so I was forced to spend the weekend in the hole. Monday morning the prisoner who'd come with me was released to general population while I remained in the hole. I griped until I was finally released Tuesday afternoon and taken to a unit that looked more like an inpatient drug rehab than a prison dormitory. The day-rooms had ice-machines, TVs, and plastic chairs. And the bunks inside the cells had springs in them.

Instead of locking us in our cells for the 4 o'clock count, the guard simply instructed us to stand in front of our cells, and counted us. After the count cleared, we walked to the dining hall for supper. It was still sunny out, so it seemed like I was walking on a college campus rather than a prison. The buildings had huge windows and were surrounded by green grass and bushes. The food was well prepared and diversely balanced. Unlike other prisons, the tables were not segregated by race and gangs; we were free to sit with whomever and wherever we pleased. From the dining hall, we were free to go wherever we wanted, whether it was the gym, the weight-pile, the running track, the baseball diamond, the library, the barbershop, or anywhere else outside or inside. I went to the barbershop and then to the library to read some Speedy Trial Act case laws.

At 8 o'clock, the facility was locked down and we were required to return to the dorms, where most prisoners sat around watching TV and eating popcorn. I had never been to a prison so pleasant. Yep! I, the escapist, had landed myself in a prison where the cell doors didn't even lock. Around 10 o'clock I approached another prisoner and asked what time we were required to lock inside our cells. "Whenever you want," he nonchalantly replied and resumed watching TV. Slightly offended by what I perceived as sarcasm, I walked away and asked another prisoner. The prisoner put his hand on my shoulder and said, "Brother, look at the doors on those cells." Baffled and hesitant, I looked at the doors wondering where in the hell the crazy old man was going with this. "Do you see any locks on those doors?" he continued. Oddly there weren't any. The old man grinned and said, "Never been any place like this, huh."

The following morning after breakfast, I went outside to lift weights and enjoy the morning air. I found myself considering whether I'd plead guilty to 20 years if I could do it at a prison like Butner. But I knew that there was no way a prisoner with my history could be housed at such a prison. Sure enough, 45 minutes into my workout, my name was called over the P.A., and I was directed to report to the lieutenant's office.

As I was making my way toward the administrative building, asking other prisoners for directions along the way, I was met halfway by two burly officers wearing black windbreakers and carrying a card with my picture on it.

"Mr. Adams," one of them said. "You can't be out here on this yard."

"I didn't know," I replied. "I just got here—nobody told me I couldn't be out here."

"No, I mean, you're not supposed to be on this compound at all," he replied. "We gotta put you back in the hole—you're too high risk for this facility."

"You're one of them guys—ain't you?" said a skinny, chain-smoking, fiftyish, black guard who stood outside my cell with a grin on his face.

"One of what guys?" I inquired.

"You know—one of them guys who killed Tupac."

"Nooooo—I ain't kill Tupac!"

"I know *you* didn't, but your homeboys did. Ain't Orlando Anderson and the Compton Crips your homeboys?"

I inquired about the guard's source of information, but he just smiled and said that he'd done research on me. He also went on to say that the guy rumored to have killed Notorious B.I.G. was incarcerated at the prison and that the administration didn't want me around him. He alluded to that as one of the reasons I was placed in the hole, but I knew that it was much deeper than that.

Out of the approximately 50 bunks in the hole, less than 10 were occupied. The prisoners there wore the same story as any other hole—a bunch of mentally and emotionally disturbed individuals vying for attention. There was a delusional prisoner who stayed awake all night loudly mimicking the sound of gunshots. Then, there was Jay Candy, a prisoner on trial for selling Crack, which he referred to as

Candy. Strangely, he used a black ink pen to boldly write *Candy Man* across the back pockets of his super small, orange jumpsuit.

The most prominent prisoner was an old, racist, white man with a boisterous voice. "See the problem with you niggers is that your dicks are bigger than your brains," he would often say. Every time a black guard walked by his cell he would say: "Bigger dick than brain." According to him, black people were the stupidest people on earth, and he tried to prove it every chance he could. For example, an inmate plumber came to the hole one day to fix a leaking pipe. As soon as he entered the unit, a black guard asked him to get against the wall so that he could search him for shanks. Ironically, the prisoner had a toolbox in one hand and a hammer in the other. "See what I mean," the racist, white man said, witnessing the pat-down from his window and a pair of Coke bottle glasses. "He's got a hammer in his hand, but the nigger's worried about him having a shank—bigger dick than brain, bigger dick than brain."

On another occasion, a white officer came through the unit with two black rookies, giving them a tour of the prison. The old bigot sardonically asked the white guard: "Where'd you get them from—Atlanta?" Unfamiliar with the racist, the black guards failed to grasp his sarcasm and continued walking. Desperate for their attention, the racist shouted: "Just because you niggers got a job and the right to vote don't make you worth a damn thing. Let's not forget that 200 years ago I coulda bought 200 of you niggers for less than 200 dollars. And trust me, niggers were worth a lot more back then than they are today."

Truthfully, the old bigot was more entertaining and humorous than harmful. He certainly didn't have a problem eating the hamburgers and roast beef that I—a black man—had given him. Between him and the prisoner with Candy Man written across his ass, I had plenty of reasons to laugh.

Since it was clear that I wasn't getting out of the hole, I made it clear to my doctor that I wasn't participating in the evaluation. Actually, I was ready to return to the southern district of Illinois and hopefully back to Jackson County Jail. However, the doctor said that I wouldn't be going anywhere unless I complete the evaluation. Therefore, I agreed to go on with the program, which was more of a sham than I was. The doctor simply took me to her office and asked me myriad of basic questions while I sat alongside a nosey guard with my hands cuffed behind my back. The questions were simple and inconsequential to the state of my psychological well-being. If I wanted to, I could have easily duped her into thinking I was crazy, but since I wanted to hurry and get the evaluation over, I told her that I was simply pretending to be mentally ill.

A few days after the evaluation, I received extremely bad news through the mail. I received a letter from one of the prisoners at the Jackson County Jail stating that the jail had been locked down for a few days while a team of cops searched the jail and "fixed the shower." I was devastated. My dejection was so palpable that the guard on shift that night asked if I was okay. He even asked if I needed to speak with the psych or chaplain. Truthfully, that wasn't a bad idea; I needed to speak to everyone—the psych, the chaplain, God, myself, and the imaginary dummy I'd been pretending to see. Clearly the universe was conspiring against my escape. It seemed that something was always getting in the way, be it a weak-eyed snitch, a cigarette-smoking cop, a naive white woman, or an unexpected transfer. It just wasn't meant to be.

CHAPTER 29

MY REPUTATION PRECEDES ME

I returned to the southern district of Illinois in the middle of May. Since it seemed that Jackson County Jail would be added to the list of jails refusing to accept me, I wondered where I'd end up next. Truthfully, since it seemed that God had plans other than my escaping, I no longer had the will or desire to escape, so it really didn't matter what jail I were to land in. Nevertheless, if I had a choice, I would've chosen Clinton County Jail. I preferred to be confined to that huge cell with a TV and a shower inside—not to mention the myriad of attractive guards, especially the older woman with the disarming eyes. When I disembarked the plane, however, I was hustled to the back of a brown van with *Marion County Jail* emblazoned on the side.

Marion County Jail was located in Salem, Illinois, an extremely small, all-white town with less than 10,000 people. The jail only housed 150 prisoners on its most populous day. Although I had no intent on breaking out, I couldn't help but case the outside of the jail when we pulled up to it. The guards were already expecting me, so I was quickly booked in and placed in one of the small holding cells in the booking area. There wasn't even a bunk in there, just a thin mat lying on the cold concrete floor. On the outside of my door, there was a metal flap on the window which prevented me from looking out into the booking area. Per the U.S. Marshalls, this is where I was to be housed until my trial.

Sleeping seemed impossible inside that cell, even for a prisoner who'd been awake all day flying across the country. The small vent above me blew cold air all night; the bright florescent lights were never shut off; doors repeatedly opened and slammed shut throughout the night as rowdy prisoners were constantly being processed in and out of the jail; and the jailers and deputies repeatedly opened and shut the squeaky flap on my window to peek in at me.

When I finally did fall asleep, I was awakened minutes later to a guard opening my tray slot and handing me what they considered to be breakfast: two powdered donuts, a cup of powdered milk, and a 6-ounce cup of coffee. I devoured the donuts and milk and tossed the cup of coffee at the wall. I hadn't been at the jail 12 hours and was already fed up with it. The breakfast was terrible, the holding cell was miserable, and I wasn't allowed to have anything—not even a toothbrush.

I was sitting on the end of the mat, thinking of a way to force a transfer, when an amiable, unconventionally attractive guard by the name of Candy opened the flap on my window and asked, "Are you the escape artist?" I responded with a restrained blush and shrugged shoulders. At that moment I wished that I was an escape artist—I certainly wouldn't have been sitting in that hellhole. When Candy (no relation to the Candy Man at Butner) closed the flap, I heard her say, "Damn he's fine," to another female guard. Suddenly, I had a glimmer of hope that something good might come of Marion County Jail.

When I appeared before the judge that following week, I sincerely griped about my conditions at the jail, including the fact that I wasn't even allowed to have a plastic spoon to eat with. I acknowledged responsibility for my conditions; nonetheless, I argued that there's a difference between security and oppression—the conditions of the holding cell were oppressive. Certainly, a spoon and a few hours of sleep weren't too much to ask for. The judge agreed and said that he would speak with the Marshal.

The following day, I was moved upstairs to a three-man cell with a TV, phone, and shower. The judge and Marshal had looked out for me, and I intended to show my appreciation by not escaping before the trial, nor would I destruct the property of the jail. Simply put, I planned to stay out of trouble. (Mind you, flirting with female staff and smuggling in comforting items were not listed under my definition of trouble. In fact, they were considered necessities for my sanity.)

There was clearly something fishy about my two cell-mates, Larry and Courtney. Courtney was a young Mullato from Centralia, Illinois, who was facing a very short sentence for a petty offense. Larry, on the other hand, was a white, federal detainee with myriad of charges ranging from identity theft to taking advantage of seniors and disabled citizens. He also had eyes just like John and Suan, and as soon as I looked into them, a red flag popped up. There had to be reason for their being separated from general population for a reason, and that the marshals wouldn't dare put me in a three-man cell with exterior windows in it unless one or both of my cellmates were informants. Considering Larry's federal charges and weak eyes, I was almost certain that he was a rat.

The following day when Candy came to work, she came to the cell to pass out cleaning supplies, and whispered: "Be careful around Larry." I silently questioned her, but she couldn't say. I assumed that she was trying to warn me that he was an informant.

Sure enough, after being in the cell for only a few days, Larry mentioned my escape from Alton. How did he know about that? He said that one of the guards had told him. Why? I suspected that they'd told him to keep an eye on me. After I admitted to being the guy who'd escaped from Alton, he told me that he had once escaped from a jail in Tennessee by paying a guard to walk him out the side door. He then asked if I wanted to escape with him, and I quickly replied "No!"

I told him that I was putting faith in the hands of the jury—which was the truth. After all of my failures, I really believed that a higher power was in the driver seat of my freedom, and that a miracle would happen in court.

Over the days, Larry continued to bug me about escaping. He said that the camera in the bathroom could be turned to create a blind spot, and that he planned to escape through the roof of the shower. When he mentioned the roof of the shower, my intuition went crazy. Nobody knew about the shower at Jackson County Jail, nobody but the feds and maybe the big dogs at Marion County Jail. Now I was 99.9 percent sure that he was working with the feds or the sheriff to get information out of me.

Still, I didn't say anything; instead, I continued to entertain his talk of escaping. When he said that he had a friend who could smuggle saws and tools into the jail, I decided to put him to the test. I told him to prove it by having his friend smuggle in a cell phone. I wrote a letter instructing my people to send a cell phone to his friend, and gave it to Larry to give to his friend to send to my people. I figured that his friend's smuggling in a cell phone would help me determine whether or not Larry was an informant.

My second week in the cell, Larry and Courtney had a fist fight. Courtney got the best of Larry, bloodied his nose, choked him out, and bit him on the back just for the hell of it. After Larry began to plead for his life, I intervened and got Courtney off of him. I was concerned only because Larry claimed to be terminally ill with cancer. Once Courtney let him up, though, he began to boast as though he'd won the fight. He then pushed the button on the intercom and told the guards that Courtney had beat him up.

The guards came and patched Larry's wounds and moved Courtney to another cell. Strangely, Larry was happy that Courtney had bitten him, and although he could have done so himself, he preferred to make the guards change his bandage. Something was really weird about this dude.

After a week had passed and my people still hadn't received the letter Larry's friend supposedly sent to them, I stopped talking to him because I was now 100 percent sure that he was an informant. Then, one evening when a new prisoner and I went to the gym, Larry stayed back, as he always did, and went through my legal documents. I wasn't certain, but when I came back, I discovered that a letter I intended to give to my lawyer was missing. In the letter I provided a spiel to John John for him to testify to. And concealed behind the stamp, I had written John John and Nicole's address.

When Larry noticed that I was searching for the letter, he said the guards had confiscated it when they did their daily cell search that night. When I asked the guards, however, they said that they hadn't taken it. Somebody was lying, and I had a strong hunch that it was Larry.

Later I told Larry that my attorney was having the tapes rewound to see who took the letter. Two days thereafter, while everyone was asleep, a guard came to the cell and told Larry to uncover the camera and stop tampering with it. By now, Larry and I were a bad gaze away from a bloody situation, so the thought crossed my mind that maybe he was planning to attack me in my sleep, and perhaps that's why he covered the camera. That evening, the guard came and got me and the other prisoner for rec earlier than usual. When I returned, they told me to gather my belongings and moved me back to the holding cell. They said they discovered a screw cap missing in the ceiling, and that was sufficient reason to move me back downstairs.

A week later my lawyer visited me and revealed the truth behind my move. It was Larry; he was not only a rat, but also a cunning liar. He didn't have cancer; he had AIDS, and had been charged for deliberately infecting unsuspecting people with it. That's why Candy warned me to be careful around him. He'd also been eavesdropping on my phone conversations, spying on my interactions with Candy, and telling the feds that Candy and I were exchanging notes. It was he who stole the letter from my papers. He gave it to the feds, and said that I was trying to smuggle in hacksaws. Worst of all, he removed a screw cap from the ceiling and blamed it on me. The sad thing about all of this was that, considering my reputation and the letters, Larry's story was extremely plausible.

Of all the people who'd made statements against me, Larry was the one that I wanted to strangle the most. Granted, most of them had stretched the truth, but at least there was some truth in their statements. However, other than my passing notes to Candy and trying to have Larry's friend smuggle in a phone, everything Larry said was a lie. More disturbing was the fact that I really appreciated the judge and marshal for moving me, and now Larry had duped everyone into believing that I didn't. I felt like the boy who cried wolf, or like the old man Steve when he was tossed in the quiet-room for my kicking on the wall.

CHAPTER 30

THE TRIAL

Early on the morning of July 14, 2008, I was escorted to the courthouse by a caravan of cops. (Larry told the feds that I had planned to have someone hijack the van.) After 54 months of detention, the day I'd been trying to avoid had finally arrived. The trial was expected to last two weeks and end in a guilty verdict on all charges. We began and finished jury selection that same day: 10 Whites and 2 Blacks, 8 women and 4 men. To my relief, they looked nothing like the close-minded, conservative, white folks I'd been seeing in my nightmares. Truthfully, I was more concerned with the Blacks than the Whites.

The prosecutor, playing on the race and gender of the jury, opened by arguing that I was a smart, calculating marijuana dealer who used others, particularly white women, to facilitate my crimes. My attorney would later counter by arguing that the government can't have it both ways. On one hand the prosecution is saying that Quawntay is this smart, calculating drug dealer who uses others to do his dirty work; on the other hand, he wants you to believe that Quawntay is so stupid that he showed up at to a truck stop to do a drug deal with strangers, and then hopped inside a van loaded with marijuana, my attorney argued. Where were the white women? Why didn't Quawntay have one of them go pick up the van? According to the government there were plenty of them sitting around waiting to do whatever Quawntay asked of them.

The government's first witness was Steve Carraway, whose testimony was true for the most part, except the parts about when we met and how much marijuana I sold him. He said that we met through his cousin Dominique in August,

2003, and that I sold him more marijuana than I actually did. Truthfully, I didn't start selling marijuana until September 2003, and I hadn't met Dominique until the middle of October.

What disturbed me most about Steve was the fact that he not only came from a family saturated with criminals, but also had less than 6 months remaining on his sentence. Still, in hopes of reducing that 6 months, he was willing to assist the government in its evil War on Drugs and send me to prison for the rest of my life. After all the marijuana I had given him on consignment, and this is how he paid me back—what a low-down, selfish negro!

The government's second significant witness was Twinky, whose testimony was also true for the most part, except when he stated that in early December 2003, he, Yeyo, two white women, and I picked up 300 pounds of pot in Atlanta and took it to the apartment that John John rented for me in St. Louis. Receipts clearly revealed that John John didn't rent the apartment until January 12, 2004. On that day I was on an airplane flying from Phoenix, Arizona to St. Louis, and Twinky and Yeyo were still in L.A. preparing to hit the highway.

Yeyo never got a chance to testify because he'd already served his sentence and been deported back to Mexico, where he resumed smuggling drugs into the U.S. Rumor has it he was later arrested in Mexico for drug trafficking and multiple murders. Ultimately, he was sentenced to life in prison.

Angel, who had three years remaining on his sentence, strolled into the courtroom with his head held high and sporting a pair of shades as if he were too cool for school. He was supposed to be the government's star witness and testify about my knowledge of what was inside the van. However, when he took the stand, he flipped up his shades, winked at me, and said that he didn't know what I knew. He basically said that he'd come to deal with Yeyo and that he never spoke to me. Truthfully, Angel didn't know me from a can of paint, and I didn't know him.

So when Leandro showed up and said that I asked him to relay a message to my friend in order to have Angel's family kidnapped, he sounded ridiculous. Leandro's testimony was the result of a tale fabricated by the Rat Pack. I had asked Leandro to call my friend and tell him to "get at" Twinky about Angel's suspected cooperation, and the Rat Pack turned it into a kidnapping plot and sold it to the feds. When the Rat Pack sold it to the feds, the feds asked Leandro, and he confirmed it as a way to support his friends' falsehood. Little did he know that they would come years later and make him testify to it.

He couldn't plead the 5th because, according to him, he didn't do anything incriminating. (He said that he never made the call for me, but truthfully, he did make the call and told my homeboy exactly what I said.) Also, he couldn't take the stand and tell the truth because he could have been charged with obstruction of justice for providing false information to the feds. Leandro basically had no choice but to testify to his lie. In fact, he even said that the only reason he was testifying was because the feds were pressing him.

Certainly, I couldn't have had anything done to Angel's family because I didn't even know Angel, much less his family. I didn't even know if he had family, nor how to get in touch with them. What was I going to do—send a private investigator to Mexico?

The only witness to testify sincerely was John John; however, his memory was a little jaded as to when and how drugs had been transported. Although I'd known him since I was about 11 and he was 18, I wasn't even mad at him for testifying. I was more disappointed because he was being selfish and, as he said, "saving" himself. And helping "The man." At least he didn't try to stretch the truth and make himself out to be a saint.

When Nicole took the stand, though, she lied more than I. For example, she falsely stated that during her first strip to

St. Louis, she caught the bus with marijuana and ecstasy pills strapped to her extremely petite, 110-pound body. She even became dramatic, stating that she rode the bus for two days reeking of "stinky" marijuana, and that she narrowly escaped the detection of drug-sniffing canines that boarded the bus.

Although I was far from the smartest criminal in the world, I damn sure wasn't so stupid as to send marijuana across the country strapped to the body of a person riding the Greyhound. Such stupidity would have been not only risky but also unprofitable. Here you have a man, whom the government accuses of dealing thousands of pounds of marijuana, allegedly strapping—at the most—a couple of pounds of pot to the back of a 110-pound woman. At $300 profit per pound, I would have been hustling backwards; after all, the traveling expenses alone would have exceeded the profit, not to mention the $2,000 Nicole was paid. Logic and common sense contradicted Nicole's testimony.

I guess she figured she'd be in less trouble by saying that she transported a few ecstasy pills (a drug I'd never seen before, much less trafficked) and some "stinky" marijuana. And as if that lie weren't enough to make her appear less culpable, she falsely stated that I threw her against the wall and threatened to kill her because I overheard her telling her aunt about my drug dealing and that she wanted to go home. This typical-white-girl testimony portrayed a false image of not only her transporting against her will, but also of me being the black beast holding her hostage.

Little did the jury know, I was the coolest thing since Popsicle, too cool to be getting angry and threatening women, let alone throwing them against walls. Nor did they know that Nicole was sneaky and deceptive, and perhaps a little mentally and emotionally disturbed. She didn't testify to that side of her many personalities. She testified that she ran out of money while transporting marijuana on her second trip, and that I had to wire her money for gas. What she didn't tell the jury that she ran out of money because she detoured through Texas to have a fling with a guy she'd met online. Nor did she tell them about the time she sneaked off with a pimp, the same pimp whom I had rescued her from because he'd beaten her up and tried to pimp her out.

I couldn't present most of the dirt I had on Nicole because my defense didn't allow me to. Instead, I was forced to let her dubious testimony speak for itself. Like the time she said that I never finished paying her for the first trip, but that she made two more trips after that because she and her boyfriend needed the money. Why would she make two more trips if she hadn't been paid for the first? Although her testimony was riddled with holes, her skin color seemed to be sufficient evidence to convince the court. After all, playing on the race and gender of the jury was the prosecutor's strategy.

That's why he brought in Audrey, who stormed into the courtroom carrying a box of tissue, and shooting daggers at me. She didn't know anything about my marijuana dealings; she was simply brought in to highlight the "white girl" theme. And truthfully, even her testimony wasn't completely accurate.

The prosecutor even brought in Nurse Tee. What did she have to do with my case? Absolutely nothing. So why did the government subpoena her? Because she was white, and her presence alone might have been enough to inflame the passion of the predominantly-white female jury.

The prosecutor was so determined to paint the "white girl" picture that he even made my poor, old white landlady fly all the way from California just to testify that I'd rented an apartment from her. Every white woman he could link to me in any way—even if it was legitimate business—he paraded them before the jury. He even went so far as to have Larry testify about my interaction with Candy. What did that have to do with 1400 pounds of marijuana loaded in the back of a U-Haul?

Since he brought in Nurse Tee and mentioned Candy, why didn't the prosecutor bring in the black guard who smuggled in the hacksaws? Or Gretchen and the wire recordings? Or the other black guard who said that I propositioned him for a cell phone? Probably because they were black, and that would have taken away from his "white girl" strategy.

What was my Defense? Lies and God-damned lies. Most of the government witnesses' testimony involved one or the other. Sure, I sold marijuana, but I didn't do all of the things that they accused me of doing—that was my defense. My only witness other than Qusai—whose name alone had the entire court terrified—was myself. I took the stand because the jury needed to hear my side; I just wish that I could have told them everything, including the truth and the real reason I was before them.

PART FOUR:
YOUNG AND MENTALLY ENSLAVED

CHAPTER 31

STRAIGHT OUTTA COMPTON

I was born September 30, 1975, in Compton, California. Although I was no different than any other infant—innocent, curious, and adorable—my genes, ancestral misfortune, and social conditions might have already had my future predetermined. In the aftermath of slavery, my great grandparents were forced to wade through the oppressive, racist South with nothing but anguish and the unfulfilled hope of 40 acres and a mule. With no financial or educational footing, they desperately fended for themselves and their children by any means necessary, with little regard for the law—which, by the way, had little regard for them. With the exception of afro picks, bell-bottoms, and gangs, my family's condition hadn't changed much by the time of my arrival. Consequently, there was very little chance that I'd be the golden child to break the cycle; after all, I had nothing but the murky foundation that existed before my arrival.

At 20 years old, unemployed, and poorly educated, my mother gave birth to me, the only boy and the last of 3 children. During pregnancy, she indulged her cravings for the then-popular chocolate beverage *Bosco*, and since I had a rare chocolate complexion as an infant, I took on the nickname *Bosco*.

My mother was blessed with both physical beauty and inner beauty. Her greatest asset was also her greatest parental flaw: she was too kind. She would give the shirt off her back and bend over backwards to help anyone, even if that meant sacrificing herself (she got it from my grandmother, and I got it from her.) She was always supportive of her children and any other child or adult in need or want. This often meant that we would have an exorbitant number of kids and adults cramped in our small apartment, struggling to get by on her limited and scarce income.

My father, Tootie, played very little role in my life. Nevertheless, his absence and inadvertent teachings would have a tremendous impact on my development. Tootie was one of the original Compton Crips; so instead of focusing on being an attentive father, he focused on running the streets with the rest of the Crips—my Uncles Butch and Donald, Lee, Mac, Salty, Tookie, and so on. During my early childhood, he would visit frequently and shower us with stolen toys. Sometimes he and I would hop in his car and cruise around Compton and Watts, sipping on malt liquor and jamming to music on his 8-track. Cruising and mingling with thugs seemed to be the highlights of our moments, and my young, curious mind absorbed it all like a sponge.

As far as I can remember, every time I saw my father, he had a gun or two within reach and a can of malt liquor wrapped conspicuously in a brown paper bag. He was always tipsy, and kept a sneaky smile on his ruggedly handsome face. As time would pass, though, it appeared that he'd gone crazy. Most blamed it on alcohol and a tough life. He'd been exposed to crime and calamity at an early age. When he was an adolescent, my grandfather introduced him to the life of crime, and they became father-and-son crime partners, robbing and burglarizing everything from houses to banks. Rumor has it that they never paid for anything but beer and gas; everything else was taken at gunpoint. As fate would have it, he was sent to prison for murder, and while most predicted that he would die by the gun, he later defied the odds and died in his sleep at a very young age.

With no father figure in my life, my mother and I were extremely close. I clung to her like a pair of jeans; she couldn't step on the front porch without me tagging along. When both of my sisters started grade school, leaving me home alone to absorb all of my mother's attention, I felt like I was in heaven. The day would begin with walking my sisters to school; then, we'd walk to the store and buy snacks. These walks were the highlight of my day.

Often my mother's beauty would attract a lot of male attention, and I would look on green-eyed as they tried to court her and rob me of her attention. If a guy wanted my approval, he had to have enough quarters and dimes to fill my pockets. On the flip-side, if things were to turn out sour between him and my mother, so did they between him and me. Whenever she would get into a fight with a guy, I would be right there wrapped around his leg, biting, scratching, pinching, and windmilling

My close relationship to my mother often provoked others to call me a "Mama's Boy." Being that I was overly sensitive and bashful, such teasing had a huge impact on my self-esteem; I perceived such insults as an attack on my masculinity. Making matters worse, I had a quiet, soft voice, so men would tell me: "Put some bass in your voice!" Also, whenever I would gripe and whine to my mother about anything, she'd tell me to "stop whining like a sissy!" Such response only exacerbated the sting to my already bruised esteem. I often felt as though I was being challenged, and began to question everyone's perception of me. With no male confidants to turn to, I would sort through my emotions, thoughts, and questions all by myself. I soon began to question whether it was okay for boys to exhibit affection.

One day the ice cream truck parked on the street, and several kids surrounded it, buying snacks. Everyone had a quarter for an ice cream except me, and I really wanted one. But instead of asking someone to buy me one, thereby expressing desire, an emotion other than anger, I remained mute. I just stood around hoping that someone would discern my desire. When that didn't happen, I became sad, and staggered into the house with my lip poked out. "What's the matter with you, boy?" my mother asked. "Nothing," I lied, concealing my desire out of fear of being perceived as being soft, needy, or a sissy (whatever that meant).

225

My dejection, infused with a strong will to do something about it, soon turned into anger, and I sneaked into my mother's room, stole one of her rare silver dollars, and used it to buy my own ice cream. Although she wasn't psychic enough to sense that I had wanted an ice cream earlier, she was able to sense that I'd stolen one of her coins. I received one of the worst whippings of my life that day. Worst of all, I didn't even get to finish eating my ice cream. That was the first and last time I ever stole from my mother.

Not long after that day, my mother and my sisters went shopping without me. When they returned with brand new Jelly shoes and none for me, I became irate. I was hurt. How could my beloved mother buy my sisters shoes and not buy any for her baby boy? She didn't love me anymore, I thought. I staggered around all day with my lip poked out, hoping she'd discern my heartache and patch it up by buying me shoes too. When she failed to respond to my silent complaints, I wanted to cry, but since crying was prohibited for young, black boys in my environment, I expressed the only emotion allowed of me: Anger. I kicked a hole in the flimsy, wooden, bedroom door, and shouted: "I want some god-damned Jelly Beans!" Little did I know Jelly shoes were for girls.

I received a whipping, but seeing the damage I'd done to the door made me feel really good. Such damage by a 4-year-old was pretty amazing, and made me feel strong and powerful. I was now convinced in the respect and power of anger. Even the Incredible Hulk said it, "You wouldn't like me when I'm angry."

If there is any truth in the theory of criminality being hereditary, my grandfather must have passed the gene to my father, who in turn passed it to me. Truthfully, the gene is merely one of rebellion, making one less likely to conform to the norms of society. In other words, I might have been a natural born rebel. But instead of being nurtured in the form of activism—like Nelson Mandela's, Malcolm X's, Martin Luther King's, or Fidel Castro's—my gene was exploited by ignorance and counter-productivity. In addition to riding around with my father, witnessing crime, I was being molded to disregard the law by many other aspects of my environment.

Every male in my family and community was a Crip. And since most of them frequented my home as guest, it sort of functioned as a hangout at time. Being the only male in a house packed with girls, I relished these moments. The Crips were the only men in my life, and therefore, my only role models. I hung to their words and mannerisms like a dedicated cadet, and my young, curious mind absorbed their inadvertent teachings like a sponge. To impress them and prove that I was cool and hip, I smoked marijuana with them, drank alcohol with them, and twisted my fingers into gang signs like they did. To them, it was pure entertainment witnessing a 4-year-old boy behave like a grown man, but to me, it was my rite of passage to becoming a man and shedding the "Mama's Boy" image.

I was so impressed by the Crips that I began to emulate them in every way possible for a 4-year-old boy. I imitated their walk, as if their hardcore, cool stroll was unique to only them; I imitated their talk, excluding the Bs and substituting them with Cs; I even emulated their appearance, sporting Stacy Adams hard-bottoms, Dickies, and blue roller in my hair. It was the late 70s and early 80s, when the Compton Crips were of mythical status. And based on the legends, I naively perceived them as superheroes, and believed that emulating them would reward me with their same level of prestige and respect.

In my young mind, I perceived no indecency or illicitness in their behavior or the social conditions of my environment. The gang culture in Compton was not only alluring, influential, and contagious, but also very much normal. And having not experienced or witnessed anything different, I accepted the tradition as that. Thus, when a bullet was fired through our house, shattering the screen on our TV, I accepted the act of violence as a common affair and expected many more to follow. Just like many young black boys before and after me, my mind was quickly being warped.

Whenever the Crips weren't around, my only male companion was my neighbor Peanut. He and I were around the same age, so we often played outside together, usually getting into things that we had no business getting into. As a child, I was somewhat destructive. I had a habit of dissecting things to try and understand how they worked and to see if I could put them back together. I was overly curious about the origin, meaning, and purpose of everything—including people and life.

Although most kids were curious, the difference between me and them was that I never asked questions. I was too ashamed and fearful of being perceived as stupid or unhip. Consequently, I became a dreamer and a thinker, and tried to come up with my own answers to the questions of life. This attitude was fundamental to my overall destructiveness.

One morning following an evening of destruction at the hands of me and Peanut, I awoke to unusual traffic around the duplex. There were white men in suits and ties snooping around, questioning people. The ambience was awkward, as it usually was when white men came around—they seemed to come around only to take away either money or people. At the moment, I had no idea what was going on, but later I learned that Peanut was murdered the night before.

I never learned the details of his death—and I probably wouldn't have understood had they been explained to me—but I began to fear that I might be next. Peanut's death made me realize that tomorrow isn't promised to anyone, not even a 4-year-old boy. From that day on, I lived with a nagging fear that I wouldn't reach adulthood.

Peanut's death affected my psyche in many ways that I never revealed to anyone. Exacerbating the ordeal, my little cousin Kenisha died after that. The fear of dying young brought on anxiety and nightmares, nightmares so surreal that I often woke up in the middle of the night hallucinating.

One particular night I'll never forget is when I awoke to the image of a dummy that resembled an adolescent Sammy Davis Jr. The mechanical lines around his mouth made it appear that he had a perpetual smirk on his face, and his soulless doe-like eyes made him seem harmless yet ominous. As I lay there frozen with fear, he pressed his palms together in front of his face and began to repeatedly chant the word "abracadabra." I screamed at the top of my lungs until my mother came running into the room clutching a butcher's knife. When she turned on the lights, however, the dummy mysteriously morphed into a heap of clothes. I tried to explain what I'd seen, but all I had to support my claim was a pile of dirty laundry sitting in the middle of the floor. My mother checked my forehead for signs of a fever, went and got me a glass of water, and told me to go back to sleep.

Another time, I awoke to the image of an intimidating Mickey Mouse frowning at me. I screamed like a sissy until my mother came running. When she turned on the light, the gangsterish Mickey turned out to be my sister Meka who had two afro puffs in her hair.

CHAPTER 32

CONFUSED & MISEDUCATED

When I was five, we left Compton and moved to North Long Beach. Although the two cities bordered each other, they differed in many ways. For example, at one time, during the 50s, Compton was a predominately-white suburb. But in the 60s and 70s when the African-Americans and Crips and Pirus took over, the Whites fled for nearby suburbs, such as North Long Beach. So while Compton had become a gang infested, chocolate city, North Long Beach remained a predominately-white middle class suburb. Therefore, to anyone who didn't know better, our move to North Long Beach might have seemed like we were moving up in the world. But we were actually moving down, for not all of North Long Beach qualified as middle class, particularly the Carmelitos, where we moved to.

The Carmelitos were low-income housing projects located in the heart of North Long Beach. What brought us there was the unbelievable cheap rent at the government's expense and the fact that my grandmother and aunts live there. For us kids, who didn't understand the significance of poverty and socioeconomics, the Carmelitos, with its abundance of kids, fields, and playgrounds, appeared to be paradise. But for the people living in the surrounding single-family homes, the Carmelitos was a rotten apple destroying the value and image of their community.

Being nothing more than a slew of old military-bunkers converted into living quarters for the poor, the Carmelitos looked like a junkyard in contrast to the well-manicured, single-family homes surrounding it. They comprised of approximately 75 two-story concrete buildings which resembled the hotels in the Milton Brothers' Monopoly game, the only difference being that the Carmelitos varied in many tacky, flamboyant colors—yellow, pink, turquoise, dingy white, and so on. They were cluttered around 20 unkempt parking lots, in no specific order as if they had been carelessly sprinkled from the sky. One third of the units were boarded up, burnt up, or simply vacant. The yards were cluttered with clothes hanging from old-fashioned clothing lines, and the parking lots were riddled with pot holes, broken glass, and stones. The Carmelitos was a mess.

It seemed that the only times the middle-class whites that lived around the Carmelitos dared to enter was when they came to buy drugs or point out an alleged robbery suspect. Just about every crime committed in a 3-mile radius was blamed on someone linked to the Carmelitos. Whenever a car was stolen (or pawned for drugs then falsely reported stolen) or a house burglarized (or the items traded for drugs then falsely reported stolen), the all-white, male, and conspicuously racist police would raid the projects in search for suspects and merchandise. It was so bad that whenever a police cruiser came through with an uncuffed white person in the passenger seat or backseat, every sane black male would go indoors and remain there for the rest of the day. Somehow, though, the cops always found their man, even if he wasn't their man.

The inexplicable mistreatment blacks suffered at the hand of the Long Beach police had my young, curious mind baffled. It just didn't make sense to me. As always, pride wouldn't allow me to ask anyone, so I relied upon my own limited knowledge and observations. Overhearing the remarks made by adults whenever cops came around, I learned that the cops were nothing but racist peckerwoods who had nothing better to do than bother black people.

I had never heard the term "racist peckerwood" before moving to Long Beach, so I had to rack my brain to figure out what it meant. I assumed that "racist" had something to do with a racecar driver–like Tom Slick–and "peckerwood" with the woodpecker in the cartoons; after all, Woody Woodpecker was the only peckerwood I knew. The more

I thought about it, the more it made sense. The cops drove fast cars, and they bothered people just like the little red woodpecker in the cartoons. *Racist Peckerwoods.* I soon came to resent both peckerwoods– the cops and the bird.

On my first day of school, I received a serious culture shock. With the exception of one or two other kids from the projects, everyone in my class was white. I had never been in a room with so many white people. Sporting a short afro dripping with curl activator, a pair of tough-skin jeans thick enough to resist a bullet, a pair of bubble yum shoes with more rubber on the tip than the bumper of a 1975 Ford LTD, I felt out of place the moment I bashfully entered the class.

Making matters worse, when I opened my mouth to speak, everyone looked at me as if I were speaking a foreign language. My Ebonics was too strange for them; furthermore, I spoke extremely slow and with a lisp. My speech was so bad that I was forced to take speech lessons in the back of the class twice a week. Although the lessons helped soften the lisp a little, they did nothing for my Ebonics, and that made me feel even more like an outcast.

As time went on, I came to realize that I, as well as most other kids from the projects, was different. We were different not only characteristically, but also socioeconomically. While we walked to school in packs, the other kids, were dropped off in sedans, vans, and station wagons. While they had lunch boxes filled with snacks, we had lunch tickets. The most conspicuous difference, aside from our skin color, was the fact that they lived in single-family houses while we lived in rundown, recycled bomb shelters. This really distinguished us. Even the whites living in the projects were blemished by them.

The unfortunate fact that we lived in the projects provided the middle-class kids reason to taunt us. We were often called "African Booty Scratchers," "Carmelitos Cockroaches" (because of the huge cockroaches that were infested through the projects), and "Welfare kids." There was no concealing or denying the truth of the taunts, no matter how hard we tried. Most of the kids from the projects were black, and the history books revealed that we were from Africa, and depicted it as a barbaric continent with people who lived in jungles; the green free-lunch ticket revealed that we were on some type of government assistance; and the fact that we were black and walked to school in packs suggested that we were from the Carmelitos, a place where housing was contingent upon being on welfare or low income. There was no hiding the truth; nevertheless, there were times after school when I would walk right past those bomb shelter as if I didn't live there. The taunting disturbed me that much.

The taunting and embarrassment had gotten so bad that I began to experience mild anxiety attacks every morning I awoke to go to school. I dreaded the thought of being trapped in that class with all those perfect kids who came from perfect families and perfect homes. Because of that anxiety, it was nearly impossible for me to grasp any education. School was merely an environment that made me feel inferior and worthless, and highlighted my socioeconomic deficiencies. It was a place where I was hardly understood, yet taunted because of that misunderstanding, as well as my skin, lips, hair, and lingo. I never verbally expressed how I really felt about school, but my actions did.

My first time playing hookie was in the first grade, and it didn't work out well. While walking to school, I faded away from the pack and told my sisters that I was going back home because I didn't feel well. Instead of returning home, though, I simply hung out in the front of the projects with my head hanging down, refusing to look up out of fear that someone would recognize me. After several hours, I looked up and saw my mother and my aunt Brenda walking my way on the opposite side of the street. Instead of running or hiding, I simply put my head down and tried to walk past them as if my mother wouldn't recognize her own child from 30 feet away. When she spotted me and called my name, I ignored her and kept walking as if she were mistaking another kid for hers. She ran across the street and whipped my behind all the way home.

Over the following couple weeks, I was walked to school to make sure I was there. But being forced to attend school didn't make it any better. I still suffered from, what I now know to be, social anxiety, still couldn't pay attention in class, still couldn't speak proper English, and still wasn't learning anything. By the time I reached the third grade, the only thing I'd learned was how to get under the desk in the event of an earthquake, and that I was a skinny, ugly, big-lipped, project dwelling, African booty scratcher whose ancestors were rescued from the jungles. With no positive black faces in the history books or my life, I accepted the miseducation as truth.

School damage my self-esteem. It underscored my socioeconomic deficiencies, something I never had dwelled on before because it had been common to everyone in my environment up until the day I enrolled in Clara Barton. That school introduced me to snobby, middle-class kids who symbolized the American dream of pride and success; by the same token, it showed me that there was no room for me in that dream. School essentially slammed the door shut on my dreams, and miseducated me into believing that I could never amount to anything greater than the stereotypical negro. And given the fact that most of the males I looked up to were now in and out of jail and absent from my life, I was forced to believe that there was a low ceiling of success for all black people, including me.

The reality of it all began to weigh on my young psyche. I became even more introverted and anxious. By the time I turned 8, I was in a state of what psychologists would have diagnosed as adolescent depression. Being that I was naturally quiet and bashful, though, such depression went unnoticed, and I made sure to keep it that way. I kept my questions and pain bottled up, and as with everything else in my life, I dealt with my adolescent depression on my own.

Now don't get me wrong, my childhood was not filled with total sadness. I had friends and fun times. I rode bikes and took them apart and put them back together. I built go-carts, recorded and listened to rap music, pop-locked and break-danced, lifted weights at the Boy's Club (until a weight flipped and busted my head), and played football in vacant fields. But none of these activities were nourished into anything positive. My mother couldn't pay for me to play organized sports, so my football dreams pretty much ended in the vacant fields.

I also had close friends. I had a biracial friend named Jimmy who had every toy that ever hit the market. In contrast to my other close friend, Travon, who was a true project kid that liked to fight and audaciously eat food from other people's refrigerators, Jimmy was a rich kid, and I couldn't help but believe that his mother's white skin was the reason. Overall, my childhood wasn't so bad. But that dark cloud of racial and socioeconomic inferiority was certainly looming, slowly eating at my passion and creating a void that seemed impossible to fill.

To fill the void and escape my reality, I stayed indoors and watched TV a lot. Aside from *The A-Team*, I preferred shows that lacked violence, conflict, and rivalry–I didn't want to watch anything that resembled my reality. I often watched TV shows and fantasized about trading places with characters. I wanted to be Ricky Schroder from *Silver Spoon*, or Willis or Arnold from *Different Strokes*. I'm sure I wasn't the only black kid in the projects who envied Willis and Arnold, two black kids who were depicted as being rescued from the projects in Harlem by a rich white man.

Searching the channels and getting lost in TV world was not only my means of escaping, but also my search for hope, identity, and pride, something I couldn't find at school. But it only added further damage to my twisted psyche and

235

battered esteem. Every show on TV, up until *The Cosby Show*, depicted Blacks as nothing but criminals, servants, and, figuratively, clowns. All of the doctors, lawyers, judges, cops, firemen, and wealthy people were white. TV's definition of wealth, power, beauty, and success was much different than what I saw in the mirror and the projects.

Ultimately, TV did nothing but confirm what the snobby kids at school had been telling me all along: black people were nothing but fourth class citizens who'd never amount to anything more than athletes, pimps, and drug dealers. With no reason to believe that I'd be an exception, I had no choice but to live up to the negative perception.

With nothing else to hang my hat on, I accepted the fact that I was nothing more than an impoverished, fatherless, black child who couldn't even speak proper English. I was convinced that my conditions were part of my identity and purpose. So in hopes of creating an air of uniqueness, and at the same time create a facade to hide my pain and insecurities, I began to openly rebel. I spent more time outside fighting, writing gang graffiti on the walls, and pretending to be a Crip. Ironically, such behavior earned me more attention and respect. I relished such attention and did everything I could to uphold my new bad-boy image.

CHAPTER 33

PRODUCT OF MY ENVIRONMENT

During the 1983-84 school semester, there was an influx of Vietnamese migrants to enroll at Clara Barton, thereby, giving the middle-class white kids another group of impoverished minorities to ridicule. However, there was one Vietnamese 6th grader who, at 5'10" 135lbs., wasn't too pleased with the taunting. He roamed the playground, bullying and doing karate on everybody. This was around the time that *Kung Fu Theater* was a popular Saturday afternoon TV show. So the fact that he was Asian and knew how to deliver a roundhouse kick had everyone terrified of him. His terrorizing wasn't limited to the white kids; the fact that we were black and from the projects didn't make us exempt. He preyed on us too. So out of fear of being victim to a flying kick, I carrying a dull icepick to school every day.

As anticipated, one afternoon during recess, the overgrown bully tried to force my friend to stop playing tether-ball so that he could play. Refusing to be intimidated by the bully, my friend stood his ground and a fight ensued. The bully had no idea that I was standing nearby watching, so while he and my friend were exchanging blows, I crept behind him and stabbed him in the back. Upon feeling the sharp pain, he immediately grasped at his wound, turned around and saw me standing there clutching the pick, and took off running and screaming. All of the other kids at recess started laughing and egging me on. Fueled by the crowd, I reluctantly chased the bully so that everyone on the playground could see that it was I who was responsible for taking him down.

Fortunately for me and the bully, a teacher intervened. Had I caught him, I would've had to poke him again just to give the people what they wanted. After order was restored, I found myself in the principal's office being scolded by 2 race-car driving woodpeckers. Being that I was only 8 years old and the bully only suffered a minor abrasion, I was spared from going to jail. However, to my delight, I was suspended from school for the rest of the week, and everyone but my mother and the cops commended me for my behavior.

I found it ironic that my mother was upset, for she had always told me and my sisters to never run from a fight. We were told to fight back or else we'd get a whipping. And if we couldn't win with our hands, we were told to pick up a weapon. But now that I followed her rules and picked up a weapon she was mad. She said that I'd end up in prison with my uncle Ronald, but I didn't mind. Prison would've only enhanced my reputation.

When I returned to school the following week, I was treated like a hero. I was no longer seen as the ugly, big-lipped kid from the cockroach-infested Carmelitos; I was now the kid who took down the overgrown bully. The attention and respect boosted my self-esteem and gave me a new sense of identity, one that gave me a sense of pride in mischief and misbehavior.

During the summer of 1984, Los Angeles hosted the World Olympics at the Memorial Coliseum. That summer, I spent two weeks at my aunt's house on 41st and Figueroa–a stone's throw away from the Coliseum. It was then and there that I first learned how to hustle. Following behind my teenage cousin Crazy J-Bone, I learned myriad of hustles that earned me several dollars a day. We hung out at the gas station, pumping gas and washing windows for gratuity; we watched tourists cars while they were inside the Coliseum enjoying the games; we hung out at grocery stores and helped shoppers with their bags; we even hauled around a push-mower and mowed lawns for people.

Hustling provided me with not only money but also a sense of self-worth, pride, and power. Instead of sitting around waiting for something to be given to me, I now had a little understanding of how to go out and get it. Whenever I was hungry and there wasn't any bread or milk in the house, I'd go out and hustle up a few dollars for bread and milk. When I blew out the adapter for my Atari 5200, I was able to purchase another one by recycling scraps of carpet I found in the back of a carpet store. I gathered the scraps, cut them into doormats, and went door to door selling them at 50 cents apiece. Sometime after that, I went to Mexico and bought $10 worth of firecrackers and sold them for $100. From that point on, no one could tell me that I wasn't a hustler.

In March, 1985, just when my popularity and self-esteem was beginning to soar, we were forced to move out of the projects due to renovation. We were relocated to a low-income complex on 109th Street and Normandie Avenue, a predominately African-American neighborhood in South Central L.A. The apartment complex was in much better conditions than the Carmelitos. They were newly–constructed and set 3 stories from the ground. They had basketball courts in the back and 2 small playgrounds. And at both ends of the street, there were schools–Washington High on Normandie and Woodcrest Elementary on Budlong.

Woodcrest became my second school, and unlike Clara Barton, all of the students, except for a handful of Mexicans, were black. We all were part of the same socioeconomic class, and although the history books were the same as those at Clara Barton–filled with prominent white men–there were no snobby white kids to rub it in our face. The color of the faces in the history books didn't matter to the kids at Woodcrest, not only because they were blind to the fact that there were still groups and classes of people who looked down upon us, but also because they seemed complacent with our conditions. I, on the other hand, knew that there was much more out there, and although I didn't believe that it was available to Blacks, I still had a bit of ambition to go after it–I just didn't know how.

Although attending school at Woodcrest was more comfortable for me than attending school at Clara Barton, I still suffered from social anxiety and A.D.D. It was difficult for me to interact with others and focus, so I often sat in class fantasizing about being somewhere else, consumed in my own world. Like me, several of my classmates were wannabe gangsters. (As fate would have it, we all would later end up in juvenile prison together.) The hardest of the wannabes, Jeff, picked on me because I was quiet and reclusive. Every day, he threatened to beat me up the upcoming Friday after school. Why Friday and not Monday, Tuesday, Wednesday, or Thursday? I hadn't the slightest idea, but every Friday, we eluded each other by leaving through different exits. Before I knew it, summer arrived and we still hadn't fought.

That summer I rambled amongst several homes–my home, my grandmother's in the Carmelitos, my aunt's in the Carmelitos, and my uncle Larry's in Compton. In L.A., I mostly stayed indoors listening to rap music, or I'd catch the bus to LAX and hustle by turning in luggage carts; in Long Beach, we'd shoplift out of the grocery store and play inside vacant project buildings; in Compton, we'd ride the back of ice cream trucks, hop on and off of moving freight trains, build go-carts, hustle at gas stations, ride bikes across to Piru neighborhoods and make them chase us, fight with kids on other streets, and ride our bikes to North Long Beach.

It was during one of these trips to North Long Beach when I was arrested for the first time. While riding our bikes past a store in an all-white neighborhood, we spotted an unattended bike in front of the store. Since we usually rode three kids per bike–one on the seat, one on the handlebars, and one standing on the back pegs–we decided to steal the bike and take it back to Compton. I hopped on the bike and started pedaling, but the chain kept popping off. As I was trying to fix the chain, three police cars swooped on us, and a white man came out of the store pointing at us and shouting: "That's them! They stole my bike!"

We were arrested and locked in a cell at the Long Beach Jail. While we were standing at the bars, on the verge of tears, the same white guy walked up to us sporting a huge, mischievous smile and a shiny police badge. The entire incident turned out to be a sting. The cop got a call that a group of black kids were roaming the neighborhood, so he set the bike in front of a store several blocks ahead of us, knowing that a group of impoverished kids wouldn't resist the urge to ride off on it.

Ironically, my short stay behind bars caused more damage than good. It helped prepare me for future incarceration by forcing me to overcome any fears I had of prison. It also enhanced my bad-boy image and gave me something to boast about in the streets.

When I returned to Woodcrest the following semester, the first person I saw was Jeff. He was sitting at his desk, frowning at me and cracking his knuckles. There was no way I'd be able to elude him for thirty-six Fridays, nor was I willing to wait until the upcoming Friday. I walked straight over to him and pummeled him until the teacher pulled me off of him. "This is not a boxing ring," said the teacher, a tall, lanky black man. "If you wanna fight, take your asses outside." Surprisingly, he shoved us out the class and said: "Don't come back until you're ready to learn."

Instead of fighting, we stood there staring at each other. Then, through a pair of busted lips, Jeff asked: "Wanna ditch and go steal some candy from the dairy?" Although I didn't eat candy, I agreed, just to prove that I wasn't scared. Needless to say, I didn't learn anything that semester other than how to steal from the dairy and about the myriad of gangs in the neighborhood.

Although my new neighborhood looked better than the old Carmelitos, it fared no better. Every street was occupied by a different gang. Within one square-mile there were at least fifteen different gangs, and they all seemed to be rivals at some point. Oddly, the street I lived on was occupied by several different factions of Compton Crips, and my apartment complex was where they hung out. Drive-by shootings were common, and somebody was getting shot just about every week. Every night, "Ghetto Birds" (police helicopters) hovered above, shining light on the apartments and into the windows. The residents never complained or called the cops on the thugs because most were friends or family.

Contrary to popular belief, most gangs, particularly those in Compton, were not formed with criminal intent, nor were members initiated into the gang by some type of ritual. Crips and Pirus were more so a network of family and friends in a particular neighborhood– like a tribe, so to speak. Simply living or growing up in a certain neighborhood automatically made one an associate or affiliate of the gang that occupied that neighborhood. In the eyes of the police and rival gangs, it didn't matter whether one was an active gang member or not–just living in that neighborhood sufficed. The police simply labeled every young, black male in a particular neighborhood as being a member whether he was or not. Accordingly, most youngsters felt as though they were connected to the gang in some way, whether by family ties, by profiling, or by stereotype. Even the school segregated kids by what neighborhood they lived in. There was no escaping it.

In any event, most dudes proudly represented their neighborhoods–even if they really weren't gang affiliated. Gangs were extremely popular and attractive, and most kids were just happy to be a part of a team or structure. Since gangs didn't have any stringent requirements, or discriminate based on age, race, or socioeconomic status, they were the easiest group to join. While most kids in other communities played sports, kids in Compton, Watts, and other areas of South Los Angeles gang-banged. Gang banging was our sport. Each gang was a different team, and each team strived to be the most notorious. Likewise, as individual members, we strived to be prominent players for our team.

When crack cocaine flooded the streets in the mid-80s, gangs became even more alluring. They were now flushed with cash, cars, weapons, and attention. Some drug dealers who weren't necessarily interested in gang banging became affiliated just for the protection the gangs provided to everyone from the neighborhood. And believe it or not, during the 80s, when unemployment was at an all-time high in South Los Angeles, everyone in the community was associated with the gangs and drugs. Drug dealing was not only accepted but also encouraged. What unemployed mother complained about her teenage son's bringing home $1,000 a night? "Just be safe," was all she said.

The only people who seemed to disagree with the drug dealing were the predominately-white police. However, in our eyes, they were simply racists who couldn't stand to see young black men making so much money. When the gang related murders were happening, they didn't care, but as soon as blacks started raking in money, the police began to militarize the community. They raided homes by crashing through them in a military tank with a battering ram affixed to the front. They robbed people, beat people, and framed people, but none of that was enough to discourage a poor man from hustling. In fact, the drama and danger associated with it made it more alluring and glamorous. Money, violence, police brutality, and corruption were all the ingredients for a gangster's paradise. At the end of the day, being associated with it or a victim of it increased one's notoriety.

Since there was no age requirement, I was allured to selling drugs at a very young age. My first real drug deal occurred in 1986. While playing 25-cent hands of blackjack with my neighbor Eric (a 26-year-old ex-con who'd recently paroled after serving 5 years for murder), I pulled out three nickel bags of weed and asked if he wanted to buy them. His eyes brightened, and a mischievous grin formed on his face (a tooth missing from a prison brawl he claimed to have gotten the best of) and he asked: "Where you get that from?"

"I found it," I lied. Truthfully, I'd stolen it from my female cousin Pig, who had a shoe box full of weed stashed in the laundry room.

"Oh, where at?" he asked. "They look just like the bags I lost yesterday." He tried to swindle me, but I didn't fall for it.

After haggling for a few minutes, he made me an offer I couldn't refuse. He said that if I were to give him one of the bags, he'd make the other two worth $10 apiece by making them more potent. I wasn't good at math, but I knew that 2 multiplied by 10 is more than 3 multiplied by 5.

Agreeing to the deal, I gave the bags to him, and he emptied the marijuana onto aluminum foil paper and poured drops of a pungent, liquid substance on it. Two days later a man came to the apartments in search of a dime bag of weed. I showed him one of the bags and told him that it was small because it was extremely potent. He opened the bag, smelled its contents, and gave me $10. That was the quickest $10 I'd ever made, and it made me feel good– manly and self-dependent.

The very next day, the man returned. When I saw him, I grinned from ear to ear, believing he'd returned for more, and I started planning how I would spend the $20. But instead of buying more, he grabbed me by my little 10year-old, pencil neck, and, with extremely red eyes and a bestial expression, said: "You little nigga–I don't smoke that shit!"

Apparently he'd never smelled PCP before–he didn't complain when he smelled it before purchasing it. But after smoking it, he returned for a refund. With his hand around my neck, and my feet dangling in the air, I quickly reached inside my pocket and withdrew his $10. There was nothing else I could have done. I certainly didn't want to scream or cause a scene because nobody but this beast and Eric knew about my dealing marijuana.

That was my first drug deal, and perhaps a sign that I was heading down the wrong path, but since I was an extremely stubborn child, I wasn't quick to give up on things I strongly believed in. And getting rich by selling drugs was something I strongly believed in.

Not long after that incident, I evolved into selling crack. Actually, I learned how to cook it long before I started selling it. I learned by observing and imitating my step-father and other older dudes. Then, whenever they weren't around, I'd scrape crumbs from their chunks of crack, and practice recooking it into rocks. After so many sessions, I started adding myriad of cutting agents to enhance the weight and size of the rocks. I did this more out of curiosity than greed. By the age of 12, people were calling me Blow-Up Bosco. The rocks I cooked melted in their hands but not on the pipe. I became so good at rocking up cocaine that adults started having me cook for them—including my step-father.

Now that I knew how to cook and had my step-father's blessing, I had access to a lot of crack. I just didn't know what to do with it. I couldn't stand out in front of the apartments and sell it because my mother would've found out. So to prevent that, I gave my re-rock to my 15-year-old homeboy Junior to sell for me. But instead of paying me, he used the proceeds to buy more crack and start his own business. Ultimately, our friendship ended with my busting him in his head with a Dayton hammer.

After being burnt by Junior, I started selling it myself, and continued to encounter problems. One of my first deals, for example, a lady in a green, early 70s Ford Mustang flagged me down as I was walking home from school. She asked if I could find her $40 worth of crack, so I ran to my stepfather and got five twenty-dollar rocks. When I returned, the lady was still sitting behind the wheel of the Mustang with the engine running. When I stuck my hand into the car, showcasing a palm full of rocks, she handed me a folded piece of green paper, hit the underside of my hand, mashed the gas pedal, and left me standing in the middle of the street inhaling exhaust fumes.

With no success on 109th, I started waiting until the weekends to peddle my crack at my homeboy's house in Compton. I had better success there, but I still encountered difficulties. Particularly, my older relatives who smoked crack always found a way to swindle me out of mine. They would either convince me to give it to them for free, or promise to pay me later but never did. Some of them—particularly Big Age—would downright dupe me.

One-day Big Age ran into the crack house and told me to give him all of my rocks and to run out the back door because the police were fixing to raid. I naively gave him my rocks, ran out the back door, and hopped several fences until I was safely inside my uncle's house. Although there were several police cars speeding up the street, and a ghetto bird hovering above, there was no raid. I'd been duped.

Clearly, dealing drugs wasn't working for me as it was for older people. Still, I saw its potential and stuck with it because I believed that it was my only opportunity at wealth. In my community, a drug dealer was the epitome of a real man; after all, he was the only person capable of taking care of his family and friends. And to me, that was the greatest sense of pride. I first felt that pride at an early age, even when my cousin Scooter and I use to pump gas to put bread on the table. Once I experienced that feeling, I became addicted. I wanted nothing else in life but to earn my own money and take care of the people in my life—I enjoyed this more than the money itself. Providing for people was my ultimate goal, and selling drugs seemed to be the only conceivable means of achieving such goal. So no matter how many times I stumbled, I refused to give up.

It wasn't until I returned to the Carmelitos when I began to make significant money dealing drugs. In the heart of a predominately-white, middle class suburb, the Carmelitos was a drug dealer's paradise. Instead of poor blacks, who struggled and fought tooth and nail for a hit of crack, the customers who frequented the Carmelitos were well-off white people who had plenty of money to squander.

Contrary to popular belief, Whites consumed more crack than Blacks did—it was just that poor Blacks were more likely to deal it. At times, there would be dozens of white folks in each parking lot waiting to be served. And they weren't coming with $2.73 like the crack heads in Compton; they were coming with no less than $20—sometimes hundreds. It was nothing for 50 different drug dealers to each make $1,000 a day. Barely 12 years old, I was content with $100.

The irony in selling crack in the Carmelitos was that most of the customers were parents and siblings of those same snobby kids who used to tease us at Clara Barton Elementary School. Crack proved that their households weren't as perfect as they appeared to be from the outside. Apparently, there were emotional voids in which only crack could fill. Now that the tables had turned, they began to experience some of the despair and deficiencies that we experienced, while we— the Carmelitos Cockroaches—were enjoying the fruits of such despair. Of course, neither of us perceived it that way, nor did we see it as an issue of race.

All we saw was the green, and all they saw was white. Since we had the white and they had the green, we were able to come together and supply each other's demand. Money was coming in so fast that I was able to buy my first car at the age of 12—and I didn't even know how to drive. My 14year-old sister, Tisha, had to drive it home for me. However, it didn't take long for me to teach myself how to drive; I simply hopped behind the wheel and started driving up and down the street. Of course, I side swiped a few cars and ran into a fence or two, but I eventually got the hang of it. Soon thereafter, I bought my second and third car, and invested thousands of dollars to customize them.

Money was rolling in so fast that I could no longer hide it from my mother and grandmother, especially my grandmother, whose hobby was looking out the window at everyone selling drugs. And now that her 12-year-old grandson was one of them, she made it her duty to keep an eye on me. She even warned me when the police were coming and gave me advice on how to conduct myself whenever encountering them. She advised me to never pull over for them in deserted areas, and to always yell and cause a scene, especially if they put their hands on me. As for my mother's concern, she stressed that I stay in school.

What my mother didn't know, though, was that before I started selling drugs in the Carmelitos, I had been skipping most of my 7 grade classes. Instead of going to class, I was hanging out at Washington High, gang banging, smoking weed, drinking beer, and playing craps with my Crip homies from Compton, Watts, and 83 Gangster. But ever since I started hustling in the Carmelitos on the weekends, I started going to class religiously Monday through Friday.

Although I still wasn't participating in assignments, I went just because I had money. I liked the awe and respect I received whenever I pulled out wads of cash to buy everyone lunch. Since I was quiet and reserved, most people didn't even know who I was, much less that I was a drug dealer. So for me to pull out thousands of dollars and buy classmates lunch, I became even more interesting and mysterious.

Other than quietly and unpretentiously pulling out wads of cash in the cafeteria, I maintained a low profile at school, but eventually I was kicked out for smoking a joint before stepping on campus. When I stepped into the class smelling like weed, the teacher called the police, and I was arrested for possession of marijuana. Shortly thereafter, I was kicked out of another junior high school for refusing to get dressed for P.E. The principal told me to leave and to never come back, so I happily strolled off campus, hopped in my car, turned up the volume on the radio, and drove away jamming "Young World" by Slick Rick. That was the last day I ever stepped foot into a public school. From that day forward, I dedicated my days and nights to selling drugs and building my reputation as a Crip.

Making anywhere from $500 to $1000 a day, I was now addicted to selling drugs. To a degree, I was no different than the consumers whom I served on a daily basis. We were both chasing a high. To obtain theirs, they carelessly entered the projects all day and night, risking being robbed or arrested; likewise, to obtain my high, I hung out in the projects all day and night, risking arrest.

It was apparent that the Long Beach police couldn't stand the fact that we were making lucrative profits from the addictions of middle-class Whites. Eradicating the Carmelitos became their top priority. They utilized every tactic just short of downright murdering us to achieve their goal, even if that meant violating every constitutional and humanitarian right sworn to mankind. The harassment was so bad that we'd instantly take off running whenever we'd see the police. This was even true for people who weren't drug dealers. Being caught by them resulted in being robbed and beaten. The ass-whipping was an unwritten policy, and the mugging was a way for them to supplement their income. And being underage didn't make me an exception.

Another one of the police's form of brutality involved their kidnapping us and dropping us off in rival-gang territory. For example, one night while driving through Compton, two L.A. County Sheriff deputies pulled me over, robbed me of my cash, and dropped me off in the Atlantic Drive

Crips neighborhood. At the time, my neighborhood and the Atlantic Drive Crips were at all-out war. The cops, hoping to get me assaulted or killed, pulled up in front of a crowd of them and told them that they had a treat for them. They then opened the back door, pulled me out, removed my cuffs, and drove away. Little did they know that, although we were now feuding, I was still cool with the older Atlantic Drive Crips, who'd known me since I was a little kid.

On another occasion, two of my homeboys and I were pulled over by two sheriff deputies after we tossed guns out the window. They found the guns, but instead of arresting us, they impounded the car and made us walk home. They were hoping that some rival gang members would spot us and take care of us. When that didn't happen, they drove by us, called us "niggers," and fired shots at us—presumably, from one of the guns we'd tossed. Although we knew that the cops were wrong, we never complained; we simply accepted the brutality as another part of the lifestyle—it was better than going to jail.

By now, I hated cops with a passion. To me, as well as most people in the „hood, they were nothing more than a gang of terrorists. And I had grown tired of running from them every time they drove up on us. Whenever any other rival gang members drove up on me with ill intent, I pulled out my gun and fired shots. With my hate for cops at its pinnacle, I saw no reason to treat them any different. So one night while standing in the cut of the project building, I saw a police cruiser slowly driving by and fired shots at it. This act of violence, along with many others, caused the city to come down heavy and hard on the projects, and the notorious young Bosco was at the top of their list.

In December, 1989, my days of terrorizing the streets came to an end. After a six-week hiatus in Compton, gang banging, getting high, and squandering money, I returned to the Carmelitos to recoup some of the money I'd squandered, and to get back into the mode of hustling. My first customers were two black dudes in a gray Chevy Lumina. When they pulled up asking for rocks, I instantly became leery of them, not only because they were black in a majority White market, but also because they were dressed like gang bangers–black and gray flannel shirts, black L.A. Raiders hats, and dark shades–at a time when it was taboo for active gang members to smoke crack–gang bangers certainly didn't go to other neighborhoods to buy crack because they usually had their own.

Concerned that they might be rival gang members attempting to ambush me, I told them to park their car and shut off the engine. While they were parking, Rat positioned himself on the side of the building with a .44 and I had a .357 tucked under my windbreaker. When I approached the passenger window, the driver put his head down and looked the other way as if he were trying to hide his face. Although this alarmed me, I still proceeded with the transaction. I gave the passenger the drugs, and he handed me the money. As I began to walk away, however, he reached out the window and tried to grab me.

Without hesitation, Rat fired shots, nearly tearing the dude's arm off. I took cover on the side of a parked car, pulled out my pistol, and prepared to fill the Chevy with holes. But when I looked up and saw the driver returning shots in Rat's direction, I instantly recognized who he was: He was no gangbanger–he was one of the rare few black cops for the Long Beach Police. How did I know? Because he had once arrested me for underage driving. I instantly ripped off my black windbreaker and ran. Running pass an army of police swooping in on the scene, I managed to make it to my grandmother's unit, where my uncle Donald was waiting for me with the back door open. He'd been listening to his police scanner and heard about a police shooting, and, as always when shots were fired, he suspected my involvement.

An hour later my mother snuck me out of the projects and took me to South Central. Unfortunately, Rat had been wounded and arrested. A week later, I stubbornly returned to the Carmelitos against my mother's advice, and was ambushed in the darkness of the night by SWAT. I was beaten, arrested, and charged with two counts of attempted murder on police officers.

I had been to Los Padrinos Juvenile Hall once before, but only for one night. Now I was staying for quite some time. Although I knew that the longer my stay, the shinier my badge of honor, I also knew that the longer my stay, the more violence and problems I'd encounter. There was no escaping it; there were no guns, Dayton hammers, or 40-ounce bottles for me to use as a weapon. Everyone in juvie was a gang member—even some guards—therefore, fighting was inevitable. I wasn't worried about the kids my age and size, but the 17-year-olds who looked as though they'd been locked up for years lifting weights had me concerned. Still, I had a name and reputation to protect, so although I was only 14 years old and 130 pounds, I was willing to fight anyone rather than be perceived as a buster.

Juvie was a place for all young gang bangers to enhance their reputation. It was an unwritten rule that all rival gang members had to fight each other. It was either fight or forever be stigmatized as a buster, and shunned and mistreated. At the time, I happened to be the only Santana Block Crip at the entire facility, so I had my hands full. When rivals heard that I was there, they tried to get me any way they could, including running out of the classrooms as we walked by in single-file lines. It didn't take me long to catch on; instead of waiting for some kid to blindside me, I began to hunt for them, including running inside their classes to fight them.

Although the guards always broke up the fights, they often let us go at it for a minute. During one of my later fights at

Los Padrinos, a guard picked me up and slammed me on the back of my head, producing a lump the size of a golf ball. For weeks, I walked around with a swollen head, and never received any medical attention. After a few weeks, the swelling subsided, but blood continued to seep from my head for the following two years, and to this day I still have a small lump and scar on the back of my head.

With the guards and my rivals against me, I began to feel a sense of alienation and sadness that I'd never felt before. Making matters worse, when I got out of the hole, that same guard often teased me by calling me the "the skinny kids with the lump on his head." My sadness soon turned into anger and I literally wanted to kill him. Every night I lay in my bunk, I fantasized about getting out and returning to the staff parking lot to blow his brains out. I actually made that my top priority upon my release. However, such release didn't come soon enough.

At court, during trial, the judge found me not guilty for the attempted murder charges, but guilty on a previous drug charge, and sentenced me to six months in disciplinary camp. I was rapidly transferred, but instead of going straight to the camp, I stayed over at Sylmar Juvenile Hall for two weeks.

Sylmar was much cleaner and more peaceful than Los Padrinos. To reduce gang violence, on Saturdays the guards would set up what was dubbed as The Chrome Dome. They'd place mats on the day-room floor, have all of the wards in unit sit around the mats, and ask if any ward had a problem with another; if so, the two could step onto the mats and settle it. Wards would anxiously await all week for this day, the day in which we could fight with no repercussions. Believe it or not, the Chrome Dome actually humbled a lot of wards; after all, getting beat into submission in front of everyone in the unit can be quite embarrassing.

I didn't have any rivals to fight during my first Chrome Dome, so I fought two big dudes who wanted to fight my smaller homeboys Baby Al and S-Dog from the South Side

Crips. Since I showed out that day, the following Saturday, the guards made an unprecedented move by bringing a ward from another unit to the event. The ward was C-Crazy from the Atlantic Drive Crips. He was a beast–for lack of a better word. He was 17 years old, athletic, energetic, and built like Mike Tyson. I had plenty of homeboys from the Atlantic Drive Crips whom I had grown up with, but since my neighborhood and the Atlantic Drive Crips were now feuding, C-Crazy came into the unit, kicked off his shoes, stepped onto the mats, and said: "I wanna fight anybody from Santana Block." With my reputation on the line, I bravely jumped up, kicked off my shoes, and stepped onto the mat.

The guard looked at my lanky, 5'10" 130-pound frame and told me to sit back down. "Is there any other Santana Block Crips in here other than this string bean?" he asked out. I did have another homeboy there with me, and he was a couple of years older and much bigger than I. "You better get in there and fight!" I demanded of my homeboy. He obliged, but seconds into the fight, he hurt his hand and quit. By now, I was pleading with the guard to give me a shot, but he refused.

Full of energy and nobody to fight, C-Crazy called out every big guy in the unit, but they all declined. He literally pleaded with guys to fight him, even promising to take it easy on them. Since everyone refused, the guard reluctantly gave me a chance. I stepped onto the mat swinging like a wild man, but he was slipping punches like a pro boxer. His strategy was to wear me down before launching his attack. Still, I just continued swinging, trying to keep him at bay and hopefully land some lucky blows. When I tired, I grabbed a chair and tried to throw it at him. This was a flagrant violation of the rules, and the guards punished me by throwing me down and allowing C-Crazy to get on top of me and pummel me. Up until them, I had been winning.

After approximately 10 weeks and 10 fights in juvenile hall, I was sent to Camp Miller, an open dormitory nestled away in the hills of Malibu. The three months I spent there were probably the most serene three months of my life. The fresh air, tall trees, and singing birds all seemed to have a calming effect on me. This was actually an escape for me, and although I missed my family, the streets, and money, I was becoming complacent in being in Malibu—after all, this was the closest I'd been to residing in a wealthy community. A part of me felt like, had I been provided a home, an income, and an opportunity to reach out and help my people, I probably would have spent the rest of my life in those hills.

In addition to serenity, I also received the most balanced and nutritionally fulfilling meals of my life. Instead of cupcakes and milk for breakfast, hamburgers and 40-ounce beers for lunch, and chili cheese fries and Thunder Bird for dinner, I was now consuming fruit, vegetables, eggs, milk, salads, beans, rice, and lean meats—plenty of it. The food combined with the daily workout we did every morning after waking up to Sinead O'Conner's "Nothing Compares" had me feeling really strong. In just three months, I went from 5'10" 130 pounds to 6'1" 155 pounds. I felt so strong and energetic that I swore to never use drugs again—I was now a health nut.

When the day came for me to leave, I had absolutely no idea what I'd do. Although I was done using drugs, I was still allured by the power and respect that gangs and money provided. I really didn't learn anything while in jail, nothing but more crime and violence, and the lyrics to Sinead O'Conner's song. It wasn't until I was back down in the pit of the noisy, smoggy city that I knew what I'd do. I got me a gun, got drunk, and spent my days looking for a big-time drug dealer to rob. I wanted enough money so that I could move up to the hills and listen to Sinead O'Conner while the birds chirped outside in the trees. I wanted enough money so that I could move somewhere I'd never have to carry a gun again or sell drugs again. I just wanted to be free–completely free.

It was the wee hours of September 17, 1990, thirteen days before I turned fifteen, when three of my homeboys–two adults and my 17-year-old homeboy Oteashas–and I were lying in the bushes of Orlie's front lawn. Orlie was a well-respected gangster turned businessman who owned the best hydraulics shop in California. Certainly, he had enough money to not only allow me to move to the hills of Malibu but also bury me in them. Unfortunately, though, he didn't send me to Malibu. Instead, he sent me back to jail where I was charged with robbery, extortion, kidnapping, and a slew of other insignificant charges.

"You're crazy; you're a walking dead man," the guards and other prisoners said of my robbing Orlie. To a degree I hoped they were right. In order for Orlie to kill me, he would have first had to refuse to testify and let me out of jail. But that didn't happen; instead, he disregarded the rules of gangsterism, and testified. Nobody believed Orlie would come to court, including himself. While on the stand, he kept saying that he was "no rat"; however, in the same sentence, he was snitching. Perhaps Orlie saved my life, because had I been released, he probably would've been obligated to put a price on my head. If not him, perhaps somebody else would have.

Having had enough with my delinquency, the judge committed me to the California Youth Authority for the rest of my youthful life, which meant that I'd be in until my 25th birthday. Whether delinquents were adjudicated in the juvenile court or convicted in the adult court, the California Youth Authority (C.Y.A.) was where they were housed until being paroled, discharged, or, in the case of those convicted in adult court, sent to the California Department of

Corrections to finish out their sentence.

There were many different C.Y.A. facilities in California, and the prisoner's crime, age, and history usually determined which facility he would be housed at. But as luck or mistake would have it, although I was barely fifteen, I was sent way up north to Preston, an old, ghastly facility which housed C.Y.A.'s most violent prisoners between the ages of 18-25.

Just like in Juvenile hall, everyone at Preston was gang related. Even the guys from the Bay Area were part of some type of prison organization or Black militant group. And it was mandatory that each member fight members of rival groups on sight, or else be robbed, jumped, and shunned for the rest of his stay. It was much more convenient and rewarding to fight rather than be stigmatized as being on the "Leva." Prisoners on the "Leva" were fair game for all other prisoners to rob, beat up, and abuse. There was no escaping the violence in C.Y.A.; either you were the aggressor or the victim. In such environment, it was utterly impossible for a child to be rehabilitated; in fact, such environment only made one more violent and criminal-minded.

Preston was so violent and hostile that a tactical team of guards constantly drove around the inside of the facility in vans equipped with riot gear—tear gas, pepper spray, rifles capable of firing bean-bags, and other grisly substances and devices—responding to outbreaks of violence. Whenever they got incidents under control, they would take the participants to single-bunk cells inside the dungeon of an ancient, ghastly castle they called "Tamarack." This was the "hole," and it was more hostile and violent than general population. Forced to live in such environment with no escape, or break, had long-lasting effects on my young, developing psyche. I was quickly molding into an extremely angry and violent young man.

Although I'd been in solitary confinement several times before, there was something about Tamarack that induced an intense feeling of loneliness, dejection, and despair. My first time in solitary was at the age of 14. I spent 72 hours in the

"Box" at Los Padrinos Juvenile Hall, and pretty much slept the time away. My second trip to solitary was at Sylmar Juvenile Hall; I spent a weekend locked in a cold cell staring out the window. My third time was at camp, where I spent 2 days sitting at attention under the constant observation of a bonehead counselor. But in Tamarack, there was no sleeping the days away. Tamarack was like a hole in an old prison movie—dark, filthy, violent, and depressing. At 15 years old, with the prospect of spending months confined in such conditions, I was forced to drown out my loneliness and sadness with anger and violence.

In C.Y.A., I witnessed some of the most reserved and peaceful prisoners morph into violent individuals. I saw nonviolent newcomers on the verge of tears—kids who wanted only to be left alone so that they could behave and make parole—turn into extremely violent prisoners and never make parole. I even saw prisoners on the "leva" get fed up with the abuse and redeem themselves with knives and other improvised weapons. The rules of life that applied in society didn't apply in C.Y.A. In order for one to survive and make it out with his teeth and eyeballs, he had to conform and adapt, even if that meant staying in C.Y.A. until age twenty-five.

Being youngest and a first-timer, I was under immense peer pressure. I was at least three years younger than everyone else, so I had to go the extra mile to prove myself. My ego was still fragile—as it had always been—so I often perceived everything done or said to me as an assault on my character. And since kindness was always perceived as weakness, I maintained a perpetual frown on my face, a facade to prevent others from seeing my soft side. A frown that I still struggle with erasing.

Everyone at Preston was required to attain a high school diploma and attend vocational classes. I was so far behind in basic education that I was assigned to a special class. My math teacher was a sweet, black woman who often clapped her hands and rejoiced whenever I solved a problem correctly. She often brought in treats and other rewards. She had a special knack for making her class interesting and exciting. Surprisingly, I made tremendous progress in her class—which resulted in a lot of clapping and rejoicing as if she were overcome with the Holy Ghost. My other classes, though, were not so interesting. They were dull and fruitless. In the afternoons, I attended a carpentry class, where my peers often pressured me into sniffing paint thinner with them, thereby, frying what little brain cells I did have.

My stay at Preston didn't last long. In July, 1991, we were transferred to Chaderjian, a brand-new facility in Stockton, California. Chaderjian was originally built as a maximum security prison for the county of San Joaquin, but somehow ended up under the control of the California Youth Authority. Each unit consisted of two tiers and fifty secure cells. The cells on the bottom tier were double-bunks, and those on the top were single-bunk. Each unit had its own cafeteria and recreation yard; therefore, other than walking to school, we never left the unit for anything.

Although Chaderjian was supposed to be less violent than Preston, it actually turned out to be worse. All of the troublesome prisoners who had been locked in Tamarack and other segregation units at Preston were now mixed in with the general population. Consequently, Chaderjian was a powder keg waiting to explode, and when it did, it was out of control. There were group disturbances and riots every week, fights and assaults every day, and serious assaults on staff members every other month. Ironically, most prisoners weren't really violent, and if placed in a normal setting, they wouldn't hurt a fly; however, under extreme frustration and peer pressure, they often resorted to violence because it was the only language others respected and understood.

Not long after arriving at Chaderjian, I began to get into a lot of trouble. As a result, I spent most of my time locked in solitary, confined to my cell all day while the other prisoners were out in the day-room or the rec yard enjoying themselves. I was barely 16 years old, and trapped in a cell. I had no communication with the outside world other than occasional letters and pictures from my mother and sisters. I developed extreme anger problems. The frustrations were mounting. And to make matters worse, the Senior Youth Counselor hated me and punished me every chance he could. He hated me so much that he tried to pay two other prisoners to jump me.

I was basically isolated to a world of anger and frustration without recourse. The senior Youth counselor hated me solely because I never submitted to him; instead, I remained quiet, stubborn, and nonchalant in the face of his threats and punishment. Ironically, although I appeared arrogant and stubborn, I was really an emotional wreck on the inside; I just did a good job of concealing it. I always experienced myriad of emotions. Instead of expressing it, though, I bottled it up until it morphed into the one emotion that I wasn't ashamed to express, an emotion that everyone accepted and respected: Anger.

Help was absent while I was going through my emotional turmoil, but my counselor, Mrs. T, did show a little concern. She tried to encourage me by loaning me personal books and magazines to help relieve some of the stress I was experiencing confined to my cell, but I barely knew how to read, much less focus and think positively. What I really needed was a psychologist and a less-hostile environment.

In hindsight, I don't think CYA was designed for me to be reformed; instead, it was merely a conveyor ensuring my confinement to the prison cell I'm in today. It was a no-win situation for me to be confined to an environment where 24-year-old men couldn't defy the odds, let alone a 15-yearold kid. I was 500 miles away from my family, confined to a world that bred and incited violence. There was no psychologist or treatment, just discipline and solitary confinement, confinement where my sadness and confusion turned into anger and more confusion.

In October, 1992, my frustration reached its zenith. I was in a cell next to my homeboy Reg-Dog from Long Beach. We both were waiting to be moved to a long-term lock-down unit. To ensure that the punishment would be worth it, and to enhance our reputation, we decided to attack the staff.

The following day, minutes before we came out for our showers, I had my homeboy set a can of chili beans on the dayroom table. Moments later, after all the other prisoners were locked in their cells, a counselor named Shervon came and let me and Reg-Dog out for showers. The Senior Youth Counselor was standing downstairs by the kitchen door watching me, Shervon stayed upstairs while my counselor, Mrs. T, was doing cell checks downstairs and another guard was observing from the inside tower. With wild desire to bash open the scalp of the Senior Youth Counselor, I scurried down the stairs and grabbed the can of chili beans from the table. Before I could finish stuffing the can of chili into a sock, he quickly slipped through the kitchen door.

Meanwhile, Reg-Dog walked over to my counselor and punched her in the face. She fell to the floor, tucked her head between her legs, covered the back of her head, and yelled for me to help. She had no idea that I was in on the attack. I lingered around the kitchen door for a few seconds, silently hoping the Senior Youth Counselor would come out and have his head split. I then ran over to my counselor. But instead of pulling Reg-Dog off of her, I whacked her a few times with the can of chili.

By now, the guard in the tower had tossed down a canister of tear gas, and Shervon had run down the stairs ordering us to lie on the ground. We had already ceased hitting my counselor, but we refused to lie down. Instead, we squatted in anticipation of real action—perhaps the SYC. But he didn't come until the tactical response team arrived. They hog-tied us, kicked us, stomped us, dragged us out of the unit, kicked us several more times, tossed us into the back of separate vans, sprayed a pint of pepper spray in my face, took us to Kern (the administrative lock-down unit), and tossed me head first into a cell, where I lay hog-tied for hours in a puddle of blood.

Although Mrs. T only suffered a broken nose and a few bruises, they treated us as if we had killed her. It took 2 days for me to receive medical attention and have my busted head stitched up. I was forced to use my underwear as a bandage. Why my underwear? Because that's all I had in my cell. At night, from 10 p.m. to 6 a.m., they'd give us a mat to sleep on, but other than that, we were never allowed anything in our cell—not even toilet paper. Our breakfast was always cold oatmeal with spit and pepper spray in it. Lunch, a green bologna sandwich and an apple which appeared to have been kicked around before being served to us. And dinner, the same. We'd assaulted the wrong person. The criminal justice system would forever haunt us.

CHAPTER 34

CHANGE

Instead of sending us to the county jail, as they had done everyone else who'd been prosecuted for assaulting staff, they kept us at Chaderjian so that they could see to our mistreatment. As a form of torture, some guards would randomly spray pepper spray through the crack of my door, A couple would quietly call me a "nigger" and threaten to kill me. They were extremely sadistic, to say the least, and my fury seemed to only fuel their sadism. I had never written home to gripe about my conditions, but after two weeks of mistreatment, I wrote my mother for help.

In response to the torture, I often kicked on the door and yelled a slew of profanities at the guards. Although doing so released a little steam, I found no solace in it. I was so angry that every little offense would send me over the edge. I was quickly becoming an old, frustrated, depressed, miserable teen. And while the guards tortured me from the outside of the cell, my conscience tortured me from the inside.

Strangely, I began to dread my conscience more than the torturous conditions. I had never assaulted a woman before, and every fiber of my being, both tangible and intangible, knew that I was wrong. I felt like shit, and tried everything I could to soothe the pain and shame. I tried to convince myself that the axiom prescribing that men should never hit women shouldn't apply for cops and prison guards; however, my heart and conscience refused to accept such a lame excuse. "What if my grandmother, mother, or sisters, were prison guards— would it be cool then?" I asked myself.

There was nothing gangster or cool about assaulting a woman, and the more I thought about it, the more I became disgusted with myself. No matter how much I tried to hide behind my self-fabricated anger, my conscience always seemed to find me. There was no escaping it, and after so many months in cruel solitary confinement, I gave in and accepted the fact that I was a scum. I looked in the mirror and said: "You're a piece of shit, and if you don't like it, then change."

That night, I quit running from my conscience, and had a long conversation with myself. I acknowledged that I couldn't change my past or take back the pain and suffering I'd caused others, but I did have the ability to change my behavior from that day forward. The first thing I did was take control over my emotions, particularly my anger. I realized that, as long as I allowed the words or actions of others to control my emotions, I'd forever be someone else's puppet.

From that day forward, I refused to let another person control me and rob me of my joy. When the guards spat in my food or called me a "nigger," I simply laughed and perceived it as degrading themselves. Their behavior merely revealed their unprofessionalism and humanitarian flaws. I found myself sincerely laughing at the notion of a 35-year-old man— perhaps a father—allowing a confined 17-year-old prisoner to inadvertently cause him so much resentment that he would behave in such a manner. What a weak-minded buffoon!

In just a matter of days, I managed to seize control over my emotions and, consequently, my actions. I simply changed my perception of other's. Instead of perceiving everything as an attack, I perceived it as a revelation of the other person's character. So when the guards spat in my food or used derogatory slurs, I perceived it not as an attack on my character, but as an inadvertent revelation of their flawed character.

Every night, I would reflect on my life and have conversations with myself. I reflected back on all of the senseless violent acts I'd committed, and I asked myself: How would I feel if such violence was perpetrated on my mother or sisters? I came to the conclusion that if I didn't like it being done to me and my loved ones, then I shouldn't do it to anyone else. I realized that my anger and violence was wrong, and that in order for me to overcome my shame for assaulting my counselor, I had to denounce senseless violence altogether. At that moment, I vowed to never commit another violent act unless my safety and others❓ safety depended on it, or at a time of war or rebellion– be it in prison or in society.

Just like that, I reformed myself by having nightly conversations with myself. My entire attitude changed, and I was now a humble, optimistic young man. Stress was now a thing of the past, and everything meant to upset me or ruin my mood seemed to bounce right off of me when thrown my way. And although I still walked through life with a chip on my shoulder, such chip was really a grudge against my weaker being, the bruised alter ego that had once weighed me down as a child. It was my way of saying: "Fuck that inferior mentality that had been programmed in my mind as a child, and fuck the invisible system that predestined my failure–I'm in control now!"

When the guards picked up on my newfound attitude, they slowly changed how they treated me. I was now a thinking man, and even they knew that a thinking man is to be feared much more than an angry man–especially one who'd be getting out some day. Also, it seemed that my refusing to respond to their evil provocations was no fun for them. It didn't take long for their spit and pepper spray to vanish from my food, for my mat to remain in my cell all day, and for me to be allowed books to read. Though I credited my change in attitude for the change in treatment, a group of new cooler black guards were also instrumental.

When I first started reading books, I realized that I was dumb as a box of rocks. It seemed like every other word I encountered required me to put down the book and refer to a dictionary. It took several weeks to read just one book, and again I still had difficulty comprehending it. As time passed, though, I got the hang of it and enjoyed it. Reading became my escape, not only from the miserable confines of my cell but also the mental confines that the ghetto had placed on my mind. Through reading, I was able to learn that there was so much more to life than what I had been taught to believe. I learned that my ancestors in Africa were not the naked, jungle-dwelling cannibals that I had been mis-educated to believe they were; in fact, they were kings, queens, scholars, and creators of ancient civilizations. This gave me a sense of pride, and induced self-respect. I also learned that there was a world outside of mine that provided opportunity other than gangs and drugs to young black men. Ultimately, through reading, I learned that my entire way of thinking had been wrong.

After four months in solitary confinement, I was taken to court and pleaded guilty to assault with a deadly weapon on a peace officer. Although I was still a juvenile, I was treated as an adult due to an error in the court's documents, and sentenced to three years in a level-four maximum security prison for adults. I went on to prison, where I continued to self-educate myself, earned my G.E.D., changed my diet and my behavior, and learned self-discipline.

As soon as I got to prison, a group of guards took me in a room and roughed me up in the name of my counselor. I believe they were more so trying to intimidate me than hurt me, because other than sore ribs and a small lump on my head, they caused no damage. As for Reg-Dog, the guards shot him with a mini-14 rifle while he and another homeboy were having a fist fight.

In addition to my zest for knowledge, a lot of my discipline and growth in prison was a result of my affiliation with the prison's Crip organization. These much older and seasoned gangsters required me to study Swahili, read books, exercise daily, learn how to manufacture and use "shanks," and conduct myself with discipline and structure.

CHAPTER 35

AN ILLUSION OF FREEDOM

On July 31, 1994, at the age of 18, I walked out of prison a changed man. When I went back through my old neighborhoods, people barely recognized me. Not only had my demeanor and attitude changed, but so had my appearance. Instead of wearing all black and dressing like a gang banger, as I used to, I wore light colors and dressed like a square. I didn't get high; I didn't hang out; I didn't stay up late; I didn't carry guns. I didn't do any of the things I used to do. Other than selling a few bags of weed to put some money in my pockets, I didn't even commit crime. I had made a 180-degree turn. People who didn't know me thought that I was a nerd.

Strangely, I found it interesting and exciting that people were duped by my school-boy appearance. Little did they know the history of the person camouflaged behind that appearance. And, ironically, after impersonating a "square" for so long, I began to develop the behavior and traits of one—I began to walk like a square and talk like a square.

Testament of my change came one night when my sister heard someone downstairs in our carport trying to steal her boyfriend's car. She and my mother awoke me and we confronted the thief. I had him at gunpoint with my mother's old, rusty .22 revolver while she and my sister were yelling at him. The old Bosco wouldn't have hesitated to fill the thief with slugs; however, the new Bosco had a conscience. The thief was only 16 years old, so I found myself thinking about the grief I'd cause his mother if I were to kill him, and I thought about my mother being in his mother's shoes. The love I have for my mother wouldn't allow me to inflict such pain on his mother, so I let the kid go and told him to go find a job or get a hustle.

By the rules of the streets, I was making a terrible mistake, for one should never pull a gun on a man and let him go;

however, I no longer lived by the rules of the streets–I was redefining them.

To escape the confines of the ghetto, and also learn a new skill that might reward me with a good job and opportunities, I enrolled in a vocational school in Torrance, California, a predominately-white suburb twenty minutes away. I took up electronic technology and computer technology, hoping to become abreast with the promising tech era.

Holding a conversation with my classmates was complicated, for years of prison had made me more socially awkward. Also, I was one of two blacks in the class, and nobody but the instructor knew about my background. So when asked about my high school days, I had to lie because I was too afraid to tell them that I was imprisoned during such years. The prettiest girl in the class–who was also a model– used to walk up to me and grab my hand, and walk and talk with me during recesses, but when the instructor noticed her interest in me, he said something to her and she never spoke to me again. I assume he told her about my past.

I soon learned that no matter how much you change or try to, your past will always come back to haunt you. On January, 12, 1995, my parole officer called and demanded that I come to his office immediately. As soon as I stepped into his office, two burly white dudes jumped from behind the door, threw me against the wall, and handcuffed me. They were C.Y.A. officers, and according to them, I'd been mistakenly released from prison. Instead of being released I was supposed to be returned to Y.A. to finish out my juvenile life sentence. I was crushed, to say the least. I had truly reformed and was on track to being a true model of redemption, and now that was being destroyed by the people whose job was to rehabilitate me. The system was screwed. I tried to play by their rules, and this is how it worked out. Never again, I told myself.

I was returned to Chaderjian, where, surprisingly, I became

the orderly in the lock-down unit. Everyone immediately discerned my maturity and growth, both physically and intellectually. Shervon commented on how handsome and respectful I had become. The only problem I had was with the senior officer in the lock-down unit, who was disgruntled because I use to sneak extra food to the prisoners. Also, another officer warned me that a group of officers were planning to come into my cell at night and attack me. I showed him a book that I was reading, *Soledad Brothers* by George Jackson, and told him that I preferred peace, but that I was willing to die to defend myself just like George Jackson. Apparently, the administration took the threat serious because they transferred me to Y.T.S., a facility in Ontario, California.

Since C.Y.A.'s purpose was to rehabilitate, I argued to the Parole board that I'd been reformed. Normally, prisoners went before the parole board once a year; however, since I was quickly completing every program the board recommended, I went before the board three times in eight months. The third time I went before the board, the meanest member—a Latina whom every prisoner loathed—was grinning from ear to ear and on the verge of tears when I finished talking. After reviewing my prior board hearings and behavior in contrast to the respectful, intelligent man now sitting before them, they were convinced in my redemption. Accordingly, they paroled me to a work-release program, and eventually paroled me for good on December 4, 1995.

When I walked out of Y.A., I stepped into a war zone. The halfway house I was released to was on 18th Street and Union, in the heart of the barrio. On one side of the halfway house, across the street, and in both directions up the street from it, 18th Street gang members hung out by the dozens. When I first got there, my job assignment required me to sweep the sidewalk every night. When rival gang members did a drive-by one night and fired approximately 100 rounds from their fully automatic weapons, I refused to ever go out and sweep again. When armed 18th Street gang members came to the halfway house looking for rival gang members, I went to Compton and got a gun, and kept it on me at all times.

Even when I wasn't at the halfway house, I kept the gun on me, especially whenever I went home. Remember the kid who tried to steal my sister boyfriend's car? Well, when I was back in Y.A., he and his friends tried to steal the car again; a feud ensued between them and my sister's boyfriend; they shot up my sister's apartment; my sister's boyfriend killed one of them; and so on. So every time I went to my sister's apartment, which was my official home and parole address, I had to keep my gun on my hip. Also a guy whom I'd robbed and shot in 1989 was now looking for me with homicidal intentions. I kept my gun on me at all times.

A month after my release, while leaving my sister's apartment and carrying my gun, two white cops pulled me over for Driving While Black and later lied that they pulled me over for not having a front license plate. When they approached the car and asked for my license and registration, they ordered me out of the car and immediately began to search me. After finding a wad of money in my pocket, they falsely accused me of robbing someone— even though there was no robbery—and began to place handcuffs on me. Fearing that they were trying to frame me with a robbery charge, I broke free and ran. I climbed a few buildings, hopped a few fences, and hid underneath a house.

After what seemed like a couple of hours, I heard the "ghetto bird" hovering above and canines barking. Moments later, a canine rushed underneath the house and tried to chew my leg off. I tried to fight the dog, but that only made it attack me more. "Stop resisting!" a cop shouted, crawling under the house with his gun pointed at me. Surprisingly, when I stopped resisting, the canine stopped biting and hovered over me with a growl as I crawled from under the house with my hands out for the cops to see. Once I was cuffed, the cops roughed me up and arrested me and called an ambulance to rush me to the hospital where I was treated for my injuries.

While I'd been hiding under the house, the cops searched my car and found a gun under the seat. I was charged with being an ex-felon in possession of a firearm, and booked into the medical ward at L.A. County Jail. The corrupt cops even charged me with suspicion of robbery, which isn't even a real charge under California law—or any law, for that matter. Since I was a young black man with cash in my pocket, they assumed that I must have robbed somebody—even though nobody had called and complained of being robbed. Once the charges hit the prosecutor's desk, though, he rejected the victimless robbery charge.

Due to my mistaken release from prison and return to Y.A., the computers erroneously stated that I'd been discharged from parole; therefore, I was able to bail out of jail. Out on bail, with a return to prison looming, and potential ghetto violence lurking nearby, I had my mind set on three things: getting money, getting lawyers, and getting out of the ghetto. I wanted to be some place I wouldn't have to carry guns and worry about police harassment.

I began to wonder whether I would have been pulled over had I been rich or white, and if so, would I have been ordered out of the car after providing a valid license and registration. Better yet, if I weren't in the ghetto, where the War on Drugs encouraged cops to beef up patrol and harass and arrest young black men for anything, would I have been pulled over and ordered out of the car for something so petty as not having a front license plate? To answer my own question, I ventured into Orange County and witnessed thousands of young, white dudes driving sports cars with no front license plates and were never once pulled over and ticketed, much less pulled over and ordered out of the car.

Something had to change. I wasn't able to change my skin color, but I was certainly able to change my address and financial status. During this time, I ventured out of town to sell drugs. One place I frequented was Oceanside, California, near Camp Pendleton. Although Oceanside was predominately white, I blended in because I was young and clean-cut with good posture like a Marine. I liked Oceanside not only because I could make $1,000 per night selling drugs, but also because of the beaches and its less hostile environment. I certainly didn't need a gun there, nor was I harassed by the police. My humble demeanor and casual appearance allowed me to get by without problems.

However, one afternoon while stopping in Oceanside to pick up some money from my homeboy, the police raided the motel my homeboys were selling drugs at. They found a gun inside my homeboy's car and threatened to take us all to jail for it unless someone confessed to owning the car. "Not only are you guys bringing drugs to my town," the lead narcotic detective said, as if we were the only people dealing drugs in Oceanside. "But you're also bringing guns." Little did he know that my homeboy had recently bought the gun from a crackhead Marine and planned on taking it out of *his* town. Ultimately, he told me that he'd let me go if we'd agree to leave Oceanside and never return. We agreed, and he saw to it that we all got on the highway and left.

Breaking my promise, I would drive to Oceanside during the wee hours of the morning, give drugs to people to sell for me, collect money, and leave before dawn. One night, a girl from L.A. and I were in a motel room when one of my friends came through and gave me some money. An hour later, the narcotics detective and his goons raided the room and arrested me for a drug deal that my friend made. The detective knew that I didn't do the deal. But to punish me for returning to his town, he lied and said that I confessed to selling drugs that night. Although he had no signed statement or proof, his word was good enough.

Once again, I was able to bail out again, and took my hustle to Las Vegas, where I developed a bad gambling problem and began to cheat casinos out of money. I scammed the casinos in several ways; I passed them counterfeit checks, counted cards, and gambled underage.

My underage scam began one night while playing blackjack in the El Cortez casino. After losing several thousands, the pit boss solicited me to fill out an application to become a VIP member. When I produced my ID, revealing that I was only 20 years old, he immediately stopped everything, returned all of the money I'd lost, and told me to leave the casino and to not come back. I was surprised because, although I had usually used a fake ID, just for the hell of it, I had never known that twenty-one was the age requirement. Even more shocking was the rule of ethics that required the casinos to return all lost money to underage gamblers. Armed with this knowledge, I went from casino to casino gambling heavily, and whenever I lost several grands, I would request a VIP application and submit it with my real ID. The casinos never failed to return my money down to the exact dollar.

One night I tried to pull the scam at Binion's Horseshoe, but was nearly beaten by goons and cited by Gaming and Control. Instead of returning my money, the goons kicked me out and threatened to bury me in the desert, and the Gaming Control agents threatened to arrest me. Though I continued to try other casinos, I was quickly running out of locations. Most of the times I entered a casino, I was met by security within seconds and ordered to leave. Apparently, my face was programmed into the computers of every casino in Las Vegas.

My last try occurred downtown at Lady Luck. After losing roughly ten thousand dollars, I requested the VIP application. Instead of counting the cash and sending me on my way, the pit boss took me to the back for a talk with one of the managers. Someone had reported the incident to Gaming Control agents, and they were on their way to the casino.

I assumed the casino was on the verge of being severely

fined, because the manager–or whoever this guy was– wanted me to tell Gaming Control that I'd misled the table about my age. He said that if I did so, he'd immediately return all of my money and give me a free stay at the hotel whenever I turned twenty-one. All of that sounded good, but the last time I'd seen Gaming Control, they threatened to arrest me, so I couldn't stand to see them again. I tried to escape by telling the manager that my parents were waiting for me so that we could catch our flight back home to California. I even pulled out my cell phone and pretended to be talking to my mom.

"Is that your mom–can I speak with her?" he asked.

"Oh no! She doesn't know about my gambling," I lied.

"Maybe she'll understand if I explain and give her a free weekend stay," he replied.

This guy refused to give up. I literally had to dupe him into thinking that my parents were willing to meet him outside the casino, and when we stepped outside I just kept on walking while he followed and pleaded with me like a sorrowful husband pleading with a disgruntled wife.

That was my last time in a Vegas casino, for in July 1996, I was taken into custody and tried and convicted on the gun charge I caught earlier that year. Before trial, I argued that I was not an ex-felon because my prior conviction for the Y.A. assault was unconstitutional based on the fact that I was a minor illegally convicted and sentenced in the adult court. However, the judge denied my motion, stating that I should've raised such claim back then in 1993, even though I didn't discover the error until 1995. The jinx from the assault continued to haunt me, and I was sentenced to seven years in prison.

Meanwhile the prosecutor in the Oceanside case threatened to add eight more years if I were to lose in trial. Although I was innocent, rather than risking it, I pled guilty to eight months. After all, I was already serving seven years– what harm was eight more months and a minor drug conviction on my record?

I went on to serve my time in a prison which was then California's most violent penitentiary, a penitentiary where the guards sported confederate bandanas, supplied white prisoners with knives to attack black prisoners, and used lethal force on the blacks whenever the violence erupted. I walked around the prison with a chip on my shoulder, never smiling and rarely laughing. I had wasted all of my teens in prison, and now I was wasting my twenties, all for a gun that I'd never even used and a drug sale that someone else had done.

To keep from going insane, I told myself that I was away at a hard knock university, and that I would get out and make a million dollars to compensate for the years. That, and studying economics and different languages, helped me get through the day and look forward to the next one.

Also helping me get through the days was Audrey. I'd met her while in Oceanside, and she was extremely supportive in a way that many prisoners envied. Once a month, she would travel from San Diego to the very top of California to spend the weekend visiting me. Her mother—also a sweetheart—was also supportive, ordering me books and a subscription of The Wall Street Journal. At the time, Audrey was still going through college, so we pretty much anchored each other, encouraging and motivating each other to put education first. With her emotional and mental support, the time flew by and I left out of prison a much smarter, charismatic, and attractive young man.

When I walked out the front gate on September 18, 2002, Audrey was there waiting for me. We flew to her house in San Diego. When the plane made a U-turn over the blue Pacific Ocean, I felt the most serene feeling I'd ever felt before. I was free, and I was going to a home in a neighborhood where I wouldn't have to carry a gun, confront burglars, or be aggressively harassed by overzealous cops.

I fell in love with San Diego. I was never once profiled or

harassed by ther4 cops, and the people I encountered were respectful and attracted to me. I was pretty much treated like a human being—probably because I looked like an innocent college kid or a ballplayer. Even when I went to dinners, parties, and other functions with Audrey, no one ever inquired about my background. Though, there were a few "Do you play basketball?" inquiries.

As I was becoming acquainted with San Diego, its gyms, beaches, restaurants, and upscale communities, I was also being allured by its vast wealth, and reminded that it takes money to survive in a capitalist society. Every time we went out, or when a bill needed to be paid and Audrey opened her wallet, I felt a sting to my ego. I'd never been the type of guy that depends on others for financial support. I've always been the guy everyone else depended on, and I had no desire to change that at the age of twenty-seven. Needless to say, I soon started back hustling.

Since I didn't want anything to do with drugs, I started scamming department stores out of expensive electronics and selling them at discounted prices. Now that I was making really good money, taking care of Audrey, family, and friends, and mingling with well-diverse groups of people, I was feeling good about myself. I was well-respected and appreciated by a rainbow of people, from Koreans to Russians. The electronics business was beginning to open up myriad of opportunities.

Then, in early September, several friends encouraged me to get involved in the marijuana business since I was respected and trusted by many large-scale suppliers. Without much contemplation, I agreed. After all, it was a fair exchange, victimless business. More importantly, it was a way for me to provide jobs and income to friends and associates who didn't know how to do anything else but deal drugs. And, ultimately, it was a way to generate money through the ghetto. I certainly didn't see any harm in it.

PART FIVE: EMANCIPATION OF A REAL NIGGA

CHAPTER 36

JUST US

Truthfully, I was before the jury for simply being a product of my environment, a man whom America clandestinely created, one who was too uneducated, discouraged, foolish, and weak to avoid the traps and break the cycle. No, I was not the golden child; I was just another mis-educated fool who fell into America's new racial caste system. And the judge, the jury, and the prosecutor were in position to ensure so.

So, no it wasn't dealing marijuana that landed me behind bars and entangled me in the system. It was a culmination of social conditions, including race, miseducation, and misguidance. Simply put, it was the odds. I just wish I could've told the jury.

On July 25, 2008, as I sat in a cell beside the courtroom, eavesdropping on the court through an intercom that they'd mistakenly left on, and listening to "Calling All Angels" by Train, the jury came back with a verdict. I was ushered into the courtroom; then the jury entered and passed the verdict form to the judge. The judge fiddled with his glasses for a second, making sure that he was seeing correctly, and began to read the verdict to the court. As to Count One, conspiracy to possess and distribute marijuana, the jury found me not guilty. Apparently, they didn't believe the government's evidence in regards to that charge. I was tempted to rejoice, for since they didn't find me guilty on the conspiracy charge, I assumed they wouldn't find me guilty on the possession charge either. Unfortunately, though, they did find me guilty on that charge, as well as others.

Consequently, I was paraded back to my cell in the booking area of the Marion County Jail, where I would await sentencing. I spent weeks racking my brain trying to make sense of the jury's verdict—it just wasn't making sense. How could they find me guilty of possessing marijuana that I did not have control over? The marijuana was locked in the cargo compartment of a van that belonged to the federal government. There was a metal cage preventing me from entering or accessing the cargo compartment. And the van was disabled, thereby, preventing me from driving away with it. So how in the world could I have had control over the marijuana if I didn't even have the ability to see it, touch it, or move it? I didn't have any hacksaws on me, so I couldn't have sawed through the metal barrier.

The jury had made a mistake, and I was certain of that. The judge had instructed them to find me guilty if the evidence proved that I had the ability to exercise control over the marijuana either directly or through others. Through others? What others? I was charged with—well, I believe that I was charged with— possessing the 1,400 pounds of marijuana while it was in the van and I was in the driver seat attempting to start it. Being that I was the only person who entered the van, there were no *others* for me to exercise control over the marijuana through. Unless the court was subtly instructing the jury that they could find me guilty for exercising control over the marijuana through the federal agents while it was still in their custody and control, there was no need for such *through others* instruction.

However, as a matter of both fact and law, it was utterly impossible for me to exercise control over drugs that were in the possession and custody of the feds. But perhaps the jury didn't know any better; after all, they were never instructed that I couldn't possess marijuana through the federal agents. In fact, being that there were no "others" aside from the agents, the jury could have reasonably believed that I could have exercised control over the marijuana while it was still in the complete custody and possession of the agents. So that is exactly what the jury did; they found me guilty for possessing marijuana while it was in the control of the government.

I am sure of that for several reasons. First, during deliberations, the jury sent out a note stating that they didn't know what marijuana I was actually charged with possessing. In fact, they suggested that I was charged with possessing marijuana other than that inside the van. Apparently, they didn't believe that I had control over the marijuana while it was locked in the back of the van. Instead of telling the jury what marijuana I was charged with, the court simply instructed the jury to look at the indictment. However, the indictment didn't even clarify what marijuana I was charged with–it didn't even give the specific date, time, or amount of marijuana that I was charged with–it simply alleged that I possessed 100 kilograms or more "on or about" January 23, 2004. Making matters worse, the court instructed the jury that any date reasonably near that was sufficient.

Secondly, according to the evidence, it was impossible for the jury to determine that I had direct control over the marijuana. Furthermore, I spoke to two of the jurors a month after the trial, and they confirmed the confusion.

Weeks after the verdict, a sexy female officer at the jail started boldly pursuing me. Every time the male guards stepped out of the booking area, she'd come to my cell, open the flap on the window and smile at me. Initially, I never really paid her any mind because I was consumed in legal documents at the time. I did, however, notice that she never came by when other officers were around.

I didn't really notice that she had a crush on me until one day I heard her adjusting the camera monitor while I was in my cell working out. At the time, the flap on my window was ajar, so I walked over and looked out and saw that she was watching me on the monitor. As soon as I stepped to the door and looked out at her, she instantly looked up at me with an "I'm busted" expression, and began fumbling with the monitor to readjust it. From that day on, I began to respond to her subtle gestures by throwing up the peace sign; she responded with smiles and winks, and shortly thereafter, she passed me some Hershey's kisses and a note.

What initially started out as us exchanging notes soon grew into a romantic relationship. She was head over heels for me, and likewise, I was crazy about her. I found it exciting how she used body language to clandestinely communicate with me while in the presence of her coworkers. She always found a way to make me laugh and smile, whether it was by blowing me kisses when they turned their heads, sticking her tongue out when they weren't paying attention, provocatively eating a chocolate candy bar, or subtly smacking her behind when she walked by. She actually made my days so much brighter, and turned that miserable holding-cell into the best cell in the jail. Every day, I awoke looking forward to seeing her.

Quite naturally, now that I had her, I had everything else that could be smuggled into the jail, such as cell phones and food she'd steal out of the kitchen for me. One particular night, while her coworker was dozing off, she sneaked inside his lunch box and stole his cookies for me. There were times when no other person was around and I'd stand at the door with my back to the camera, a blanket draped over me, and an erection protruding through the tray slot while she crouched on the other side. She was a real thrill seeker, to say the least.

The cameras never were a problem. Whenever she'd pass stuff to me, I'd block the view of the camera in my cell. For example, when she slid things under the door, I'd stand at the door with my back to the camera and my feet obstructing its view of the bottom of the door. Whenever she passed things through the tray slot, I'd tuck my pants legs into my socks, unbutton the crotch of my jumpsuit, and stand at the door with my crotch inches away from the tray slot and my hands on the door for the camera to see them, and she'd open the tray slot and drop the items into the crotch of my jumpsuit.

Whenever I used my cell phone, I'd beat the camera by pacing the floor with a blanket draped over my head and body as if I were cold. At night, I'd lie on my back, raise my knees, and pull the blanket over my head. This is how I was able to talk to two of my jurors. Initially, I had a paralegal speak with several of the jurors' weeks after the trial; then, when the paralegal told me that two of the jurors didn't believe that I was capable of controlling the marijuana alone, I contacted them myself. One of them said that she would not sign an affidavit while the other was indecisive. The indecisive one—a young white lady—and I went on to exchange personal text messages for quite some time thereafter. I was hoping to persuade her in the future, if need be.

Meanwhile, I filed a motion for a new trial based on the evidence submitted at trial. Needless to say, my judge denied the motion on December 12, 2008, and sentenced me to 35 years behind bars. To support such harsh sentence, the judge relied on my two faulty prior convictions: The Oceanside drug conviction and the, forever haunting, CYA assault conviction. I tried to argue that the latter conviction was unconstitutional because it had been rendered in violation of the law; however, the judge, like every other judge before him, essentially determined that such argument should've been presented in the court that rendered such judgment. According to him, it was still on my record, so it was valid.

Thirty-five years isn't a life sentence, but there isn't much of a difference. It might not be enough to ensure my death behind bars, but it's certainly enough to ensure society a 60-year-old, miserable, psychopath to deal with. It was also enough to bring tears to the eyes of many others, including my paramour at the jail. And it was certainly enough to arouse the spirit of Kunta Quawntay. And being confined in a cell in the booking area with the support of my paramour, I was in the perfect position to execute an escape.

Whether for escaping, gathering information, enjoying the company of my paramour, or being entertained, I had the best seat in the house. Everything and every person entering and leaving the jail had to come through the booking area. From that cell, I learned more about the jail than the people who worked there. I also became better acquainted with the officers, who, after realizing that I was the coolest thing since Popsicles, treated me as if I were one of them. They'd leave my tray slot and window flap open all day, and we'd talk, joke, laugh, and debate.

From that cell, with my paramour's help, I was planning to literally walk out of the jail. But as I was making preparations and figuring out ways to cover her tracks, I began to have a change of heart. After so long, I began to realize that most of the guards at Marion County Jail were genuinely good people; they gave me a new perception of small-town white folks. For people from a town without blacks or other minorities, they seemed far from racist. They were simply small-town country folks who worked hard on weekdays and partied on weekends. Interacting with them, I was able to discern how one's environment plays a major role in one's development.

Strangely, my experience in that country jail-cell had a lasting impact on my psyche. Ever since then, I began to respect and appreciate the simple things about people—their character. I also came to appreciate country music, a genre I'd never listened to until the guards set a radio outside my door and played nothing but country. Ultimately, my interacting up close with the workers at the jail allowed me to respect and judge them by their intentions rather than my fears. Ironically, their behavior toward me made me rethink whether there was compassion in the hearts of some people who worked in the criminal justice system. Such thoughts gave me the confidence that perhaps the Seventh Circuit Court of Appeals would also be fair and humane. After all, considering the character of the guards at Jackson County Jail and Marion County Jail, and the jury's not-guilty verdict on the conspiracy charge, these small-town white folks were proving my fears wrong.

My confidence was soon so high that it almost felt divine. I was now absolutely certain that I would come back on appeal. The money-laundering conviction was a no-brainer; there was absolutely no evidence supporting it. Plus, I still had my Speedy Trial Act claim, and the evidence supporting the possession charge was nil. I was so confident in my return that I was willing to go to prison and fight rather than escape. My paramour working at the jail agreed that I should try my chances on appeal first. We decided that it would be best that I go through with my appeal, come back at least on the Money Laundering, and, if displeased with the outcome of the overall appeal, then escape. I was that confident in my return.

As expected, October 29, 2010, three bias, uncompassionate judges for the 7th Circuit Court of Appeals vacated the Money Laundering. However, they affirmed the possession conviction. Their opinion, filled with irrelevant disinformation, was more so slander than fact. I asked them whether I had the ability to control the marijuana while it was locked in the back of the van, and they rambled on about insignificant falsehoods such as the allegation of my throwing Nicole against a wall. What relevance did that have to whether or not I had possession of the marijuana inside the van? None! It was simply a way for evil people with power to advance the devil's cause. It's one thing for a 20 or 30-year-old to slander and inflict harm upon people—that can be blamed on ignorance or immaturity—but it's another thing when a 50-year-old public servant does it.

The judges even had the audacity to accuse me of being stingy. I became irate when I read that. That was tantamount to accusing God of being evil. Throughout my life, I have given the shirt off my back to assist others in financial need, and even to this day I still continue to do so–even to the detriment of my own wants or needs. In any event, what did my degree of benevolence have to do with whether or not I had the ability to exercise control over the marijuana inside the back of the government's van? Absolutely nothing. It was just a way for three close-minded judges to show their immaturity and unprofessionalism.

Even their reasons for affirming the conviction was based on falsehoods. For example, they stated that I had the ability to exercise control over the marijuana in the sense that I could've fashioned myself a joint from it. I know that I've been called Houdini and have pulled off miraculous things, but how in the world could I have fashioned myself a joint from marijuana that I couldn't even see, much less touch?

I was in the passenger compartment of the van. The marijuana was secured in the cargo compartment of the van. There was a metal partition separating the compartments; therefore, it was utterly impossible for me to access the marijuana from the passenger compartment. The only way I could have possibly accessed it, was by exiting the van, walking around to the back of it, unlocking the cargo doors, and climbing into the back. But with no evidence to suggest that I had the key or ability to unlock the back doors, I couldn't even do that.

Possession means to have control over an object. The only thing I had control over was the key, and that key gave me no more control over that van and it's contents than it did the Oval Office and its contents. I couldn't start the van and drive away with the marijuana, nor could I magically crawl through the metal partition and fashion myself a joint. And I certainly couldn't walk around to the back, magically open the doors, and unload 1,400 pounds of marijuana at a public truck stop with three dozen federal agents positioned around waiting to arrest me. I had no control over that marijuana. Thus, the judges were wrong. At the most, I should have been charged with attempting to possess the marijuana.

Nevertheless, the court refused to acknowledge this because it would have meant setting me free, and such an act is contrary to the purpose of the War on Drugs, and conflicts with the goals and agenda of the affluent and covert bias public officials who fear equality, justice, and freedom for all. After all, this is America's definition of justice—which really means *just us*—certain groups of people are excluded. Unfortunately, I happen to belong to that excluded class of people.

FREEDOM

F reedom. Chasing freedom, that ever so elusive freedom. It seems that I, as well as many others, have been desperately seeking true freedom since birth. Over the centuries, generations have come and gone, suffering and dying, with dreams of freedom, only to never attain it, many never even knowing what it really means to be free, much less having experienced what it feels like. I imagine the lives and conditions of African-Americans during the ages of slavery, Jews during the Holocaust, and Black South Africans during Apartheid. I then imagine the emotional scars, the psychological damage, the socioeconomic conditions, and the mental shackles that persisted and continued to haunt them after allegedly being freed. This makes me wonder whether physical freedom exists only for certain groups of people, and whether there is something more to the meaning of freedom.

Flashing back on the days of slavery, I can't help but wonder if my current form of captivity is part of the same scheme. Slavery, peonage, KKK terrorism, Jim Crow, confinement to plantations, confinement to the other side of town, confinement to ghettos and projects, vagrancy laws, Stop and Frisk, the War on Drugs, and the myriad of other laws and tactics designed to limit freedom and prosperity are certainly grounds for suspicion.

Some might opine that I am exaggerating by such comparisons, but the eerie resemblance of slavery to mass incarceration, and Jim Crow to the War on Drugs, is too blatant to be just a figment of my imagination. For example, many rural White communities are thriving from the mass incarceration of Blacks due to the War on Drugs. And prisons, just like plantations, are filled beyond capacity with captives who are forced to work for little or nothing at all. Some prisons, such as Angola in Louisiana, actually were plantations before being converted into prisons. In many of these prisons, racist guards routinely brutalize "niggers" in blind spots and cover it up with lies and doctored paperwork. And just like the days of slavery, there's always a "jiggaboo" negro overzealously assisting in the oppression.

Also like slavery, prison can warp one's psyche so severely that he or she may find it extremely difficult to ever be normal or productive in life. Imagine being confined to a dull, unproductive, monotonous world where there are no tomorrows, a world where dreaming is painful, and flashing forward produces nothing but a bleak, blank screen; thus, one is forced to reminisce on the joys of yesterday to find something to smile about. With absolutely no control over today or tomorrow, a prisoner is merely a slave standing still and thinking backwards. Just like the ancient slave, the modern slave is hopelessly existing under the twisted psychological and physical control of people who deem themselves entitled, superior beings.

Even when allegedly freed, the prisoner still faces difficult challenges, just like the ancient slave. He or she lacks the right to vote, to bear arms, to run for office, to travel to different states and countries, to work certain jobs, and to live in certain communities. He or she is essentially declared an outcast, and accepted only by that same unstable community that led him to prison—you know, the one that's populated with outcasts and over-policed by overzealous cops that are pressured to meet a certain quota of arrests and citations in a politically correct manner. And, having been warehoused in a useless, dehumanizing prison that teaches nothing but how to wash dishes, peel potatoes, and fend off vicious attacks, he or she is bound to return. The War on Drugs and slavery are both part of the same conniving scheme—I'm sure of that.

"Well, if you don't like being a slave," many close-minded Americans will say, "don't break the law." After all, according to the 13th Amendment, slavery and servitude are the consequences of breaking the law. But just because a few wig-wearing guys believed that crime justifies the loss of freedom and the continued existence of slavery doesn't make it right. Being labeled a criminal doesn't necessarily make a person evil and deserving of the loss of humanity and God-given rights; it simply means that the person has stepped beyond the bounds of the law. Does that make a person evil or wrong? No. Sometimes the law itself is evil and wrong, and breaking it is not always detrimental to society. Often, laws are enacted as a way to control and/or oppress the people and to generate revenue. Consider the vagrancy laws enacted immediately after the Emancipation of Proclamation. Not long ago, there were laws which prohibited blacks from sitting at the front of the bus. Does that make Rosa Parks a criminal and deserving of the loss of humanity and freedom?

Law doesn't determine what's right or wrong. Law is simply a means for the legislative branch—not the people—of the government to push their personal agendas. For example, Ronald Reagan's War on Drugs, which has cost the country millions of lives and trillions of dollars, wasn't enacted for the benefit of society. Frankly, it was pushed forward for the purpose of a clandestine agenda that continues to exist today. When Reagan declared his war only 2 percent of Americans viewed drugs as a problem. This fact alone makes me wonder whether Reagan, like the drafters of the 13th Amendment and the Jim Crow laws, foresaw an opportunity to re-enslave Blacks under a different name. It was during this time that the word *criminal* became synonymous with *Black*, and orange became the new black. Perhaps the law is just another means of the same old, evil ends—deprivation of physical freedom.

Are drugs so much of a threat to society that it was worth declaring a "war" which to date has labeled more than 33 million Americans as criminals, skyrocketed the prison population from 350,000 to 2,300,000, and essentially made 25 percent of the black male population outcasts, all in just thirty years? It's difficult to imagine how such victimless offenses in which willing participants are bartering substances amongst each other and getting stoned could cause the government to declare a war and create so much havoc. Tobacco and alcohol cause 10 times more deaths and illnesses than drugs, but dealing in them is legal. Isn't that ironic? It's also ironic how drugs didn't become so much of a problem until after Reagan declared his War on Drugs and his administration allowed CIA-sponsored drug dealers to flood the black community with crack.

What's even more ironic is the fact that Whites deal and consume more drugs than Blacks do, but Blacks are arrested and sent to prison nearly 20 times the rate of Whites. Whites make up nearly 75 percent of the drug offenders, yet Blacks account for nearly 75 percent of the people sent to prison for drugs. The War on Drugs is more about over-policing and criminalizing the Black community than eradicating drugs from society. Certainly, the consumption of illegal drugs hasn't dipped since Reagan declared war. But the number of black prisoners has skyrocketed.

Sure, Whites get arrested for drugs too, but not anywhere near the rate Blacks do. Considering statistics and media imagery, one would think that being a white drug dealer or consumer makes one less of a criminal and far less a threat to society. Look at the recent laws decriminalizing marijuana across the country, where White businessmen are becoming rich overnight and glamorized for dealing marijuana. Although marijuana is still illegal under federal law, the feds have turned a blind eye and vowed not to interfere. While I'm serving a 35-year sentence and have been declared a threat to society for the exact same conduct, the media are sensationalizing these white pot-dealers as harmless pioneers in the "Green Rush."

For example, sometime during the fall of 2014, the USA TODAY showed a picture of a smiling white man standing next to 2,000 pounds of marijuana which he was selling for 6 million dollars. Is his selling 2,000 pounds of marijuana less of a threat to society than my attempting to possess 1,400? One thing is for sure, considering the price, his marijuana was much more potent and expensive than mine was. But it is I who sit behind bars with a 35-year sentence, and he is the man with a six-million-dollar smile on his face.

Also, consider the manner in which the government filed charges in my case. John John, a black man, who rented cars and an apartment for me to transport and store marijuana, was charged with conspiracy; whereas, Nicole, a white woman, who actually admitted to using such cars to knowingly and intentionally transport marijuana, was not charged with the marijuana conspiracy. I can't help but wonder if race played a role in the government's decision to charge John John with the marijuana conspiracy and not Nicole. Cooperation and criminal history didn't have anything to do with it, because they both had prior felony convictions, and they both cooperated. Race had to have been the decisive factor.

In the mid-90s a study revealed that during the late 80s and early 90s the federal prosecutor in L.A. charged more than 2,000 people for violating Crack cocaine laws. All but eleven of them were black, and none were white. This was true although most crack cocaine offenders at the time were white. Instead of being subjected to the harsh mandatory minimums under federal crack laws, though, whites were being referred to State courts, where they were more likely to be sentenced to probation or drug rehabilitation programs.

One would think that such blatant racism is prohibited in the criminal justice system. However, according to the Supreme Court, in McClesky v. Kemp, it is totally acceptable as long as the prosecutor doesn't frankly admit that race played a role in his selective prosecution. In other words, prosecutors have unlimited discretion to charge whomever in any manner, even if race is a decisive factor. Considering the intrinsic racism in the criminal justice system—particularly in the War on Drugs—and its eerie resemblance to slavery, it is safe to assume that my fate had been manipulated by some evil scheme long before my arrival, and that a prison cell was being made for me before I even became a criminal. As the fruit of a tree of ignorance, poverty, injustice, and miseducation, I didn't stand a fleeting chance of breaking the cycle and dodging the trap. I was born to lose and spend the days of my life chasing freedom, just like generations before me.

But even though the justice system is greatly flawed and arguably designed to oppress certain classes of people, I have to accept responsibility for my own mishaps. As a confused, impoverished, misguided, insecure, ghetto child in desperate search for identity, meaning, and purpose, I was duped, by ghetto illusions and mind-warping media imagery, into hanging my hat on the brittle hook of gang-banging and distributing the cocaine that the Reagan Administration allowed to saturate my hood.

I often blame myself for being duped. But why should I beat myself up for falling for the trick? After all, I was just a kid who didn't know any better. And even as an adult, a time when men should be wiser and make sounder decisions, I still wasn't in the position to make better choices because I was still enslaved, both physically and mentally.

I guess I feel better by shouldering the burden because I, as an adult, allowed myself to be imprisoned behind the invisible walls of fear, doubt, and misperceived poverty, the same walls that enclosed my young inexperienced mind and heart as a child, the same walls that restricted my growth and confined me to a world of limitations by duping me into believing that money was the means of attaining freedom and happiness, and that dealing drugs was the only means of attaining wealth. Consumed by such walls, I essentially imprisoned myself, for the restrictions of such walls were all in my mind.

Confined to such walls of limitation, I conducted myself accordingly, even when such conduct conflicted with my heart, soul, and innate traits. In hindsight, I now know that my true character was actually confined and concealed behind those self-defeating walls, and the more I reacted to my fears and twisted beliefs, the taller and thicker the walls of my self-imprisonment became. And the stronger the walls became, the more difficult my struggle and fight for freedom.

Generations of chasing freedom. That's what I've been chasing—chasing freedom. Freedom from oppression, freedom from injustice, freedom from poverty, freedom from prison, and freedom from the invisible walls.

I've come to realize that freedom means much more than being released from penal confinement, and much more than the right to vote and sit at the front of the bus. Loss of freedom comes in many forms—fear, greed, racism, injustice, poverty, ignorance, miseducation, and so on. (Even those who oppress others are bound, bound by hatred, ignorance, and fear.) So even if the jury would've acquitted me, if the judge would've released me, or if I would've successfully escaped, I probably still wouldn't have been truly free. I likely still would've been wandering through life with shackles on my mind, being provoked, motivated, and controlled by man, propaganda, and shallow desires like 90 percent of the population. And just like the blind fool I use to be, the many who have come and gone, and the ancient slave singing *We Shall Overcome*, I would've still been chasing freedom by standing still and thinking backwards.

Freedom is much more than the protections of a constitution drafted by slave owners, the sight of the blind Lady Justice, and the opportunity to work and pay bills and taxes. Living in the suburbs and being embraced by one's neighbors don't equate to freedom. Freedom is much more profound. It is the rational self-control of the mind and the unrestricted ability to express and enjoy the heart's desires.

It is the ability to smile, laugh, and enjoy life without being burdened by fear or shame. Ultimately, it is the power to control one's own mind and desires as opposed to being controlled by the mind and desires. Freedom is sheer self-control.

When people are free, they are neither controlled nor motivated by fear, greed, hate, anger, or propaganda. Therefore, racism, oppression, injustice, and manmade laws do not deter them, and prison bars and poverty cannot silence them. No matter the fight or resistance, they press forward with courage and humility.

While Mandela fearlessly fought the racist regime of Apartheid from the confines of a prison cell at Robben Island, he was free. When Fidel Castro sat in a prison cell, planning his exit and next revolts, he was free. Dr. Martin Luther King Jr. was also free while he continued to march and orate against racism in the spite of threats from the KKK and the FBI. And although she was permanently confined to conspicuously illicit negro skin, and denied the basic rights of humanity by the wicked laws of slavery, Harriet Tubman was free as she courageously risked capture by travelling south to free the slaves at night.

When people are free, they are in tune with their divine meaning and purpose in life. They understand that their time here on earth was given to them for a reason—a cause. Therefore, they are bound by no man—or law. They are rebels with a cause. They are soldiers and generals for humanity, and nothing can stand in their way. They are free!

So in my chase for freedom, I've come to learn that what my soul has been seeking doesn't rest in the control of a man wearing a black robe, nor does it rest in the final words of 12 random citizens. My key to freedom is within; it is within my heart and soul, and it can be obtained only by taking full control of my mind and desires, by finding and living up to my meaning and purpose in life, and clearing my conscience of all guilt. I've come to realize that it is the ultimate purpose of every blessed man to improve the conditions of his hood, his community, the world, and humanity as a whole. That is the law of the universe. No prison bars, oppressive laws, or traps can stand in my way. Nor can any haters who lack compassion and humility deter me, for they are just pieces of furniture subject to be moved or stepped around.

So after wasting my first 14 years destructively confined to the ghetto, and 23 of the following 25 confined behind bars, standing still like a useless slave, I've accepted the fact that I'm too handsome, intelligent, courageous, charismatic, and influential to be living my life like a dog chasing cars up the street. I have grown tired of being provoked by fear, tricked by the wicked, and controlled by the system. After 4 decades of being a slave, I am removing the shackles from my mind. I have found my meaning and purpose in life. So "Massa" can have his rusty, blood-stained shackles back—I'm taking over now.

I'm free!

CONCLUSION

Although the plot of this story mostly involves my desperate and determined escapes, the purpose of my story is to reveal how and why I became confused, hopeless, desperate, and thereby confined, both physically and psychologically. By the same token, I hope that this is a story of hope, revealing how a determined mind can find a way to overcome anything, including prison walls, and how a determined soul can escape the invisible walls and bars of self-imprisonment, and reconstruct a man in accordance with the laws of humanity.

In this story, I reveal how I was miseducated and confused by a dysfunctional society and prison system, and how that miseducation and confusion imprisoned my mind, heart, and soul. I wanted to show how I—like so many other young black men who are miseducated, confused, and misguided with a superficial sense of identity and culture—tried to free myself by earning fast money, empty pride, and unhealthy notoriety, and exhibiting other behavior that not only galvanized the bars around my soul (thereby further confining and concealing my innate traits and meaning and purpose in life) but also led me down a path to physical imprisonment. Clearly my conditions played a major role in my development, and my unhealthy cognitions limited my choice of behavior to that which was the norm of my dysfunctional environment.

To some, it might seem that I fault racism, poverty, and injustice for my unfortunate fate. But, rest assured, I don't. Although the stench of America's racism still resides in the cracks of the law and capitalism, preventing mental and socioeconomical wounds from healing, and thereby allowing it to continuously eat away hope, ambition, and zest to live productive and prosperous lives, I refuse to allow it to control me. I must not allow another's evil to be master over my mind. So, regardless of the scars, and regardless of my conditions, I still have the ability to fight and be free.

In the last chapter of this book, I touched on the fact that no person is truly free until he or she finds and attempts to fulfill his or her meaning and purpose in life. Specifically, I tried to point out that we all have a meaning and purpose, and until we begin to fulfill it, we will be bound by the superficial ideology of man, and helping to advance his agenda rather than the agenda of the universe and God.

In order to find my meaning and purpose in life, and thereby attain true freedom, I first had to demolish the walls of my self-imprisonment, walls that were created by the ills of a dysfunctional society and years of confinement. I had to change my way of thinking, to overcome my fears and greed, to rid my conscience of the burden of guilt and shame that my years of doing wrong had placed upon it, and to find myself hidden behind the walls. In other words, I had to allow my soul to break free.

So, although I'm still confined to a prison secured by concrete walls, iron bars, barb wired and electrocuting fences, armed towers, and miserable close-minded guards who are themselves emotionally and mentally bound, I am free. I have no burdens or worries, for I am in absolute control of my thoughts, feelings, desires, and actions; I am no longer spurred by propaganda, greed, despair, or fear; and I have found my meaning and purpose in life, and I am committed and determined to fulfill it. And no matter how tough the struggle may be, I have the drive to push forward, fueled by my own vision and the reflections of my ancestors—who persevered through a struggle much worse than mine.

So, as I end this book, I am reminded that this is not the end. The world is just a tiny part of the universe; there are infinite amounts of tomorrows. If we free our minds, we'll see.

AFTERWORD

I won.

In addition to that mental and spiritual freedom - true freedom - I ultimately gained physical freedom.

As I did shirtless pushups on the cold concrete floor of my prison cell, a guard knocked on my door and told me to "Pack up. You're going home." After 16 years, 6 months, and 1 day, I was finally being freed. The guards opened my cell door and escorted me up to R&D (Receiving and Discharge). When I stepped through the doors of R&D, the Unit Manager stood there with a mischievous grin on his face. "You must be psychic," he said. "Remember when you told me to allow the transfer to proceed because it must've been part of God's plan?" He asked, handing me a copy of the judge's order.

The judge's order read: Release Mr. Adams immediately, but first make him spend 2 weeks in quarantine to protect the public from COVID.

It all began 7 months earlier when I filed a motion to the United States District Court for the Southern District of Illinois asking that my sentence be vacated due to ambiguities in the law that were inadvertently created with the passage of The First Step Act of 2018. Discerning merit, the judge ordered counsel to represent me and file a supplemental motion for the proceedings. With little faith in the argument, and total disregard for my advice, Counsel filed a frivolous supplement that set the stage for the government to respond with a contentious argument that portrayed me as a career criminal who'd murder half the population if released.

Surprisingly to most, I replied to the government's response by firing my attorney. I filed a motion to the judge asking that I be allowed to proceed pro se. My attorney was fumbling the ball, and I'd had enough of losing at the hands of others. If I were to blow my shot, I wanted to blow my shot.

The government brought in two more assistant U.S.

Attorneys to help them respond to my reply. And that's when I started to sense success. When the government changes attorneys, their opponent must be on to something. It's like changing pitchers in a baseball game when Barry Bonds or a homerun hitter is at bat. The government replied to my reply, and I replied to their reply.

Time slowly ticked as we all awaited the judge's decision. April slowly came and I became very optimistic. I was so optimistic that I would tell the other prisoners that I believed the judge would grant my motion and release me on Friday. I'd say this every Monday, Tuesday, Wednesday, and Thursday only to find myself sleeping in the hard prison bunk Friday night. But there was this strong intuitive feeling that kept telling me that I'd be going home Friday. I'd do this every week. "I'm going home Friday," I'd say to the other prisoners. Why Friday? I don't know. Maybe because I'd have an entire weekend before having to report to a probation officer. Months of Fridays passed and I was still in prison.

Then one Thursday in early July I sat at the old-fashioned typewriter in the prison dayroom helping another prisoner draft a motion for the courts. "What's going on with your case, Bosco," he asked.

I told him, "You know what? I think the judge is going to grant my motion tomorrow and let me out of here. Immediate release."

About five minutes after I said that, a guard came out of the guard's booth and called my name. "Adams, go pack your stuff. They want you at R&D."

The only time a prisoner goes to R&D is when being released or transferred to another prison. This was July 2020 when COVID had the Federal Bureau of Prison essentially on lockdown. All transfers were at a halt. I had to be going home.

I ran up to my cell, packed some paperwork and pictures of my daughter, gave away everything else, and raced up to R&D. When I got there, the officer asked me where was my property at?

I told him, "I'm leaving it all. I'm not taking any of that stuff home with me."

He told me I wasn't going home, and that instead, they were resuming transfers, and that I was one of the first to be part of this new experimental transfer process. The plan was to place prisoners in solitary confinement for three weeks, load us on a bus six feet apart, ship us to another prison, place us in solitary confinement at the new prison for three weeks, then release us to general population. We were being guinea pigs for prison transfers.

While in R&D, I saw the Unit Manager and asked him if he could put a stop to the transfer because I wasn't trying to be transferred for many reasons. One, because I had a motion in court that I was optimistic about and didn't want to be in transit and potentially miss the opportunity to file any necessary supplements or responses that the judge might suddenly require. Also this was when we thought COVID was the death sentence. I certainly didn't want to catch this mysterious virus and kick the bucket.

The Unit Manager said, "I'll try to see if I can put a stop to it. But the warden is gone until Monday. When he returns, I'll see what I can do."

They took me to solitary confinement and locked me in the cell with nothing but a mattress and blanket. This solitary was worse than average solitary. To ensure we didn't catch COVID-19, they fed us on paper plates, and the paper plates and trash would pile up in the corner. Nothing was coming out of our cells. Not even us prisoners. They refused to let us out for showers. Instead, they gave us soap so that we could birdbath in the sink. Nothing was exiting the cell.

Monday came around, and the unit manager, true to his word, came around to my cell and asked if I was still interested in stopping the transfer. I said, "Nah, don't even worry about it. Fuck it. Whatever's happening is part of God's plan. The universe is directing something here, so just let it be."

Then three weeks and one day later, on a Friday, I was in the cell beginning to stress. Why was I still in that terrible cell awaiting transfer? When I stress, I try to find meaning and purpose in the moment, for all struggles are meant to direct us. Why in the hell was I being transferred anyway? It didn't sit well with me. Why was I even being transferred if it were meant for me to go home? Was the judge not going to grant my motion? Was she going to deny the motion and force me to spend 19 more years behind bars? Was that why I was being transferred? After all, I was going to a medium custody facility for the first time since my attempted escapes. Was it meant for me to reincarnate Kunta Quawntay and start back trying to escape? Yes. That's what was happening. My motion was going to be denied and I was going to a medium prison to escape again.

Stop thinking negatively, I told myself.

I took off my shirt, and started doing push-ups. And that's when the guards knocked on the door. I was going home. That's why I'd been placed in solitary confinement for three weeks. For prison officials, it was quarantine to prepare me for transfer, but for the universe, it was three weeks of quarantine to prepare me for the judge's order that would, unbeknownst to all of us, require me to spend two weeks in quarantine. That's why the Unit manager was smiling and calling me psychic. I'd already done the 2 weeks. I was going home. On a Friday.

I got my life back. I wasn't going to die in prison. I was going to be able to spend time with my daughter while she was still a kid. It was a real sense of freedom.

Since it was late in the day and nobody was expecting me to get out, I didn't have any clothes. The officers in R&D, working overtime due to my unexpected release, donated some hand-me-down clothes to wear out of the prison. They placed me in the back of a squad car with no cuffs or shackles, drove me to the airport in Scranton, Pennsylvania, pulled over, handed me a plane ticket, and told me to get out.

Just get out? You mean, really? I could just get out of the back of the car and mingle with these people? I got out and went inside to the counter where I was helped by a woman named Sherry. I gave her my ticket and prison ID. My flight was boarding, so she ran with me to get where I needed to be. I barely made the flight.

We stopped over to change planes in North Carolina. I walked around the entire airport looking for a pay phone so that I could call my mother to let her know that I was out, but I couldn't find one. Back in the air, I was sandwiched between two ladies. They had iPhones. I had never seen them before. I asked one of them to call my mother and notify her that I was on my way home.

I landed in Los Angeles. My mother and sister picked me up and they took me to Denny's parking lot where my daughter sat in a car unaware of my release. I snuck up on the side of her window and surprised her. She started crying tears of joy. This was the first time we'd seen or held each other beyond prison. She was now 15 years old.

I'd made it. I was now free mentally and physically, and home with my daughter. I would go on to gain full custody of her, raise money to independently produce the movie *Bosco*, and start living for the first time.

Now that I am out of prison, I have changed very little in my memoir. I want to keep it raw because I wrote it in solitary confinement. I want people to feel what I was experiencing, feel the anguish, feel the pain, feel the little bit of hope that came and went at times, feel how I can be subjective at moments back then, and then compare it to how I am now more objective. I want you to read this and feel that journey, the ups and downs.

ACCESS TO AUTHOR

If you wish to follow Quawntay or post questions and comments about this book, visit him at:
www.quawntayboscoadams.com
quawntaybadams@gmail.com

Made in the USA
Columbia, SC
19 June 2024

36970620R00172